KILLING ZONE

KILLING ZONE

HARRY McCALLION

BLOOMSBURY

This book is dedicated to Bob T,
B Squadron, 22 SAS

First published in Great Britain 1995
Bloomsbury Publishing Plc, 2 Soho Square, London W1V 5DE

Copyright © Harry McCallion

The moral right of the author has been asserted

A CIP catalogue record for this book is available from the British Library

ISBN 0 7475 2013 5

10 9 8 7 6 5 4 3 2

Typeset by Hewer Text Composition Services, Edinburgh
Printed in England by Clays Ltd, St Ives plc

CONTENTS

1

MY EARLY LIFE

'If a woman asks you to marry her, spit on her.'
The only words of advice my father ever gave me.

To say I was brought up is like saying the Second World War started in 1939 and finished in 1945 and leaving it at that. I was dragged, kicking and screaming, through a time that only barely resembled childhood, into a premature adulthood. This story does not start with my birth.

I have only faint memories of my grandfather Henry, after whom I'm named. An elderly man with a white beard, he told me stories of the Great War during which he'd served with the Argyll and Sutherland Highlanders and been decorated for bravery. He could have made the Army a career but chose civilian life after the armistice. He was a stern martinet with the strictest of moral views who was respected in the community, and this, combined with his fine war record, prompted many to urge him to stand for local office but he steadfastly refused. First and foremost he was a family man and, like many Catholics, he believed in a large one.

My mother, Mary, was the third eldest of a family of five: two boys and three girls. From almost the time she could walk, she was the bane of her father's life. Where he was austere and conservative, she was a rebel, a tomboy who preferred to wear jeans and a leather jacket rather than a skirt, and could hold her own in a fist-fight with any boy her own age. Confrontation soon came. Mary started to smoke at a very early age in direct defiance of, and probably because of, her father's warnings. At the age of twelve she walked into the house and lit a cigarette in front of him.

Grandfather, who would not even let his wife smoke in the

house, was being defied by his daughter. His reaction was swift and brutal. He slapped the cigarette from her mouth, stripped her naked, hung her by her arms from a door and thrashed her with his broad working man's belt until she was unconscious. Only the intervention of my grandmother saved her from further punishment. The scene was set for years of confrontation. If Grandfather thought that by whipping my mother he would break her spirit, he was badly mistaken. The physical abuse she suffered simply made her more determined, more obstinate and more of a rebel, characteristics she passed on to all her children, although it would be three years before she again tried to smoke in front of him. My mother told me: 'At fifteen I thought I was as hard as nails and able to take my father. I swaggered into the sitting room with a lit cigarette in my mouth. My father looked up from his chair.

' "What's that you've got in your mouth," he said quietly.

' "A cigarette. If you don't like it we can go outside and sort it out."

'A slight smile played on his face. "Are you offering to take me outside?"

' "That's right, outside."

'He sighed. "OK. I'll just put my boots on."

'Like an idiot, I stood there and watched as he laced up his heavy working boots.' She shook her head with the memory, then smiled. 'He kicked me out of the house, down the stairs, into the yard and back up again. I would never physically challenge my father again.'

The realization that she could not overcome him drove my mother to seek another method of rebellion in the shape of my father, Allan. He was a hard man in a city of hard men. He was not tall, but lightning-fast, vicious, relentless and, even in his early years, willing to resort to any weapon that was at hand. He was also a man with plans to escape the grinding poverty of Glasgow, for the lush pastures of England, which suited my mother admirably. Allan also saw himself as a reincarnation of Al Capone. In his mind he would build a criminal empire in England with his brothers, Henry, Wally and John, who were cut from the same cloth – unstable, immoral and extremely violent. Around them they would eventually gather others with similar talents.

My mother became pregnant, then married my father. She was sixteen. Six months later, in early January 1953, I was born. According to my mother, just after my birth I contracted a serious illness. The local doctor was called but told my parents that there was nothing to worry about. My mother was not convinced, and my father decided to take me to hospital, where they diagnosed scarlet fever. The hospital doctor told him that had I not been admitted that night I would almost certainly have died. His reaction was typically simple and brutal: he went to the local doctor's surgery the next day and hospitalized him.

We lived in Lime Hill Road in the Gorbals. My earliest memory of my father is from when I was four. A bus route passed directly in front of our tenement block, and one day the door burst open and my mother rushed past me, a giant in the uniform of a bus conductor some way behind her. He was shouting, 'Send out your man.'

Allan walked purposefully down the small garden path outside our front door. He must have been at least a foot smaller and a stone lighter than his challenger, but my father was an expert. He never wasted words. Talking to somebody you were going to do was a waste of energy and simply put them on guard. The conductor was still shouting threats when my father jumped up and head-butted him. Blood exploded over the man's face as he began to fall. My father grabbed hold of his lapels and pulled him on to two more savage head-butts as he slid to the floor.

My father lived by the maxim 'if you put a man down, make sure he stays down'. He began to kick the man rapidly in the face and body. Then he slowed and walked round his crawling victim to deliver well-aimed kicks to the kidneys and groin. The bus conductor tried to scramble out of the garden towards his waiting bus. My father followed him, still kicking, even as the man screamed for mercy and help. He got neither. The driver and passengers watched in silence as he was kicked back on to the bus. Only then did they reboard it. My father rang the bell.

With the bus gone he looked left and right, challenge in his eyes. Our neighbours simply shrugged. The bus conductor had insulted my mother and taken on my father. In their brutal world, it had been a fair fight. My father walked back to where I stood in the corridor, a smile of satisfaction on his

3

face, ruffling my hair as he passed. Mum cleaned up the blood on the pavement.

My father was often absent but I was too young to realize this was due to his frequent periods of incarceration. At first his were crimes of violence, but theft and robbery would soon follow. Although he saw himself as a master criminal, his first attempt at theft was farcical. He had been working in the shipyard and was stealing lead, which he smuggled out down the sides of his boots to avoid snap inspections by security guards at the dock gate. He stole a small amount each day and sold the lot at the end of the week to a scrap merchant. His greed and daring increased. One night he filled his boots with several pounds of lead, but as he walked towards the main gate he found it increasingly difficult to lift his feet. He struggled towards the gate like a deep-sea diver, dragging each foot forward inch by inch. Passing workmen stopped to watch; some even cheered him on. By the time he reached the gate he could no longer lift his legs at all. He stood there panting with exhaustion as the security guard burst into uncontrolled laughter. He was searched and got six months.

The very first fight I can remember being in was shortly afterwards, when an older boy made a remark about my father and his lead boots. I head-butted him and kicked him when he fell. I was a good learner. When my father returned he decided to move us to England. We all went, along with his father, mother and brothers. By then I had two brothers, Allan and Martin, and a sister, Veronica. We settled in a small town in the north of England.

It didn't take long before everyone except my father's parents was involved in one criminal act after another. Their violence brought them to the attention of both the police and other criminals and before long they had a little empire, working as enforcers, as well as carrying out robberies and burglaries. Some of their jobs were more than a little cheeky. They burgled a shoe warehouse next door to a police station, claiming they were bailiffs recovering bankrupt stock. Their getaway van broke down and they had the audacity to ask a passing policeman to help them. He gave them a push, and they got clean away.

Various local hoods liked to be associated with the family because they offered a degree of protection from other violent criminals. A burglar called Henderson turned up at our home one afternoon wearing a new suit, which everybody admired. He regaled us with the story of how he'd broken into an empty house, gathered up all the valuables and then had a bath and changed into one of the owner's suits before leaving. There was a murmur of approval from the assembled men; they liked nerve. Suddenly the smile on Henderson's face was replaced by a look of horror.

'Oh, no!' he groaned, and jumped up and began to pace the room, a clenched fist to his forehead.

'What's the matter?' my father asked.

'I've left my old clothes back at the house I burgled.'

'So what?'

'I've left my wallet in my trousers.'

Hardly were the words out of Henderson's mouth than there came a knock on the door. It was the police. He went quietly, pleading with my father not to let anybody else know how stupid he'd been.

The youngest of my uncles, John, had a short but violent criminal career. It started with my father having a fight in a bar in the town centre – over what, nobody can remember. He won and left the bar shortly afterwards with Henry and Wally. John had arranged to meet them there later, and when he arrived the man who'd been beaten by my father had a go at him too.

One account has the man attacking John with a broken bottle, another that somebody else intervened on John's behalf. Uncle Henry told me that John always carried a German bayonet strapped to his forearm and that as he was attacked he used it in self-defence. What is beyond any doubt is that by the end of the incident a man lay dead. John was arrested and charged with murder, for which he was to serve life. My mother maintains that he was railroaded into prison and that had he not been a member of such a notorious family he would have escaped with a relatively minor charge.

The police were frequent visitors to our house, either turning up in the middle of the night to take my father away, or early in the morning to search for stolen goods. On one occasion I was playing outside when a man dressed in a suit and tie walked up to our front door. Seeing me he paused and squatted so that his face was level with mine. He had brightly polished shoes.

'Hello, young lad. What's your name?'

'Harry.'

He produced a lollipop and handed it to me.

'Well, Harry, was your daddy home last night?'

I shrugged. 'Don't know.'

'What about your Uncle Henry – was he in your house last night?'

'Don't know.'

'What about your Uncle Wally?'

'Don't know.'

My inquisitor tried a new approach. 'Are those new clothes you're wearing?'

I nodded.

'When did your mother buy them?'

'Don't know.'

A look of anger spread across the man's face, but he forced a smile. 'You don't know very much, do you, Harry?'

'I know enough not to talk to coppers,' I said. Before he could reply, I walked back into the house. Barely six years old, I had been drilled to say nothing to strangers about my family and to suspect everyone was a police officer.

Violence was the first, rather than last, resort for solving problems, even in the family. One rainy afternoon three squad cars arrived at the house. The police talked to my father for quite a long time: unusually they were looking for my Uncle Wally. In the kitchen he spoke to my mother briefly.

'I'm going with them. Henry's been shot.'

Wally and Henry had been involved in an illegal enterprise that had required the use of a sawn-off shotgun and some hired help. Henry had apparently masterminded the enterprise and split the proceeds after it was over. Wally was not impressed with the division: Henry had kept sixty per cent.

'I want half,' Wally had demanded.

'I planned the job and financed it. I deserve sixty per cent,' said Henry.

'That doesn't matter. We're partners. I took half the risk, I deserve half the profits.'

'No way.' Henry was adamant.

'If you don't give me my full share, I'll shoot you.'

Henry said it was like something out of a B-movie Western. He stood up and looked his brother straight in the eye over the small table.

'If you shoot me, it will be in the back.' Turning, he started to walk away.

When he recounted the story to me many years later, Henry smiled half in wonder, half in exasperation. 'The bastard shot me. I didn't believe he'd do it.'

Wally was arrested for attempted murder. Henry's life hung in the balance, as the shotgun blast had hit him in the back of the head. Fortunately the load had been pellet (had it been shot he would almost certainly have died instantly). Even so an operation to remove them was judged too risky, as some had penetrated Henry's skull and lay dangerously close to both his brain and spinal column. When he eventually regained consciousness, the decision was reached to leave them. To the day he died Henry had twenty-two pellets embedded in his head.

Family loyalty now took over. The brothers might fight and even shoot each other but, faced with the common enemy, they closed ranks. Henry refused to press charges against his brother. Undeterred, the police charged Wally with illegal possession of a firearm. Henry gave evidence for the defence, claiming to some restrained mirth in the packed courtroom that his brother had found the shotgun and it had gone off by accident just as he was rising to report the matter to the police. Despite his best efforts, Wally got three years.

It was at this stage that my father found a new woman to share his life, or at least his bed. He turned up with her one afternoon and calmly announced that my mother was free to stay or leave but that the woman would be sleeping with him from now on. My mother went berserk and tried to attack the intruder with a knife. I remember the screaming, the insults, the children crying, my father physically restraining my mother. She left within hours to seek sanctuary with relatives. It was the start of a downward spiral for my family. Terrible as life had been, it was to get worse. Fortunately, though, I was to escape the worst of it.

I went back to Glasgow and came under the wing of my grandmother, Martha, who became the main influence for good in my life. She was a caring, softly spoken woman who was every inch a lady. She lived at 33 Allander Street in Possil Park, a deprived area. It was a three-storey tenement block in which each landing had two front doors, each of which led to a two-bedroomed flat, with a living room, kitchen and toilet all off a central corridor. Gran and I lived on the middle floor.

I was enrolled in St Teresa's Primary School. The next two years were to be the only time of stability I ever knew during my childhood, but the area was rough and my school a hard training ground in the art of street survival. Nearly everybody belonged to a gang as individuals were always preyed upon. My earliest confrontation, the first day I was at school, was with three members of my class, who stopped me in the corridor.

'Got any money?'

'No.'

'Don't believe you.'

'I haven't got any money.'

I tried to walk past. The biggest boy, called Salter, hit me smack in the mouth. The McCallion temper that I was to struggle to control all my life exploded. I started to throw wild blows at all around me while screaming at the top of my voice. More by luck than anything else I managed to fell Salter. The others ran away from the madman. The next day I was approached by other boys who wanted me to join their gang. I'd been accepted.

Everything in the area was territorial. Our small world encompassed a few blocks of Allander Street. The top end of the street was unknown to me, as to venture past our boundaries invited immediate attack from the children who lived there. We in turn would chase and beat up any unprotected boy we found in our territory.

My first really bad fight came a few short months after I arrived. It started with a stone-throwing session between our street and boys from the next one, but as it progressed more and more children became involved until a pitched battle broke out. It was a chaotic affair. We charged down the hill to scatter them, and then they regrouped and chased us back. Older children were sucked in, and bricks and stones were replaced with bottles and improvised wooden clubs. I found myself in a heaving mass of bodies. Before me a face appeared, contorted with anger and fear. A fist swung towards my head, knocking me backwards. As I fell I saw a gleam of silver in my attacker's hand. I started to rise and was aware of something wet running down my face. I was bleeding badly.

I staggered away, just as the sound of police whistles could be heard in the distance. Gran nearly died of fright when she saw me. She washed me and took me by bus to the Glasgow Royal Infirmary. I'd been cut with a sharp blade which was to leave a four-inch scar just above my eyebrow. I was stitched up and sent home with Gran, who promptly sent me to bed with no supper – her harshest punishment. I wore my stitches like a badge of honour to school the next day. I was proud to have a scar, just like the big boys.

Our school was at the top of a hill. Below us was our church, a magnificent structure that looked more like a cathedral to me, and the centre of our small community. Each Monday we would be asked which mass we'd gone to the previous day: the early-morning mass at eight o'clock or the late mass at noon. Those who admitted going to the late mass would be interrogated as to why they'd stayed in bed and not made the effort to attend the early one. Heaven help you if you admitted actually missing mass altogether – it was considered a heinous sin.

Our religious instructor was a kindly old dear, in contrast to some of the teachers, who had the motto 'spare the rod and spoil the child' tattooed on their hearts. She'd often tell us that the road to heaven was like a long, greasy pole you had to climb and always be in danger of sliding down to hell. But if we were good Catholics, God would give us a helping shove up the pole. Discipline at school was strict. Any infringement was punished by the belt – a broad, thick leather instrument of torture that was administered across the palm of the hand. It was considered a weakness to cry or flinch when you received your punishment but the first time I got it I nearly fainted with the pain.

Every Friday afternoon the priest would visit Gran. They'd talk for an hour or so and then she'd give him a contribution towards the Church. Poor as we were, the Church still got something. How Gran managed I don't really know. She had a war widow's pension and I suppose my mother and the Social Security must have helped. Despite the shortness of money we ate reasonably well.

Saturday we would often spend visiting my cousins, the Crichtons, who lived on the outskirts of the city. The two eldest, Robert and John, were near my age and we would spend the afternoon playing football, at which I was never any good, and then have a meal together. Gran and I would get the last bus home, just as the pubs were closing. The buses would be full of drunken, roisterous men and women and impromptu singalongs were commonplace. We'd all join in, helping whatever budding performer had chosen to sing by shouting out the chorus at the top of our lungs. People stamped their feet and clapped to keep up the tempo.

Gran and I would spend Sunday together. It was a special day. She would make soup, almost a meal in itself. Perhaps because I'd never had enough to eat before, I used to love watching her prepare it. She would soak a ham-bone in water to create a stock the previous day, and leave dried peas to soften in cold water. On the day of cooking, she would finely grate the other vegetables and then add chopped leaks and lentils. The result was so thick you could almost stand a spoon up in it. It tasted delicious.

One Sunday I was playing outside in the back garden. All the gardens stretched a long way behind the tenements, separated from each other by rows of iron railings. Two yards away I saw a classmate, Jimmy Ryan, crying. I climbed over to ask what was wrong.

'I'm hungry,' he sobbed.

I knew his mother lived alone with him, and I asked if she'd gone out.

'She's locked me out.'

I was too young then to realize Jimmy's mother had a terrible reputation with men. I took him up to Gran. She knew. She washed him and sat him down for tea with us. He stayed until bedtime then made his way back home under the shelter of Gran's arm. When she returned she tucked me up in bed, under a blanket and a pile of coats to keep me warm.

'Thanks for feeding Jimmy, Gran,' I whispered.

She kissed me on the forehead. 'I don't have much, Harry, but nobody's ever left my house hungry.'

Years later, on one of my visits to Gran while on leave, she told me that Jimmy Ryan and two other men had tried to rob the bookie's at the bottom of Allander Street. A man was stabbed to death. Jimmy was caught and sentenced to life imprisonment.

At school I had a new teacher, James MacRae. Before, learning had been a chore, but under his firm but fair hand it became something special for me. I especially loved Scottish history. 'Big Jimmy' taught us about times gone by, of battles and wars, kings and conquerors. He taught with a passion that swept us along. He never stood still, moving and gesturing as if he himself were there, fighting alongside the Scottish heroes of our past: Bruce, Wallace, the Marquis of Montrose, but most of all the 'Black Douglas'. The Black Douglas was a man so feared by the border English that their ladies used to frighten their children to sleep with the warning that if they didn't, he would get them. Legend has it that as one fine English lady warned her child, a voice from the darkness behind her said: 'But my lady, the Black Douglas is already here!'

Close to our school was the Botanical Gardens, a beautiful tropical garden. The glasshouse was hot, damp and always deathly quiet. Through it ran a gravel path with wooden seats every twenty feet or so. I would often retreat there after school and sit under the palm trees reading the stories that Jimmy MacRae had told me of in class. It was my secret place where I could slip into the past and live the lives of long-dead heroes.

Although he probably never knew it, Jimmy MacRae was the closest I ever came to having a father-figure, the role model I so desperately wanted. It was his teaching, more than anything else, that would inspire me to search for adventure. From him also I developed my own brand of honour. Terrible as some of my actions were to be in adult life, I never hurt a woman or child, turned my back on an enemy or deserted a friend. I hope the Black Douglas would have been proud of me.

The lack of a strong father's guidance in my earlier life meant that now I ran wild most nights. Gran would let me out to play after supper and I would return for bedtime at ten o'clock. In those four hours I would roam the street with my gang of school friends, terrorizing anybody that came into our area, and being terrorized in turn by older and more vicious gangs of boys. The streets were exceptionally quiet; there was no traffic to speak of, except the occasional coal lorry. I learned how to play cards and gamble, about girls long before my first biology class, and, most of all, the value of being part of a group. There was crime, of course, but my generation was spared the horrors of the drug culture that was to follow in the late sixties.

On Saturday nights I was allowed to stay out until half past eleven. At the bottom of Allander Street runs the main thoroughfare of Saracen Street, and on Saturdays there would be organized fights outside the Saracen's Head. Not the boys' stuff we got up to, but grown men, man to man. There was only one rule: no weapons. Apart from that, anything went. Crowds would gather to watch and I used to make a few pennies running to get them pie and chips from the nearby fish shop. Sometimes even the police would stop but in those days they never interfered.

The police were both feared and respected. When we played football in the street, the very sight of a uniform would cause us to scatter. If you did something really bad, like break windows or street-lights, they would very often give you a severe slapping, a 'doing over' as we called it. Then they would take you back home, where you'd get another slapping for bringing the police to the door. Our community was a very insular one. Problems like wife beating were usually sorted out within the family, or if it was trouble with a neighbour, man to man. Few would ever dream of calling the police, unless it was to something like a burglary, and then it was usually because the gas meter had been broken into and the gas company had to be informed. Despite the poverty, the violence and the deprivation, it was still considered a considerable stigma to have a son or father arrested or, worse still, imprisoned.

In the summer of 1960 our family was reunited. My mother had remarried an Englishman called Walter Cunningham. He was a steel erector by profession and so we would be continually on the move, following one construction job after another. I would no sooner find my feet in one school than I would be forced to leave for another. I was always the new boy, never in one place long enough to make friends. By the time I was eleven I had, by my own count, gone to more than twelve schools. The construction industry wasn't solely to blame; my mother had made a terrible choice for our second father.

Cunningham was a weak man: in body, spirit and moral fibre. After a six-month honeymoon period, the fights between him and my mother started. They were awful in their intensity: screaming, foul-mouthed insults were exchanged with a ferocity that was almost beyond imagination. Then came the physical violence. Cunningham would attempt to beat my mother, who would defend herself with any weapon that came to hand. Sometimes if he caught her without a weapon, he would leave her battered, bruised and semi-conscious. But more often she would get her hands on something like a poker and beat him senseless, standing over his still-jerking frame and impugning his masculinity. How they managed never to kill each other was a source of amazement to me.

When he couldn't inflict any physical damage on my mother, my stepfather would turn his attention to us, and in particular to me. On one occasion when my mother had fled the house during a violent argument, he told me to put some coal on the fire. As I dragged a bag of prepacked coal to the grate I heard a scream from my stepfather. It had been raining heavily and the bag had left a black, oily smear on the carpet. I stood to say I was sorry but he smashed me to the floor with clenched fists, blacking both my eyes, then put his boot on my neck and forced my face into the black mess.

'Lick it up.'

Only when I started to vomit did he relent.

When my mother returned, she nearly went insane. The entire family was packed up and on a train to Glasgow within hours. The cycle of break-up and reconciliation was to last until I was fifteen. I would always go to Gran's. Then Cunningham would find my mother, promise that things would be different, and they would get back together again. Soon the fighting would start again and it would be back to Glasgow for me.

I became prone to extremely swift and violent mood swings, but worse, the temper I had perhaps inherited became almost uncontrollable. It was as if there was a raging animal inside, always threatening to overwhelm me. Only on the quiet nights as I sat with Gran, and watched television or listened to her talk about my grandfather, did I feel safe and calm.

On one of my returns to Glasgow I discovered that most of my contemporaries had graduated from fist-fights to more serious affairs. Organized gangs like the Tongs, Fleet and Cumbie ruled the streets. Some of them were several hundred strong. When I was coming home from school one day a gang member made fun of me because my Scottish accent had been diluted by frequent stays in England. My reaction was to attack him with a flurry of punches and kicks. It took three other boys to pull us apart. A few days later I was returning to Gran's flat. As the landing light was out, I walked up the steps, guided by memory and instinct. The close was almost pitch-black. A voice from the darkness above me asked:

'Are you Harry McCallion?'

'Yes.'

There was a blinding flash of light, then a blackness more complete than any I had ever known. I woke up in Glasgow Royal Infirmary, my head heavily bandaged. The doctor was of the opinion that I'd probably been hit with a hatchet. By sheer good luck it had entered at an angle and caused a glancing rather than a penetrating wound. I was left with a five-inch scar and bad concussion but no permanent damage. Neither I, nor the police, ever discovered the identity of my attackers. I was thirteen and already had more scars, physical and emotional, than a man three times my age.

During one of my frequent visits to Gran's house we watched John F. Kennedy's inauguration on her small television.

'They'll never let that man live,' she prophesied.

'Why, Gran?'

'Because he's a Catholic.'

Everybody remembers where they were when Kennedy was shot. I was sitting with Gran. She nodded sagely and looked across at me. 'What did I tell you?'

Gran was years ahead of Oliver Stone.

When I was fourteen we moved back to the same northern town my father had originally settled in. He was in jail, but Uncle Henry was still there working as a bouncer in a local nightclub. He was a frequent visitor to the house and I loved to listen to him tell the story about Wally shooting him. Each time he told it, it sounded funnier.

It was here that matters finally came to a head between my step-father and my mother. As usual it started with a fight – a bad one by even their standards. Cunningham had my mother on the floor and started to kick her. I tried to intervene. He picked me up above his head and threw me like a rag doll against the wall. My sister ran from the house to the only person she could seek protection from, Uncle Henry. The police were called but by the time they arrived Cunningham had fled and I had lapsed into unconsciousness for the second time in my young life and been taken to hospital.

Twenty-four hours later, Uncle Henry picked me up. He was a fine-looking man, at five foot ten the tallest of all the brothers, and with a huge spread of shoulders and large hands. Always neatly dressed, on this day he wore a light-brown, three-quarter-length Crombie overcoat, dark trousers and shiny brown brogues. His appearance meant a lot to him. He was a man who liked women and knew they were attracted to him. He never bought cheap clothes, preferring to wait until he could afford the best and latest fashions.

'Look like a million dollars and people will treat you like a million dollars,' he once told me.

That morning Henry was unusually quiet as he drove me home. He would ask occasional questions about Cunningham, how long this had been going on, and whether he had hit me and my brother and sister before. I answered frankly. His face was an impenetrable mask.

Arriving back at my home, even I, used to the unpredictable violence of my stepfather, was shocked. It looked like a battlefield, furniture up-ended, debris scattered all over the floor. In the middle of all this Mum sat, her arms clasped around her body, rocking slowly and crying. Her face bore the marks of a savage beating. Henry told me to go and make some tea. He sat in front of her, and from the kitchen I heard him say quietly: 'This can't go on, Mary. You know that.'

It was several minutes before my mother answered. 'I know, Henry, I know. But what am I to do? I've got four kids to bring up.'

'This isn't the way, Mary. No matter what lies ahead, it can't be as bad as this.'

At that moment Cunningham walked in.

Henry rose to meet him.

'I think you'd better leave for a time, Walter – until things settle down.'

I think even Cunningham was appalled at the scene that confronted him. His face looked drawn and lined. 'I just want to talk to my wife. Just talk, that's all.'

Henry shook his head. 'Now isn't a good time. Leave it a couple of days, Walter.'

Cunningham started to get angry. 'This is my house. Who are you to tell me what to do in my house?'

'I know this is your house, but these are my brother's children. This can't go on, Walter, it just can't go on.'

Cunningham was a silly man, vicious, petty-minded and a bully, but his next words were the stupidest he ever uttered.

'Right, you, outside.' He gestured towards the back garden.

We were all stunned. I looked at my younger brother, Allan. His mouth hung open with disbelief. Henry too had a hard time understanding it. His face, normally impassive, struggled to control a smile of disbelief. When he spoke his voice was very quiet and restrained.

'I don't think you really want to do that, Walter. Now why don't you just spend a few days away and everything will sort itself out.'

Cunningham became incensed. 'This is my house!' he screamed. 'Nobody tells me what to do in my house.' He walked to the back door. 'Now outside.'

'OK, Walter, if that's what you really want.'

It was then that I realized the difference between a truly hard man and a blowhard. The really hard men never lost their tempers or raised their voices – they had no reason to. Henry was a very hard man. He'd even worked, at one stage, as an enforcer for one of the big London firms. Seconds after he walked outside we heard the first scream from Cunningham. I grinned with savage delight as they got louder and eventually became whimpers. Minutes later Henry returned and as he walked through the door he checked to make sure there were no blood spots on his immaculate Crombie.

'He's decided to go and visit his relations for a few weeks and give you time to think, Mary.' That was all he said.

Henry was a frequent visitor over the next two weeks. It was the last time I was to see him. He eventually became part-owner of a club and died of a heart attack in 1989 with a barmaid on one knee and a pint in his hand. I think he would have liked to have gone that way. In that time my mother came to the decision to finally break completely with Cunningham, who returned after two weeks but was a broken man. He faced a family that loathed him and decided to leave for good. After packing what possessions he had he made his way to the front door. I went to see him off.

'You're lucky I'm only fourteen, but one day soon I'll be a man,' I told him. 'If I ever find you I'll kill you.'

He never answered. Fear of Henry probably prevented him from hitting me again. Turning, he walked out of our lives for ever. In adult life I would spend two army leaves searching for him. Fortunately for both of us I never found him. Now we were on our own.

Without a man to contribute to the family income, we were dependent on Social Security. There was never enough: never enough food, never enough heat, never enough clothes. For some reason I couldn't fathom, my mother kept moving from town to town. For her this was simple. She packed everything we owned, which wasn't much, and put us all on a train. When the ticket inspector came, she'd explain that a family member had died and that she had got on the train so fast she'd forgotten to get a ticket. She'd provide her name and address and on we would go.

We moved through several big northern towns, Manchester, Bradford, Doncaster. When we arrived she would contact the Social Security and we'd get some kind of accommodation, usually bed and breakfast, then a council house of some kind. Furniture was sparse, or non-existent. Most of the time we slept on mattresses on bare floors.

We'd be lucky if we had a single electric fire. It was during the winter that my brother Martin, standing warming himself in front of one, was severely burnt when the shirt he was wearing caught fire. He was rushed to hospital and kept there for a week. When I went to collect him he told me in an excited voice all about his week: the clean clothes, toys, and new friends he'd made. Then he burst into tears.

'Why do we have to live this way, Harry?'

I put my arm around his shoulder. 'I don't know. I really don't know,' was all I could say. We walked the rest of the way home in silence.

We'd been on our own for nearly a year when my mother had a complete breakdown. She'd been living on drugs for a long time: sleeping tablets to make her sleep and other pills to get her going again the next day. Eventually her mind just refused to accept the situation and she simply withdrew into a world of her own. For long periods she sat humming to herself and when she did speak it was in a little girl's voice. It was appalling to see and we had nobody to turn to. I feared if I notified the authorities we'd all be taken into care. It was up to me and I took over the household, sending the others out to school, where they would be fed, and getting my mother to sign her benefit books so that I could buy some food, which my younger sister and I cooked at night.

The crisis lasted over a month, but eventually my mother returned to reality. We continued to move, as if by doing that we would somehow find something better. I grabbed what little schooling I could along the way.

Four months before my sixteenth birthday, my mother disappeared. We simply woke up one morning to find her gone. I was alone with a family to feed, no money, nothing in the house to eat or even sell. I felt as if I was a hundred years old. I gathered my brothers and sisters about me for a council of war.

I considered getting on a train for Glasgow and going to Gran's, but feared that as we were children the guard might detain us for the authorities. Anyway, we didn't know where Mum was or when she'd be back. The most important thing was to get some money together for food. There was no way we could do it honestly. We stripped lead and copper pipes from empty houses and sold them to scrap merchants. It's not something I'm proud of, but it meant the difference between going hungry and eating. With the money I bought mostly vegetables and made my own version of Gran's soup. It was nowhere near as good, but it kept us from starving. Mother returned after a week. She never told me where she went and I never asked.

Shortly after she returned, a man knocked on the door and I answered it.

'Do you know who I am?'

'No, but your face is familiar.'

'It should be. I'm your father.'

The first thing that went through my mind was how small he was.

He stayed for the afternoon and spent most of the time talking to my mother alone. Then he left with hardly a goodbye to us, and I never saw him again. As far as I'm aware neither he nor Cunningham ever helped my mother. They simply left her to struggle along on her own. My father died alone at Christmas 1981, from a sawn-off shotgun blast to the head. The gun was found close to his body. It could have been suicide or murder. I never found out, and never really cared.

I left school on my sixteenth birthday, with no formal qualifications. A week later I started my first job as an apprentice welder in Hatfield Woodhouse, just outside Doncaster. My working clothes consisted of a pair of old overalls that Cunningham left when he walked out on us. My job consisted mainly of welding hydraulic pit props for the nearby coalmines. I worked a full eight-hour day for less than four pounds a week. Most of the time I had no lunch, and during dinner break I'd hide myself away in my welding booth, in case my workmates saw the shame of my poverty. Because I only had one set of overalls the grease and dirt of the factory would soak through the thin fabric during the week and infect my skin. Try as I could at night I couldn't get the grease off my body, and I soon started to get skin disorders: acne, blackheads and dermatitis.

Wednesday was pay day and we all ate well. The meal was never spectacular – usually Spam sandwiches – but to us it was a feast. We were by now living on a caravan site with five of us crammed into a three-berth caravan. Recognizing that I needed to eat during the day, my mother did a deal with a local farmer to buy some fresh eggs with part of my pay. For the next year I got two boiled-egg sandwiches every day; it was almost as bad as not eating at all. It would be many years before I could look at a boiled egg without feeling sick.

When I turned seventeen, I decided to join the Army. Inspired by a book I'd recently read, I decided to join the Royal Marines. Fortunately for me I couldn't find the Navy recruiting office and asked for directions from the Army office.

'Why do you want to join the Navy?' asked the sergeant.

'I don't. I want to join the Marines.'

'Ah well, come in here, lad. We've got all kinds of commando units.'

Thus I was with a single sentence enticed away from a career with the Royal Marines. Seated in front of the sergeant I listened as he explained about commando gunners and commando engineers. Behind his head was a large picture of a man suspended from a parachute.

'Who are they?'

He looked behind him. 'The Parachute Regiment. You don't want to join them.'

'Why not?'

'They're the toughest in the Army. Only a third of volunteers get through their course – it's murder.'

'That's what I want to join.'

Try as he could to dissuade me I was adamant: it was the Parachute Regiment or nothing. I would have to undergo a medical examination and a date was set for two weeks' time. The doctor who examined me was a middle-aged man who tut-tutted as he examined my chest, took my pulse and blood pressure and weighed me. When I'd put on my shirt he told me to sit down and observed me over a pair of black-rimmed glasses.

'I can't pass you fit to undergo training,' he said bluntly.

I felt as if the world had collapsed around me. 'Why not?'

'Two reasons. First you are well under weight. Second you have dermatitis. It will have to heal before you can even begin to consider putting any kind of heavy pack next to your skin.'

'How long will it take?'

He shrugged and wrote out a prescription. 'Four to six weeks, for the skin complaint. As to the weight, you'll have to put on at least three pounds.' He shook his head. 'I'd say you were on the borderline for malnutrition. Now have someone apply this ointment to your back every night after a bath.' He handed me a prescription. 'I'll see you again in four weeks.'

The deprivation that I'd endured through my early life had left its mark. When I walked out of the surgery a feeling of total helplessness came over me. For an hour I walked around the busy city centre, trying to come to terms with it. Then my resolve hardened. I would join the Army. For the next four weeks I bathed every night and applied the ointment the doctor had prescribed. Food was more difficult. I ate everything I could lay my hands on, including bags of sugar. I did every menial job that was advertised in the local newspaper shop, dug gardens, delivered leaflets, anything, to help me buy food. Four weeks later I returned. He nodded at the improvement in my skin, then weighed me and shook his head.

'Only two pounds.'

I felt close to tears.

He looked at me on the scales and smiled.

'Not really enough, but adequate. I'll allow you in. A few weeks of Army grub will soon put meat on your bones.'

Minutes later I was upstairs in front of a lieutenant-colonel and being sworn in as a soldier in the British Army. Because I'd no qualifications I was required to go to the Army's assessment centre at Catterick. It meant an overnight stay and it was quite an adventure being with other recruits, having good food and a clean bed to sleep in. We sat the exam and I was amazed to discover that I'd come second. The major who had presided over the exam called me back.

'Why have you never sat any O levels?'

'By my own count, I've been to at least twelve schools since I was eleven. I was never in one long enough to sit any exams.'

'That's a pity, you obviously have a good mind. When you finish training you should take some qualifications.'

I'd take his advice one day; it would be over twenty years later, but I'd take it.

I was to report to the Parachute Regiment Depot, Browning Barracks, in two weeks and until then I was on leave.

On returning home I found that my mother had a new man in her life. Donny Boyle had known my mother for some time, and now he'd moved in. We didn't get along, although he seemed to be on great terms with everybody else. I probably resented the intrusion of another male in the house. Every man who'd assumed the role of father had hurt us. On the first afternoon I was back my anger boiled over and a furious row broke out between me and Donny. What amazed me was that my entire family sided with him and all turned on me, screaming abuse. If they'd thrust a dagger into my heart they couldn't have hurt me more.

I stormed out into the mid-afternoon sun, feeling more alone than I'd ever been in my life. I must have walked for an hour or so, not knowing where to go and what to do. Finally, more in desperation than anything else, I rang the recruiting office where I had joined up and told them my problem. The sergeant told me to make my way to the railway station and he'd meet me there. He found me sitting alone on a bench and sat beside me. I told him my predicament.

'I can't go back, I just can't.'

'I don't blame you, son. I wouldn't either. Anyway you don't have to. You can report early to the Para Depot if you want.'

'Can I? My course doesn't start for two weeks.'

'That's not a problem. I've already rung them and they've got accommodation waiting for you until your course starts.'

'Great. I'll go.'

He handed me a rail warrant. 'Have you any money?'

I shook my head. He handed me thirty shillings and made me sign for both. 'The thirty bob is an advance from your first wages, OK?'

I nodded. 'Thanks a million.'

'Come on, son. We'll find out when the next train is.'

He stayed with me until the train for Aldershot was about to leave, then shook my hand.

'You make sure you get through that Para course, and remember this: you're in the Army now. You'll always have a bed, a roof and a meal and someone to listen to you. You're part of our family now.'

For the first time in many years I felt as if life had something to offer me. I got on the train and left Bradford and my family behind. It would be four years before I would see any of them again.

I arrived at Aldershot and managed to hitch a lift on a passing Army Landrover to Browning Barracks. In some ways I took a lot of emotional baggage with me into Army life: I had low self-esteem, I suffered from paranoia, I was ill at ease in company. But worse than all of these was the anger that simmered just below the surface, coiled and deadly, threatening always to overwhelm me.

I walked up to the guardroom entrance and knocked on the window. A huge Para corporal emerged, muscles bulging against his shirt, red beret set at a jaunty angle, the silver cap badge of a parachute flanked by outspread wings glinting in the light. I weighed less than eight stone and was wearing a thin nylon jacket over my only shirt, a pair of black cotton trousers that were an inch too short and a pair of old shoes with the soles hanging off. The corporal smiled down at me.

'What do you want, son?'

'I'm a new recruit,' I stammered.

He looked me up and down, a bit surprised, then light dawned behind his eyes. He pointed a finger at me.

'McCallion?'

'That's right.'

'We're expecting you. Had some trouble at home, eh? Never mind. Families – least said soonest mended. That's what I always say. There's a bed in the accommodation block for you and if you hurry you can get a bite to eat in the NAAFI before it closes. Where's your luggage?'

I held up a plastic carrier bag. In it were two pairs of socks, a pair of underpants and some shaving gear Cunningham had left.

2

THE PARAS

'Paratroopers are human Alsatians.'
An Phoblacht (Republican News) – early 1970s

The door burst open. Framed there was a broad-shouldered man, the two pips on his epaulettes indicating that he was a lieutenant in the British Army. He surveyed us for a second, then spoke.

'There is only one reason you are in this depot. To learn how to kill the enemy. How to kill the enemy – nothing else. Carry on, Sergeant.'

We had just met our platoon commander, Hector G. Still only civilians in uniform, we were shell-shocked. None of us knew what we had let ourselves in for and we had little time to reflect. The training was intense from the start: up at 0500, clean the barracks, a hurried breakfast and full muster parade at 0830. Then a five-mile run, weapons training, drill, lunch, assault course, more drill, more weapons training, tea, then at least two hours to get our kit and locker clean enough for the next day's inspection. As I was by no means fit – I felt close to death on the runs – most nights I collapsed exhausted into my bed at the first opportunity.

Sergeant Vaughan was a veteran of twelve years' service. The corporals were a hard bunch, often brutal, but fair: Wally Beard, a career NCO destined to rise quickly through the ranks only to be tragically murdered in the Warrenpoint massacre; Roger C, who would later serve in the SAS; and Steve F, who had just returned to the Paras after a tour with the SAS. They were men; I was still a child. Until this point in my life I had never mixed socially with a large group of people and I found it extremely difficult. Although most were about my age, or a little older, they seemed far more mature. The one man with whom I struck up a close friendship which was to endure all my life was Bob B, a Scot from Fife, who'd been a TA corporal. Bob always ran short of money at the weekend and with monotonous regularity would borrow ten shillings off me every Monday morning. I never spent the money when he returned it after pay day but put it aside, knowing he would ask for it.

Despite my unease in the company of others I loved the training. I loved being warm and having regular meals and warm clothes even if they were all the same colour.

The Physical Training Instructors who took us on our daily runs were even more brutal than the platoon staff. Everybody shouted at us. There was no attempt to gain trust or respect; everybody seemed to want to break us, to get us to ask for a transfer to another unit.

After every run the PTIs lined us up in three rows and we would be made to chant, over and over again at the top of our voices: 'For the right to kill, we must suffer. For the right to kill, we must suffer.'

We were constantly given new weapons to strip and reassemble, including the SLR (self-loading rifle), GPMG (general-purpose machine-gun) and the Carl Gustaf anti-tank gun. The first day I was issued with a Sterling sub-machine-gun it fascinated me so much that I couldn't resist putting an empty magazine on it and cocking it continually to see how its action worked. I was spotted by an NCO, who called me across to him, took the weapon from me, checked it wasn't loaded, then hit me across the head with it. I was only barely conscious when he handed it back but it was a lasting lesson in weapon discipline. I never cocked a weapon again unless it was to clear or fire it.

Our first real test was called Junior Wales: two weeks in the Brecon Battle School learning basic patrol techniques. Our physical training didn't suffer; in fact it intensified. But the hardest test was ahead for all of us in P Company. Apart from the selection courses for special forces, it was the hardest physical test in the Army. There was the added edge that we, as recruits, would be pitted against fully trained soldiers who were doing P Company to get their para wings and join the Airborne Brigade.

It began with a five-mile run across a long valley on the hottest day of the year. At the summit of Miles Hill, I looked back over the expanse of sand called the 'tank tracks' and saw our route was marked by collapsed bodies, and this was only day one. The entire afternoon was spent in the gym, going round and round an indoor assault course. I'll never know how many circuits we did.

The next day we had the 'log run': eight men strapped to a telegraph pole running at top speed up and down high hills. Going down was worse, because if you fell you were dragged and trampled on until you regained your feet. In the afternoon there was the only event I enjoyed: milling. Two men wearing boxing gloves pounded the hell out of each other for three minutes. There was no skill, just brute force and aggression. I was up against a military policeman, Corporal Steve F. The ex-SAS man got me holed up in the corner so much that I ran across the ring when the bell sounded, hit him with two outstretched fists in the chest and went on throwing furious punches. I'll never know what kept him on his feet. Even with the oversized gloves we were using damage could be inflicted. My opponent's eye swelled up and a cut appeared above his right cheek. He not only lost the fight, but had to leave the course.

Day three found us doing what, for me, was the hardest test. The airborne assault course was made up of planks, see-saws and obstacles suspended forty feet in the air on scaffolding. It started with a climb up two parallel bars some sixty feet high. We then had to shuffle across, negotiating two obstacles placed on each bar by balancing on one foot. In the middle we had to bend down, touch our toes and call out our name, rank and number.

After that we had the assault course proper, running along a foot-wide plank, jumping over gaps and stepping on to and off see-saws. The trick was to look directly ahead at all times and to keep moving as fast as you could. If you slowed down or stopped to look down you were lost. The final test was the most nerve-racking of all. Two recruits at a time would run along ten planks and hurl themselves across an open space into a vertically suspended net. I waited in some trepidation for my turn. Two regular officers on P Company were ahead of me. On the command to go, they ran and jumped, both bouncing back from the net. Below, two members of staff were placed to break any fall. They caught the first man, but missed the second. He hit the floor with a sickening thud and began to scream. He was still screaming as they put him in the ambulance. He'd broken his back.

It was my turn. As I took a deep breath, I felt my heart pounding like it wanted to jump out of my chest. I started my run as fast as I could, my eyes fixed on the net, then I was in space, the net hit me and I clutched at it with outstretched hands but bounced right out. I was falling. Hands tried to grab me, caught my shoulders, my left foot hit the floor heavily. I heard rather than felt it snap. I didn't scream but tears welled. I tried to stand up, desperately willing my leg to hold me. It wouldn't. In minutes I was in a Landrover and on my way to hospital, where they X-rayed my ankle but were unsure if it was broken. I was sent back to camp to await their findings.

The pain in my leg was intense. Through the dinner break I rested, hoping it would be strong enough to hold my weight in time for the next exercise. I hobbled out at 1400 dressed in my PT kit. Hector G took one look at me and sent me back. The slow, shuffling walk back across the square was one of the loneliest I ever made. I lay down on my bed, fighting back the tears of pain and frustration. A corporal walked in.

'What in hell are you doing lying on your bed, you wanker? You can't fool me. If there was something really wrong with your leg they'd have kept you in hospital. Get off that bed and sweep the floor.'

He threw a broom at me. With difficulty I tried to move round the room using the broom more as a crutch than a cleaning instrument. My ankle was throbbing like mad. I had hardly started when a medic burst in.

'McCallion?'

I nodded.

His face contorted with horror. 'What are you doing on your feet, man, your ankle is broken in two places. They're getting a stretcher across to take you back to hospital.'

I looked at the NCO defiantly. He couldn't meet my eyes. My P Company stint was over. I felt as if my world had collapsed.

When my leg was in plaster I went to see Hector G. He told me he was sorry to lose me. Our paths would cross many times in the next few years. Hector became a highly decorated officer with the SAS, leading the assault on the Iranian Embassy in London in 1980 and winning the Military Cross in Oman, the MBE in Ulster and a

Mention in Dispatches in the Falklands. He was one of the handful of officers I met in the Army whom I truly respected.

It took three months for my leg to heal, then I, and five other back squads, joined another platoon to continue training. The platoon sergeant, Bunny Harvey, lined us up in the corridor and asked us why we'd been sent back to his platoon. When each man had given his reason, he surveyed us with thinly disguised disdain.

'I don't like back squads, whatever the reason you have for being here. You should have got through first time. I've got a good platoon, and back squads are always a problem. Give me one excuse and you'll be back-squared again. Now go find the section corporals and they will divide you among the sections.'

The sergeant's words were prophetic. For the rest of our training we had to try twice as hard as the other recruits just to stay even. My only consolation was that Bob B was with me as he too had suffered an injury on the airborne assault course. Bob was a few years older than me and had the advantage of previous training in the TA. He was lean and tough and had a biting, sardonic humour which was often directed at himself, but it was his words of encouragement which saw me through a difficult time.

For the next five months I battled through. It was a lonely time for me, and the new platoon seemed an unfriendly place compared with the first one. They seemed to resent me just as much as the platoon sergeant. Mail calls were particularly bad. I never got a letter, except one from my friendly tax man. I got into fight after fight, holding my own in most but sometimes getting a terrible beating. I gave up trying to be one of the boys and concentrated on getting through the training.

I passed P Company, then Advanced Wales. We were never left in any doubt about our primary role in life: to kill. On one simulated exercise we ambushed a patrol of terrorists, one of whom dropped near my feet, apparently wounded. I was told by the training major to interrogate him. I did and managed to get the location of the enemy base from him. I rejoined my ambush party.

'What are you going to do to him?' asked the training major.

I hesitated and he kicked me in the ribs so hard I was bruised for weeks.

'You kill him. Do you understand? Kill him. We'll have no squeamishness here.'

I shot him with my blank ammunition. It was a lesson I learned well.

Finally, parachute training in Abingdon. This consisted of eight jumps, two from a Second World War barrage balloon with a cage suspended beneath it, followed by six from a Hercules C130 transport plane. Receiving my wings was a proud day for me. Then it was back to the depot for a few weeks and our passing-out parade. All my contemporaries had their families to see them walk from the square as fully trained paratroopers. I had nobody, but that didn't matter much to me – the Army was my family now.

On 2 January 1971 I was marched up the short distance from Browning Barracks to Montgomery Lines to join 2nd Battalion Parachute Regiment. I was still only seventeen.

I was posted to A Company's second platoon. The platoon sergeant hated me on sight and made no secret of it. Looking back, I can hardly blame him. I was probably every sergeant's nightmare – a big-time 'crow' who didn't know when to keep his mouth shut. I had opinions which continually got me into fights. But it was all a front as I was just a scared kid. I felt totally insecure and unable to confide in anyone. Whenever I tried, the person would tell everybody what I'd said to them, which just fed my paranoia and fuelled an anger that at times I could hardly control.

I desperately wanted to be accepted yet the harder I tried the less I seemed to be. I was continually the butt of jokes and the target for every bully in the Company. I fought, but I was still only really a child in a man's world and easy prey. The Parachute Regiment of the early 1970s was a hard place where you had to learn to stand on your own feet with help from no man. Perhaps, in desperation, I took the wrong path. It didn't happen overnight but in time I became even more brutal than most of my peers.

The 2nd Battalion was waiting to go on a tour of Ulster and everybody was looking forward to it. They'd already served a tour in the Province. They called it the 'disco tour' as there had been no gun battles or riots and most of their time had been spent chasing the local girls. We expected the next tour to be the same. Two men had been killed: one was stabbed to death in a bar fight; the other fell off the ferry drunk and was never recovered.

We were having lunch in the mess hall and at my table were some very hard men, some veterans of the Borneo campaign. Many members of 2nd Battalion would have made the Waffen SS look like boy scouts. The orderly clerk came in, his face taut with anger.

'Anybody heard the news? The IRA bastards have just murdered three young Scots soldiers in Ligonel, just outside Belfast. They were off duty and drunk. All shot in the back. They never had a chance.'

There was no outburst of anger – just silence. I looked at the faces of the older soldiers around me. I read on them the same thing: 'Just wait till we get across.' The IRA didn't know what they'd let themselves in for. Many historians who write about Ulster talk of turning points. For me and everybody at the table, that was the major turning point. There would be no more 'disco tours'.

We arrived in Ulster in late May and were first posted to Magilligan Camp, just outside Londonderry. At first the tour seemed to be a carbon copy of the earlier one: discos and drinking. We were probably the last soldiers to be able to walk around the Bogside in uniform and unarmed. We would be relieving our 3rd Battalion in Belfast in a few weeks. They seemed to be having a torrid time: gun battles and disorder almost every night. We couldn't wait to take over. Then came some sobering news. A terrorist had walked into the Royal Ulster Constabulary station in Springfield Road and planted a bomb in a suitcase. The explosion killed a Para sergeant, Mick Willets, who used his body to shield some civilians. He was posthumously awarded the George Cross.

Two months later my Company was in Belfast, stationed in Sunnyside, just off the Ormeau Road. It was a different world, with bombs going off frequently. We had been in the capital only two weeks when we suffered our first fatality: a member of a patrol from C Company was shot to death in an ambush in Andersonstown. The next four weeks passed fairly quietly for us, but our B Company in Ballymurphy were having trouble with gun battles and sniping attacks.

Our location, on the upper Ormeau Road, which we shared with a TA unit, was a quiet backwater where regular Saturday-night discos were held and there I met a very attractive girl called Lorna. Women were still a mystery to me. I had few social graces and found it hard enough to hold a conversation with a man my own age, never mind a girl. Lorna did most of the talking. I sat absorbed by her eyes of deepest blue. At the end of the evening she invited me to her parents' home for dinner the following week. As the night approached I was both excited and nervous. I had a lift to the address and when I got there I received my first surprise. The house was built into the side of a hill overlooking the city and unlike anything I'd seen before. Lorna's mother, a gracious, softly spoken woman in her late thirties, greeted me. Daddy was something different. A big, ham-fisted giant of a man who'd dragged himself up from nothing to become one of the largest building contractors in Northern Ireland. His eyes never left me the whole time I was in his house.

The meal was a nightmare. So many knives and forks and spoons. In my house you were lucky if you got a spoon. There were eight of us at dinner, including Lorna's older sister and her boyfriend, who was an architect, and a middle-aged couple. Lorna's mother was a diamond. She whispered words of advice whenever my confusion became too great and directed the conversation to cover any mistakes I made.

As we said goodnight Lorna told me she was going on a week's holiday but asked me to ring her. When I did her mother answered. Lorna was still abroad, she explained. Her father had decided that before she went to university an extended tour of the continent was in order. I never saw her again.

One of the more unusual duties I had to perform was to guard a paratrooper in Musgrave Park hospital. Leon McKevitt, who had been all-Ireland middle-weight boxing champion before joining the Army, had an enormous expanse of shoulders, huge biceps and a neck any bull would have been proud of. He was in hospital recovering from a gunshot wound. It had happened while he'd been on leave at a party in Dublin. One of his relatives started to threaten what the IRA would do to the Parachute Regiment in Belfast. Leon had promptly dispatched the unfortunate man to the local hospital but he'd returned to the party in the small hours armed with a handgun and shot Leon. Our orders were not so much to stop the IRA getting at Leon as to stop Leon getting out to settle the score with his relative.

At the beginning of August the Battalion killed its first man outside Springfield Road RUC station. As a van was driving past a sentry heard two bangs; whether he was actually shot at or the van backfired is not clear. The guard commander, a sergeant, grabbed his rifle, ran into the street, knelt down and fired two rounds into the van, killing the driver, Harry Thornton, instantly. One member of the Battalion recovered part of the dead man's skull and used it as an ashtray. Rioting broke out in the immediate aftermath of the shooting.

Then, early on the morning of 9 August 1971, we were ordered from our beds and told to assemble. Our platoon commander, who had some unpronounceable Polish name, addressed us.

'The government has decided to bring in internment without trial. The first arrests begin in one hour. You will now be divided into squads for your own individual lifts.'

I was in the platoon commander's squad of four. We were to go into Andersonstown and arrest a man called Fox. We took off in a Landrover, driving slowly through the dark and deserted streets. At the house I was sent round to the back, while the officer and the other two members banged on the front door. I waited. The night was so still. I wondered what was taking so long. Some twenty minutes later a window in the house next door opened and a woman poked her head out.

'Were you with that lot who took away Mr Fox?'

I looked up, thankful to see some life in that dark place. 'Yes.'

'Well, they left five minutes ago.'

She shut the window with a resounding bang.

I walked round to the front of the house. The Landrover was gone. I was alone in one of the hardest Republican areas of Belfast, on what was to become one of the bloodiest days in the history of Northern Ireland. I didn't have a clue what to do or even which way to walk to safety. In my mind I tossed a coin and turned right, the way the Landrover had come into the estate. I made my way slowly through the darkened streets, the sound of my footsteps echoing off the walls of the houses I passed. A man in his early twenties, dressed in denims, and with long, dank hair over a hatchet face, appeared in an alleyway ahead of me. He gave me an evil smile.

'On our own are we, Para?'

'Not really,' I cocked my rifle. 'I've got this for company.'

He eyed me up and down for several seconds then stepped back into the darkness of the alley. I walked on, spinning round every two or three steps to see if I was being followed. Eventually I came to a hill and saw a ring of three-ton army trucks below me. Landrovers buzzed in and out of the ring like angry bees. I ran the last hundred yards faster than I'd ever run before and arrived inside the protective ring, my chest heaving. I spotted my platoon commander talking to the Company OC. I marched straight up to him, slammed myself to attention and said: 'Thanks for telling me you were leaving, sir.'

Then I did a smart right turn and walked away. I was explaining what had happened to the rest of my section when he came across to me. He didn't apologize, but gave me a telling off for embarrassing him in front of the OC. We returned to Battalion HQ for breakfast.

We didn't have long to wait for the local Catholic population to react. Barricades sprang up everywhere, and petrol bombing and sniping broke out all over the place. We'd hardly finished our meals before we were dispatched to our first riot, in Ballymacarret in south Belfast. The local unit had been pressed for over an hour when my platoon debussed and charged. We hit the rioters hard. They'd never been up against paratroopers before and we scattered them like confetti, leaving a mass of smashed bodies behind us. Chris H, who despite his smallness had earned the nickname Fearless, had led the attack, firing rubber bullets as fast as he could. It was some sight. By the time we left Ballymacarret there were no more rioters to deal with.

There was hardly time to catch our breaths before we were back in action, this time on the Falls Road in west Belfast. For the rest of the day we fought up and down the street under a continual rain of petrol bombs, twenty men against over three hundred rioters. By mid-afternoon we were exhausted and starting to take casualties from the incessant petrol bombing. The platoon commander was running up and down frantically telling us not to open fire. Beside me on the barricade was Chris H, a lance-corporal from the Signals Platoon, and Matt T, a nasty little Scots soldier. Matt threw a withering look at the departing officer's back.

'I thought we could shoot petrol bombers?' His voice was filled with disgust.

'Aw, shoot the next one that comes around the corner,' the Signals lance-corporal said almost conversationally.

That was good enough for Matt. Most probably the words were little more than bravado, but he took them literally. Lifting his SLR, he began to wait. He didn't have to wait long. A youth of about seventeen appeared, petrol bomb in hand. He launched it at our position and disappeared back around the corner so fast Matt couldn't get a bead on him. Almost immediately another rounded the corner, a little more daring than the first, and raced a good distance towards us before throwing his bomb.

Across a distance of less than thirty yards their eyes met and something in Matt's face must have convinced him that he was about to open fire. The youth spun round, as if in slow motion, and started to run back towards the safety of the corner. Then Matt fired, hitting him in the base of the spine. It was as if the lower half of his body was suddenly ripped away, throwing him into the air. He landed on his back, then slowly began to roll over and over, his mouth open in a noiseless scream. A slow smile crept over Matt's face.

'Got him,' he said softly.

Everything began to speed up as several youths ran out and dragged the injured man away. The petrol bombing stopped as if by magic. There were cries of outrage from the crowd. I jumped up on the barricade and held my rifle above my head. The howls got louder, sounding more animal than human.

'Get down.'

The platoon commander appeared, his face white with anger.

'Who opened fire?'

'I did,' Matt replied.

'Who gave you the order to open fire?'

A bright smile spread over Matt's face, he pointed to the lance-corporal.

'He did.'

Both were ushered away to the nearest RUC station to give a statement.

The riot on the Falls Road petered out after that. The Company had a sweep of some two hundred pounds in the pot for the first confirmed kill. Matt rang the hospital constantly to find out if the man he'd shot had died so that he could claim it. Unfortunately for Matt's bank balance, the petrol bomber survived, although he was crippled for life.

We were pulled back to Springfield Road RUC station for some much-needed rest and food but we were in action later that night in the area surrounding the police station. It was a terrifying experience. Mobs of over a hundred rioters prowled the narrow streets with their back-to-back terraced houses. We took a terrible hammering. Steel bars sharpened at one end like spears rained down on us in the darkness. If I'd been carrying a rifle instead of a baton and shield, I would almost certainly have opened fire. How none of us was killed amazed me. The only way we could contain the frenzied mob was to fire tear-gas. This was again done without the consent of the officers. Even as we were being pelted with every kind of missile imaginable, two officers stood in the middle of the street demanding to know who had fired the gas.

Back in the Springfield Road we collapsed, close to exhaustion. We had been in almost constant action for nearly twenty-four hours. I fell into a troubled sleep, only to be woken two hours later. Our B Company in Ballymurphy was nearly out of ammunition and I was to help escort a resupply. We set off in force through the now empty streets, littered with barricades and burnt-out cars. Occasionally as we passed a side-street the rattle of a dustbin lid on the pavement warned of our passing. The sound of firing was everywhere. Perhaps some was directed at us but in the dimly lit streets it was difficult to tell. Eventually we arrived at Henry Taggart Memorial Hall, B Company's base. They were on a high, and as soon as I walked in I understood why.

Six bodies lay sprawled at the bottom of a raised stage. One of them was a woman, hit at least three times. On every reunion I've attended the number of bodies in the hall has climbed. The last time I heard the story it had risen to twenty-two. B Company personnel had survived at least two determined attempts by armed civilians to overrun their camp and had shot the hell out of them. In all, B Company, and Support Company, who gave the close fire from the nearby Springmartin Estate, killed eleven people in Ballymurphy over the bloody three days that marked the start of internment, among them a Catholic priest.

The IRA claimed that they had lost only two men in the whole Province. Locals claimed that all those killed were innocent people shot down in cold blood. I talked to many of the men involved both at the time and very soon afterwards. They said unequivocally that they shot only at armed people. The woman killed was said to be manning a Bren gun. I have to believe what they say. It is my firm conviction that in the immediate aftermath of the introduction of internment, many locals simply grabbed guns supplied by the IRA to have a go at the British Army. It was merely convenient for the IRA that most of them had not been sworn in as members.

The man who shot the Catholic priest told me that he only shot him after he picked up a weapon from beside a wounded gunman. This was confirmed to me by at least two other people who had seen the shooting. One told me that the priest had made no effort to actually go to the wounded man but had searched for the weapon and was only killed when he tried to retrieve it. In such circumstances fact and fiction always get mixed up with the passing years, so that now, twenty-three years later, the truth is impossible to distil. But that night I was in no doubt at all: we had given the armed forces of Republicanism, whether the IRA claimed them or not, a very bloody nose.

For the next two weeks we helped patrol the hard-line Catholic areas of the Falls, Springfield Road and Ballymurphy. Although the violence had died down the hatred on the streets could be almost touched, it was so intense. All of it was directed at us from the Catholic side. The women used to build themselves up into an almost hysterical frenzy, screaming their abuse. I had been brought up a Catholic, although to be perfectly honest I had always been more than slightly sceptical – I never saw a hungry priest in Glasgow.

We had occasional riots, but nothing as bad as the days ushering in internment. In one 'riot' in Ballymurphy we were faced with a mob of mostly middle-aged women. Our driver, who had the wonderful name of Boris Budle, was eager to get stuck into them. From the back of the crowd a voice piped up: 'I see him. There's the one that stole my daughter!'

Boris jumped up on to the bonnet of the Landrover, then his face blanched.

'Oh fuck, it's the mother-in-law.'

He retreated to the safety of the base.

We spent an increasing amount of time on guard duties in the sangars, sandbagged army observation posts. Many times during the long periods of guard duty, I would relieve the boredom by singing. My voice has the soothing tones of a buzz saw carving metal, and my impromptu solos prompted the locals to deliver a note to the base OC.

'Please stop the singing sentry,' it pleaded.

We left Ulster in the final days of September. The tour had, as far as we were concerned, been a success. We had over fifteen confirmed kills but had claimed many more. There was one final twist. We shared the overnight ferry home with civilians. As the bar was closing most of us were drunk and one of the civilians, a Catholic, was shouting abuse at some B Company men, calling them murdering scum. Officers and NCOs tried to get him to restrain himself but to no avail. Finally they left, unwilling to be present when the trouble started. He was still shouting when I left the bar. Legend has it that somebody, although nobody knows who, threw him overboard sometime in the night. Whether it actually happened I can't say certainly, but given the attitude of the 2nd Battalion at the time, I wouldn't have been at all surprised.

We had less than five months before we were due back in Ulster: time for a spot of leave, a couple of exercises and some training before we would be, once again, back in Belfast. I started to slip into the Para culture, helped considerably by Fearless. He was an unusual man and could have been an officer but at the time I met him he was completely anti-authoritarian. He'd been a soldier since he was fifteen. At eighteen, he'd been the youngest junior NCO in the Parachute Brigade but he'd reverted to the rank of private because he didn't want the responsibility.

On leave our average day off started with a late breakfast, a walk down to the pub, which opened at 11 o'clock, and drinking until afternoon closing. Then we would, if it was a good day, take a bottle of wine into the park. Our conversations would range over topics I'd never thought of before, that is when we were not trying to get any available girl into bed. We'd grab a quick meal at 4.30 and be back in the pub an hour later. By 7 o'clock we were well gone and usually rolling around in a fight of one kind or another. Fights were frequent as there were twenty thousand or so soldiers in and around Aldershot. There were very few women, or at least very few who would dare go into one of our pubs. It didn't take much to get trouble started; the pubs, take-aways and taxi ranks were slaughterhouses. Most Sunday mornings you woke up with your face stuck to the pillow with your own or somebody else's blood.

A typical outbreak of mayhem happened in the Bake-and-Take restaurant one Saturday night. Fearless had a long-standing feud with a member of 3 Para. He'd spotted his enemy at the other end of the counter and launched a pre-emptive assault. I turned to see two members of the opposing battalion struggling with my little friend. Dropping my take-away, I rushed to his aid and threw a punch at the larger of the two men. My fist hit the side of his head with a satisfying thud, his head spun round with the force, then with the deliberation of a Sherman tank taking a bead he turned slowly towards me. It was Leon McKevitt!

Letting go of Fearless, whom he'd been trying to restrain, he threw a punch at my head which missed by a fraction of an inch and sounded like a meat cleaver carving the air. Fortunately for me, two members of 9 Squadron (Para Engineers) pulled me back. Fearless wasn't so lucky. Leon's next punch hit him squarely, breaking his nose in two places. A mobile patrol of Royal Military Police was spotted at the bottom of the road and we all scattered.

For several days I was aware that Leon was making enquiries about the young lad who'd hit him. Having discovered my name, he circulated the word that the next time he saw me would be my last. A feeling of impending doom descended on me when I spied Leon's rolling gait as he came towards me. He spotted me immediately. Deciding the only option I had was to face up to the monster, I held two hands in front of me to forestall any immediate attack, and said: 'Listen. I know I was wrong and I'm sorry.'

Leon's eyes had narrowed. I felt that he was measuring the shortest distance between my chin and his fist.

'I looked round and saw two men on to my friend,' I said.

'I was trying to break the fight up.'

'I know that now. But at the time it looked like two on to one. What would you have done?'

Leon's head tilted to one side as he considered his response. A slow smile spread over his face. 'Ach, to be sure. I'd probably have done the same thing.' He threw an arm around my neck. 'Forget it. That's a good right hand you have there. You should take up boxing.' With those kind words of advice he guided me towards the nearest pub for a pint.

Before I knew it I was back in Belfast, this time in the nasty Republican area of the New Lodge. We were based in Girdwood Army Camp, where my whole platoon was crammed into a single, one-storey aluminium hut of about ten feet by sixty. Thank God the IRA didn't have mortars in those days. From the very beginning it was a hard tour. Sixteen- to eighteen-hour days were the norm, and sleep was a precious commodity in days and nights that merged together. Most of us didn't know what day of the week it was most of the time. Only three weeks into the tour I was so tired I felt that I could sleep standing up. When I got back to camp one evening I staggered towards the toilets and showers and in the semi-darkness bumped into a figure smelling of shampoo and scented soap.

'Who's that?'

I recognized the Company Sergeant-Major's voice.

'McCallion, sir.'

'What's wrong, McCallion?'

'I'm dog-tired, sir.'

'Well, McCallion, it's tough at the top.'

'It's tough where I am as well, sir.'

For me the tour was a nightmare. One emotion still dominates my recollection of the time – fear. Not of the IRA or patrolling the streets; quite the opposite, it was a relief to get out. The fear was generated by the platoon I was serving with, the Mortar Platoon of Support Company. Among them were some of the worst bullies I'd ever served with in my entire army career. They made my life hell for four months. None of them will ever really know how close they came to driving me too far, and the dark, violent thoughts with which I rocked myself to sleep. The worst of them was a tall, good-looking man with a sarcastic sense of humour. He was a natural leader, a man who was respected, someone who would go far. He was all the worse because he was intelligent enough to know that what he was doing was wrong. In the years that were to follow, every time I felt like giving up I would remember his grinning face and from deep within me find the strength to continue.

The tour was marked by three major events for me. The first happened almost by accident. I was in the rear vehicle of a two-vehicle patrol. We patrolled in stripped-down Landrovers as it enabled us to return fire and dismount quickly, a technique the regiment had perfected in Aden. A car containing two men swerved between our vehicles. The driver looked nervous. I told the vehicle commander to stop the two men at the junction of Lepper Street and New Lodge Road, and pulled them over. The passenger was an enormous brute of a man who had a seaman's identity card on him. While it was being checked, I searched him. Nothing. In his pocket was a packet of cigarettes and almost as an afterthought I looked inside. There was a hand-written note on thin paper which read, 'Remember how you got the hacksaw blades into us last time. Well this time we want you to hollow out the centre of a packet of cream crackers and insert . . .'

I didn't bother reading any more. It was obviously instructions to smuggle equipment to terrorists in the nearby Crumlin Road Prison. We arrested and separated the two men before taking them to Battalion HQ at nearby Glenravelle Street. I accompanied the prisoner, sitting behind him in the back seat of his car with a sub-machine-gun. Another patrol member sat beside him in the front passenger sea. We told him to drive slowly behind the front Landrover. As we were approaching the base he jammed the brakes on and attempted to get out of the car. I reached forward as he was half out of the door and grabbed the back of his jacket collar, pulling with all my might. He slammed back into the car. The sub-machine-gun I was holding smashed into the back of his head, opening up a large gash. He threw a punch at the man sitting next to him, missing by inches. I cocked my weapon, and he froze like a startled rabbit.

'One more move and I'll put a round into you,' I said.

His hands came up in surrender.

'Why did you try to escape?' I asked.

'You've got to try, haven't you?' he replied.

We continued the rest of the short journey without interruption. I handed him over to the desk sergeant. He was again asked why he had tried to escape. He pointed at me.

'Because he was hitting me!'

I was shocked at the blatant falsehood.

'You bloody liar.'

Before the conversation could go further our sergeant came into the room, took one look at our prisoner and shouted, 'Don't let that man go,' before running back up the stairs as fast as he could. He was back in minutes, a wanted poster in his hand.

'Yes, it's him all right,' he said.

Our man was an officer in the Provos wanted for a double murder. He had lured two RUC detectives to a shop and machine-gunned them to death. He was sentenced to life imprisonment, with a recommendation that he serve at least thirty years.

Day to day on the ground we had the local IRA Active Service Units terrorized. We knew who they were and we threatened to shoot them on sight. One patrol murdered an IRA man's dog and shoved its back legs through his letter box and a note in its mouth threatening that he was next. Many of the top gunmen in the area moved out, fearing that they would get similar treatment. Two soldiers, including a major, had been killed in the New Lodge just before we'd arrived and we were determined that would not happen to us.

The second big event of the tour was a gun battle with Protestant paramilitaries in the Shankill Road area. Every battalion has its penal platoon, where all the unit's malcontents eventually washed up. In 2 Para it was the Machine Gun Platoon. It had some good soldiers, but they were in the minority. Midway through the tour I was on patrol with the RUC's mobile response unit when we were directed to the Woodvale Road, just off the Shankill Road, where the newly formed UDA had put up roadblocks. No sooner had we arrived than it was decided to call out the Brigade Reserve. This just happened to be the Machine Gun Platoon of 2 Para.

The UDA had erected their barricades in response to the Army's reluctance to dismantle the IRA barricades in the Bogside in Londonderry. This area, known to the locals as Free Derry, was no-go to British troops as armed IRA gangs patrolled it openly. The Protestant extremists were threatening to seal off the Woodvale area until the Army removed the Bogside barricades. It was mostly bravado. Their barricades were made from civilian cars, borrowed from their owners with the promise that they would be returned undamaged. Almost as soon as the Machine Gun Platoon arrived, the platoon commander and the platoon sergeant disappeared to consult with the local UDA commander and the platoon was left in charge of a junior NCO.

I was talking when a single shot rang out.

'Gunman!' shouted the man who'd opened fire.

A man in a combat jacket lay sprawled on the pavement at the bottom of the street and almost immediately he was surrounded by other semi-uniformed men.

'They've got guns!' another voice shouted.

The junior NCO started to give a fire-control order at the gunmen below him but was interrupted midway by the platoon commander, who had rushed back. Had he not, I have no doubt that many more people would have died that night. A brief consultation took place, then we were ordered to advance. It was more of a ragged charge, men screaming as they plunged down the darkened street. It was exhilarating, running headlong towards an enemy, not knowing what you would find or when they would open fire. From behind us came the sound of another high-velocity shot. Some halted to find out what had happened, the rest of us continued. The smallest member of the platoon had been attacked and knocked to the floor as he ran past an alley. He'd shot his assailant in the shoulder.

We arrived at the end of the street. The crowd had scattered. On the pavement a man lay, blood gushing from a hideous wound in his neck. He was trying to breathe but bright-red, frothy blood kept spraying from his mouth.

We came under fire. Bullets ricocheted off the walls around us.

'There, on the roof. There, on the roof.'

I saw a gun flash and fired. Then all hell broke loose. The entire platoon began to fire and manoeuvre down the street. It was awesome to behold. Whatever gunmen were there disappeared like snow in the summer sun. I was called back to rejoin the RUC patrol, who had remained at the top of the street. They were none too happy about the night's events and it showed. As we drove away the Machine Gun Platoon were ramming their APCs into the barricades to dismantle them. Behind me one UDA man lay dead, another badly injured. We claimed three other hits but they were never confirmed.

The tour continued. After one major arms find, the IRA mounted a series of shootings and bombings against us but only succeeded in wounding one of our corporals and two small children in crossfire. We were told that 3 Battalion PIRA were going to launch a major attack on us during the last few weeks of our tour. We struck first. Our Battalion intelligence sergeant, who was decorated for his work in the New Lodge, led a devastating series of raids. We netted most of the IRA's most wanted and experienced men, cutting the head off the organization. With three days to go, hardened IRA men from the nearby Ardoyne were drafted into our area. The scene was set for a showdown, and the third highlight of my tour.

As night fell we moved into the New Lodge in force. It was blacker than a witch's heart and as still as the grave. All the street-lights had been put out, and not even the dogs were barking. I moved down the pavement, edging from door to door, feeling rather than seeing my way. My breathing was hoarse and my heart beat so loudly it must have been heard two streets away. Around me in the darkness nearly forty paratroopers were converging on the five blocks of flats that dominated the area. I was nearly at the junction of Lepper Street, the exact place where the first British soldiers were killed in Ulster, when the first gunman opened up.

Five high-velocity rounds cracked from the roof of the building ahead; the terrible coughing roar of a Garand rifle. One of them smashed into the wall beside me and sprayed brick dust over my head. I fired back. The Paras returned fire, then others opened up above us, one with a long burst. My eyes strained to locate the gunman. From the top of Artillery Flats a second burst of automatic fire echoed off the narrow walls. I saw this one. As I returned fire the whole area seemed to disintegrate. At least thirty men concentrated their fire on the gunman; nothing could have survived. Once we had fought our way into the flats, we found a discarded Garand rifle, two pistols and blood everywhere.

'Don't mess with the best, because the best don't mess,' as one member of the Company put it. It was later established that we'd killed one and wounded two that night. The area subsided into a sullen quiet.

The advance party from our relieving unit, the Royal Marine Commandos, had arrived. I escorted one of their patrols around the area. One quiet, tall marine surveyed the high points in the New Lodge with the eyes of a hawk. He was the unit's top sniper and would kill six gunmen in four months to win the Military Medal. I came to know and respect him as a member of B Squadron 22 SAS.

It was during this tour, when I was just nineteen, that I decided to marry. Shortly after my date with Lorna I'd met Pat. The IRA had blitzed the centre of Belfast and people gathered to see the damage. I was on guard duty and had asked one of the middle-aged women in the crowd if there were any good-looking girls she could introduce me to. Her neighbour's daughter was a nurse, she told me, and surprisingly the following day she brought Pat to the camp to meet me. Our relationship had developed from there and continued into my next tour. I'd continually asked her to write to me. Close to the end of the tour a lengthy letter arrived telling me she was pregnant – not by me, but by a black medical trainee. Pat was a woman in trouble, and my sense of honour prompted me to offer her the protection of my name.

During this time I made the mistake of asking for advice from another member of the mortar platoon and within hours the gossip was all over the camp. That night on guard duty I received a new piece of graffiti in the sangar: 'Harry McCallion's bird lets niggers shag her and has little black babies.'

It explained the mentality of some of the men I worked with. Most of the time I could hardly bring myself to talk to some of them and after that tour killing became very easy for me. I only had to imagine one of their faces, then pull the trigger.

We returned to Aldershot and took over a Brigade spearhead battalion, ready to go anywhere in the world where trouble sprang up, even the centre of nearby Camberley. Two members of B Company were badly beaten up by a gang of bikers and their injuries were severe enough to require a stay in hospital. The Regimental Sergeant-Major called the Company, minus officers, on parade at the end of the day's training. RSM Reg Melody was ideally suited to his role in the Parachute Battalion. He was a powerfully built man with a granite jaw and a flattened nose that somehow added to, rather than subtracted from, his rugged good looks. He was a Para's Para, hard as nails and as straight as a die. His door was always open and he cared for us as if we were his own family. Even though he scared the living daylights out of most of us, we worshipped Reg. After the incident in Camberley, he addressed B Company: 'Gentlemen, it has come to my attention that two members of your Company have been hospitalized by a gang of motor-cycle thugs. In my day, such a thing would not be tolerated. Now, far be it for me to suggest any act of vengeance, but there are two three-ton trucks parked at the end of the yard. Their drivers have been told to go to town. Anybody who wishes to join them is free to take a ride.'

With that he departed. Every available member of B Company got on to the trucks. The bikers never bothered another Para, or anybody else for that matter, again.

Three days later the whole Battalion was called on to parade. A situation had developed in Ulster that required the deployment of the spearhead battalion to be used in a major offensive called Operation Motorman. Every major IRA stronghold would be saturated, including the 'no-go' areas in Londonderry. My Company was going into Ballymurphy.

Two days later we were back in Belfast. We'd only been away from Ulster for six weeks. On the night the operation was launched, we set off in convoy, heading for the west of the city. Somehow we got lost. From nowhere a Landrover appeared and uniformed men directed us through the Protestant Springmartin Estate to Ballymurphy. I thought they must have been a local army unit but as I drove past I realized some of them were masked and wore armbands with UDA emblazoned on them. We drove into Henry Taggart Memorial Hall in Ballymurphy, the scene of B Company's battle during the internment riots. The unit we were relieving, The King's Regiment, were a shambles. Having lost five men killed in Ballymurphy in less than two months, they looked shell-shocked and demoralized. I could hardly believe we were part of the same army.

Within two hours of taking over the area we'd located a major arms dump containing nearly a dozen weapons situated thirty yards from the base within sight of an observation post. We saturated the streets, leaving the locals in no doubt that there had been a change. I was out for nearly six hours without a break and when we were called back in, my platoon sergeant told me to take over as sentry for twenty minutes in the back sangar, just until things were sorted out and he could get somebody to relieve me.

The post had been unmanned since our arrival. I walked up the wooden steps into the sandbagged observation sangar and as I opened the door a smell hit me, almost causing me to vomit. Shell dressings stained with dried blood lay scattered about the floor. What looked like human brain was spattered against one wall. It was a hell of a welcome back.

The Battalion had been *in situ* barely two weeks when eighteen-year-old Private Bell was killed by a single-shot sniper in Ballymurphy. It was his first patrol, and the round that killed him passed over the heads of my own patrol as we were leaving Henry Taggart Memorial Hall. The loss of such a young soldier was a savage blow so early in the tour.

On one patrol I became suspicious of a man standing watching us from an open doorway and the sergeant in charge decided on an immediate search. We detained him and rushed into the house. Upstairs we found a stripped-down Garand rifle and ammunition. It turned out to be the man's first mission for the Provos. His brother had been killed by us during internment and he was looking for revenge.

B Company in Ballymurphy were having trouble because they'd taken over a school as a base and some of the local women wanted it back. A hundred or so mainly middle-aged women decided on an impromptu protest outside the base. The OC, a very small man, stood behind a long line of his troops dressed in full riot gear, urging them not to overreact. A single stone was thrown high into the air and everybody watched as, with agonizing slowness, it descended. The OC was still calling for restraint when it hit him smack on his head. He shouted something, exactly what is uncertain, but it sounded like 'Get them.' The crowd was dispersed in minutes.

Our sister battalion, 1 Para, were having trouble on the Shankill Road. It came to a head one bloody night of rioting in which they shot four UDA men. I was a member of the patrol sent up as reinforcements. Almost as we entered the Company base, in Tennant Street, a UVF gunman opened fire at a sandbagged observation post on top of the squat, two-storey, red-brick building. The sentry fired back, hitting the man in the chest, and an Armalite rifle was recovered. There were no more shooting incidents that night. I little realized that in the future this RUC station would play an important role in my life.

The Motorman Tour lasted only two and a half months and even people like me, who enjoyed Ulster, were tired of the place. I was looking forward to some well-earned leave. My new wife had spent only a few weeks with me, and I needed some time to find accommodation. But before I'd even dropped my bags my wife handed me a letter telling me I was required back in Ulster for the trial of the IRA man I'd arrested. I had less than twenty-four hours' leave.

The trial was in the old style, with a jury of twelve good men and true. Later Diplock Courts would be introduced, with one judge hearing all the evidence because of the difficulties posed by intimidation. The IRA man who had returned seeking to avenge his brother's death refused to recognize the court, so the judge conducted his defence for him, giving him every possible advantage. Throughout the trial the terrorist lounged in the dock, yawning and feigning indifference. He faced three charges: possession of a Garand rifle, possession of an Armalite rifle (whose location he'd given during RUC interrogation) and membership of the IRA. We expected him to get four years maximum.

When it came to sentencing the defendant, the judge, almost painfully, reminded him that we lived in troubled times, saying: 'Sentences must then reflect those times. On the first charge, possession of a Garand rifle, I sentence you to six years' imprisonment.'

The IRA man's shoulders slumped.

'On the second charge, possession of an Armalite rifle, I sentence you to a second term of six years, to run consecutively.'

The defendant's knees went and two prison guards supported him.

'On the third charge, membership of the IRA, I sentence you to another five years.'

There was a low groan from the dock.

The judge looked up and continued: 'But this will run concurrently. You will therefore serve a total of twelve years in prison. Do you understand?'

The IRA man nodded dumbly. As he was half carried, half dragged towards the cells, he suddenly found his voice, shouting: 'Up the Prov.' The doors leading to the cells cut off his words. Behind me the RUC officer in charge of the case leaned forward and said: 'That's his IRA career over before it's begun.'

I was just thankful that I could get back to Aldershot for some leave. While I was waiting for a lift back to the army base and then to the airport, I met, very briefly, the Reverend Ian Paisley. He was a huge man, and unlike his public image, very quietly spoken and polite.

After leave we returned again to the steady routine of Battalion life. We were due to go to Malaya in five weeks but before that Aldershot was rocked by news of a brutal abduction. On a warm summer's afternoon a dark car screeched to a halt outside the Kentucky Fried Chicken take-away restaurant in the High Street and a cardboard cut-out of the chain's founder, Colonel Sanders, was seized. But before the car roared off, tyres screeching in true gangster style, a note was thrown on to the doorstep of the eating house. It read: 'We have kidnapped Colonel Sanders. We demand four large Kentucky Fried Chicken suppers, with Cokes, for his return. Place the dinners in the park opposite at 3pm or the Colonel gets it.'

In response to the kidnappers' demands the store put the following note in its window:

> We will not submit to extortion.
> Return the Colonel at once.
> The police have been informed.

Aldershot's population held its breath. They didn't have long to wait. The next morning an envelope was received containing the Colonel's severed ear and a note which read: 'We're not bluffing. This is your last warning. Pay up or else.'

The Aldershot Police spokesman talked, grim-faced, to the local paper: 'We are obviously dealing with some very dangerous people. Anybody who would sever the ear of a helpless cardboard dummy is capable of anything. Our enquiries are focusing on Montgomery Lines and in particular 2 Battalion of the Parachute Regiment.'

Indeed they were. A full-scale search of the barracks was initiated at the weekend, when, it was supposed, the kidnappers would be off guard. Several ladies were discovered sleeping within the Battalion's lines and escorted out, but no Colonel Sanders. The heat was on. The kidnappers could at any moment be discovered and face the full wrath of civilian and army law. They reacted with a ruthlessness that would shock the whole of Aldershot. On a dark Sunday night a package was thrown through the doorway of the take-away but not discovered until Monday morning. The horrified sales staff uncovered the dismembered remains of the Colonel. Attached to it was a final note. It said simply: 'You were warned.'

Despite an extensive investigation by both the military and civilian police, the kidnappers were never discovered. They remain at large to this day, their identities shielded by the Parachute Regiment's code of silence, and my lips are sealed.

With 1972 drawing to a close we went overseas to Malaya for jungle warfare training. The days were hard, but we looked forward to the nights. Nobody could navigate in the jungle when the sun went down – that was until one officer decided to try. In a deluge of rain we were strung out for miles. To lose touch with the man in front of you for a second in the pitch-darkness meant you were lost. Screams cut through the night as men fell away from the path. I slipped in the mud and grabbed the nearest tree for support. Something bit or stung me. I jumped back with a yell of pain and surprise and bumped into the men behind me. In seconds we were a mass of arms and legs, tumbling down a slippery slope. Eventually everybody was told to stay exactly where they were and make the best of things until first light. It was a miserable night. We were unable to erect hammocks or even ponchos and sat under our individual groundsheets, wet, cold and miserable, tormented by every passing insect or leech that fancied a bite.

My arm started throbbing. When I saw it in the first rays of morning light I nearly collapsed with shock: it had swollen to nearly twice its normal size. I reported to the Company medic and was earmarked for immediate casevac. I was not alone. Our night-time walk had cost two broken arms, a broken leg and a badly sprained ankle. The entire Company had suffered terribly from insect bites and leech attacks. One poor bastard had twelve of the things on him. Never moving in the jungle at night was a lesson the SAS had learnt years ago, and one I would not soon forget.

Back at base camp I had my arm inspected by two doctors. I was curious about what had bitten me.

'Possibly a centipede. Vicious little monsters, centipedes,' I was told.

'Could have been a scorpion. They have similar venom.'

'You have several puncture marks which could have been the sting.'

'Might even have been a tree or plant. Some of them have pretty potent saps that can cause this type of reaction.'

My head was turning from one doctor to the other like a demented ventriloquist's dummy.

'That's possible, but it's definitely not a snake bite.'

'Yes, definitely not a snake bite. None of your puncture wounds remotely resembles a snake strike, and besides' – the speaker smiled down at me – 'had it been a snake you probably wouldn't have made it through the night.'

I was in hospital for nearly a week before my arm was back to normal but I was released just in time for our R&R.

We had a Battalion parade before we were launched on the unsuspecting citizens of Singapore. Our CO gave us a quick talk about what the Battalion was going to do the following year, including another tour in Ulster. He ended with some of the do's and don'ts he expected us to observe during our leave, then left the stage to the RSM. Reg asked the officers to fall out and called us closer to him.

'Now listen to me.' His gaze embraced all four hundred of us. 'In Singapore town at the present you have the American 6th Fleet.' He made a dismissive gesture with his right hand. 'No problem. You have the 2nd Battalion Irish Guards. No problem. You have 45 Commando.' He waved his hand slightly from side to side. 'Bit of a problem there, but not much. And you have elements of the Italian Army. Even less of a problem.' We burst into laughter. He waited for it to subside before continuing.

'The point I am making is this: the town is full of troops of all nationalities, not to mention some home-grown thugs. I want all of you to stay in pairs, pairs at least. Now, if any of you end up in hospital I will come to visit you and the first thing I will look at is the bed next to you. If your buddy isn't in it, then I'll find out who he is and personally make sure he joins you.'

When we hit the town it was full of Americans who made the mistake of confusing us with the Irish Guards, a mistake many of them didn't remain conscious long enough to appreciate.

There were other dangers: whores and catamites. The first thing most of the men did was hit the whore-houses. It was an education. The house in question, Tokyo by Night, was one of the best in the city. It was well run, and the girls were young and beautiful. All negotiations were done with the *mama-san*, a formidable old lady with an iron will and a quick brain. When my friends had departed she came to stand beside me at the bar.

'You no want girl?'

'No, *mama-san*,' I said respectfully, not wishing to offend her. She was a woman of advanced years, and her bouncers were two of the biggest Chinese I'd ever seen.

'Why you no want girl? You like boy?'

I was horrified and it showed. 'No. No. It's just that paying for it doesn't appeal to me, that's all.'

She nodded, smiling at my discomfort. 'You play chess?'

I said yes and a board was produced and we began to play. She was good, a bold attacking player, and was inside my Sicilian defence before I knew it. She won the first game easily. Beers kept coming as we played and she matched me drink for drink. I won the second game when she miscalculated a pawn sacrifice. We were well into the third when my friends returned. I asked them to wait, but it didn't take long for her to beat me again.

'What's your name?' she asked as I rose to leave.

'Harry McCallion.'

'We play again, Harry McCallion, next time you come. OK?'

'You're on, *mama-san*.'

I never learnt anything about women on that trip, but by hell my chess improved.

The catamites were absolutely gorgeous until about 3 a.m., when the stubble started to show. One of our number succumbed to their charms and regaled us all with tales of his night-time activities. He even wrote home to his wife that she need not worry about him straying as he was only 'going out with the boys'. I decided to die curious.

Back in Aldershot, we started build-up training for Ulster. This time we wouldn't be in Belfast but in the rolling hills of South Armagh. It was to be an eventful tour. The Battalion had a massive area to patrol. A Company (mine) were in Armagh and Portadown; B Company in South Armagh; and D Company in Newry. By far the hardest and most dangerous area, Crossmaglen and Newtonhamilton, was given to Support Company, assisted by Patrol Company (C Company).

Our briefing concerned the terrorist threat in Armagh and Portadown. Portadown was a mainly Protestant town with hard-line UVF and UDA murder gangs operating from it. There was a small Catholic enclave, around Obins Street, where a small but effective IRA unit operated. The area between Portadown and Armagh city was known as Murder Triangle. Sectarian killings were commonplace on the lonely country roads and one of our main tasks was to eliminate the gangs responsible or make it more difficult for them to carry out their nefarious activities.

Armagh was a completely different prospect, a mainly Catholic city with a strong and effective IRA unit which carried out frequent attacks against the security forces. Our main enemy in the city, unlike the rest of the Province, would be the Official IRA. The Officials had declared a ceasefire the year before but this didn't seem to cramp the style of their units in Armagh city. They had carried on killing and bombing with abandon, sometimes working in conjunction with the Provisionals.

The controlling influence behind these attacks were the Grew family, Seamus, Desi and Oliver, who had the support of other Republican families like the Grillys and Carrolls, many of whom were linked by marriage. Through this extended family they controlled most of the terrorist activity in the area. They were well armed and could command thirty or more gunmen. As the years passed the family would change allegiances often, from the Official IRA to the Provos and the INLA – anybody in fact that would allow them to continue with their murderous careers. Our second priority would be to attempt to capture Seamus Grew, who was wanted on serious terrorist charges, and disrupt his Official IRA murder gang.

My first impression of Portadown was very pleasant. Unlike most of the hard-line Republican areas I had served in, most of the people would at least talk to us, Obins Street excepted. Armagh was just the same as any Republican area: hostile – especially the Dramague Estate. In Armagh we were nominally under the operational control of 2 Fusiliers, who didn't much like us. We, in turn, thought little of them. It was a recipe for disaster.

Our initial weeks were to set the tone for the tour. B, D and Support Companies were shot at several times in the first week and their aggressive return of fire convinced their attackers they should resort to bombs. After that first week there were no more shooting attempts. In Portadown we were called out continually to deal with bombs and bomb hoaxes as the small IRA unit in the town mounted a major offensive. Theirs were crude but effective devices and the large number of hoaxes was meant to lull us into a false sense of security. It almost worked.

The second week of the tour opened with the worst possible news. A two-Landrover patrol from Support Company's Anti-Tank Platoon was blown up outside Newtonhamilton. Two members of the patrol were killed and a third badly injured, although he made a complete recovery. A parallel foot patrol caught a man running away from the scene. He was arrested and when he tried to escape, shot in the head. Amazingly he survived. The Para sergeant who shot him was tried for attempted murder and found not guilty. This all happened as we were mounting our first ambush in Armagh city.

Information had come in that there was a terrorist weapons hide in a field just outside the Dramague Estate. An eight-man party, under platoon sergeant Mick W, was to try to intercept the IRA as they picked up the weapons. We were dropped off and made our way to the ambush site, which was less than ideal. It was in a school playground, and a large wall topped with a wire fence blocked us off from the Dramague Estate. Only two or three men at the most could get on to the wall at any one time. We settled into the routine of watching, resting and guarding our rear. About two hours passed before we heard the sound of intense firing from our left flank, in the centre of the estate.

A Fusiliers' patrol had been ambushed and one man shot. The radioed information was going berserk, so it was hard to tell exactly what was going on. A member of our party, Sammy G, spotted movement to our left. Three men were on the wall, including Mick W, who had my rifle with its Trilux night-sight. I was at the base, listening to their whispered conversation. Three men dressed in uniform and wearing berets were walking across our front. Our men couldn't be sure that they were not a UDR patrol, or even from 2 Fusiliers. Certainly one of them was carrying a bolt-action .303 weapon but they were still issued to the Army at the time. The others too were carrying weapons, but in the darkness it was unclear what they were.

Mick told everybody to hold their fire. Suddenly the three men stopped but as one stepped forward, Mick recognized a Thomson sub-machine-gun in his hand just seconds before the terrorist laid it down. Mick fired. Almost immediately we heard screaming.

'I'm hit. I'm hit, my guts are hanging out.'

Bob and I tried to get to the wounded man but try as we might there was no way we could scale the wall. The screaming was still intense when our radio operator gave a contact report and requested that a Fusilier patrol respond. The reply was unequivocal: we were to withdraw immediately. And there was no way we could budge them. We withdrew to our pick-up point and were lifted back to Gough Barracks. In the debrief we had several surprises. The first was that Mick had hit two men with his single shot. One, James McGerrigan, was dead, and the second was badly injured. The next surprise was the attitude of the Fusiliers. Unit rivalry apart, it seemed to us that they believed we had shot innocent people. It put a damper on our celebrations but unknown to us the Fusiliers inserted a covert OP (observation post) after our ambush and the next day the IRA tried to move weapons close to where we'd shot McGerrigan. The OP opened fire, killing Tony Hughes, Official IRA quartermaster for the area, and wounding several other men. Two cars full of weapons were recovered. In twenty-four hours we'd dealt the Official IRA in Armagh a hammer blow. Two of their men were dead and at least four wounded. In addition we had captured most of their front-line weapons. They wouldn't bother us for the rest of the tour. Lest the Officials in the area get confused about who killed McGerrigan, we drove into the area the next week and pinned a beret to the site with a note telling them, and inviting them to have a crack at us. They didn't take up the offer.

The military police were now investigating McGerrigan's death.

To say that they gave everybody on the ambush a hard time is an understatement. They seemed convinced that we'd committed some kind of skulduggery. Even when McGerrigan was given a full IRA funeral and the .303 Lee Enfield he was carrying was discovered, they were still trying to pick flaws in our statements. Our action was only vindicated after the tour. John Nixon, the second man Mick had shot, was convicted of weapons offences and sentenced to eight years in jail. Mick W never received any recognition for his ambush, despite the fact that it led to the almost total destruction of an IRA Active Service Unit.

While we were enjoying success in Armagh, Support Company were suffering in Crossmaglen. Landrover patrols were abandoned after the two deaths outside Newtonhamilton and the Company tried to dominate the area with foot patrols. In late May a report was received that four armed men were digging beside the road just outside Crossmaglen. A patrol from C Company was asked to investigate. After landing from a helicopter they made their way across country to the vicinity of the digging. The sergeant-major told the patrol's second in command to wait and went closer to investigate. He was standing directly over the disturbed earth when the terrorists detonated the mine, killing him instantly.

The second in command called in the contact report and more troops were rushed into the area. Even as the ambush site was being secured, a mobile patrol from the 17/21st Lancers arrived in armoured cars. What happened next is unclear but it seems that two of the cavalrymen found a command wire and followed it. There was a second explosion and both were killed. The terrorists had withdrawn only a few hundred yards and waited for the follow-up operation before detonating the second, larger explosion. In future all such sites would be approached with care and troops dispersed to cut-off positions – to stop the enemy escaping the killing zone – before any clearance operation. It was a bitter and difficult lesson to learn and it cost two young lives, but learn it we did.

In Portadown, at the beginning of June, A Company's Lance-Corporal Ian B was called to a suspect device in a café. By now the huge number of hoax calls was nearly driving us to distraction; they meant long hours spent standing on street corners waiting for bomb disposal, only to find that the device was nothing more than rolled newspaper with wires attached. On this occasion B asked for bomb disposal and was told they would be with him in an hour. This became two hours, then four. B decided to take matters into his own hands. He walked into the shop, opened the bag left on the shop counter and saw a mass of wires. He asked his driver for some pliers. As none could be found he brought out his clasp knife and began to saw through the wires. Halfway through his task he saw the dynamite attached to them, then an alarm clock. He continued cutting, finally severing the wires linking the dynamite to the alarm clock. As he was removing it from the bag, the alarm went off. B said he nearly had a heart attack! His life had been spared by a fraction of a second.

Bomb Disposal were horrified. B had us all in stitches with his description of the look of total disbelief on the team leader's face when B described how he sawed through the wires. The Company OC gave his junior NCO a good telling-off. The local RUC station gave him a plaque for bravery. B wouldn't always be so lucky. He was sergeant in charge of an ambush party in South Armagh in 1980 that ambushed and killed two of their own men. B went absent without leave some time later, was busted to private and eventually left the Army.

Shortly after his foray into the realms of bomb disposal, my patrol had a head-on confrontation with the UDA in Portadown. Following our arrest of several of its members a band of nearly fifty, wearing a mixture of combat clothing, their faces concealed, surrounded our two Landrovers. One hooded man told us to lay down our guns. Despite the tenseness of the situation most of us burst out laughing at the thought. As they edged towards us I cocked my rifle, an example followed by the rest of the patrol. The hooded man shouted from the safety of the crowd: 'Don't worry, they won't fire.'

'If you believe him, you're even more stupid than you look,' I replied. 'Who wants to be the first to try?'

Behind me, one braver than the rest rushed forward. Billy C, a nasty little Jock Para, felled him with a well-timed butt stroke. The crowd was trying to build themselves up for a mass rush and what would have happened was anybody's guess. But before they could do so two more of our Landrovers appeared, loaded with Paras. The UDA mob scattered and we removed our prisoners to the RUC station. This was our last confrontation with Protestant paramilitaries in the area.

The tour ground on. We had our little victories, arrests and weapons finds, but towards the end the Battalion suffered its fourth and last fatality. Ian Wallis, a sergeant in Patrol Company, was blown up and killed outside Crossmaglen. He was an outstanding soldier, well liked and respected by everyone. His loss was keenly felt by us all.

I was one of the escorts for the incoming CO of our relieving unit, 2 Battalion Scots Guards, in Portadown. He told the senior RUC officer that he intended to carry on where we had left off. The RUC man's reply is as fitting an epitaph for our tour as any: 'You'll have to be big men to fill these men's shoes.'

The loss of so many fine men in South Armagh depressed me greatly. I was building up a terrible hatred inside me for the IRA and its supporters in the Catholic community. Priests in the areas I had served in had been in cahoots with the terrorists. I decided I could no longer associate with the Catholic Church and changed to the Church of Scotland. Eventually I would come to the conclusion that all organized religions were as bad as each other, but the very word 'Catholic' in those days was enough to put my teeth on edge.

Shortly after I returned from leave I was seconded to special duties, the formation of what was to become 14 Intelligence Company. When it had first entered the Province the Army never envisaged that the campaigning would be a long-drawn-out affair. When it became so, military chiefs decided they needed their own eyes and ears on the ground, which led to the formation of the Military Reaction Force (MRF). The unit was formed by volunteers from each battalion that served in the Province, who were asked to supply four men. From these recruits a hard core of regulars would remain to train and supervise the next batch. It was an unmitigated disaster.

The MRF was ill-conceived, badly trained and had little, if any, proper control over their operations. It turned into nothing more than a murder gang. I know of at least one shooting in Andersonstown – a fifteen-year-old boy was shot dead from a passing car – which was the work of the MRF. The operator claimed that the youth was carrying an M1 Carbine. The MRF team were using a green Ford Cortina. The IRA ambushed a similar car a few minutes later and killed a completely innocent couple. This had nothing whatsoever to do with either the SAS, who were as yet not involved in the Province, or any government policy. It had everything to do with bad soldiering. They had gone rogue.

Matters came to a head after the shooting of three men with a Thomson sub-machine-gun at a Falls Road bus stop. The soldier involved was prosecuted but not convicted and the MRF was immediately disbanded. This led to a rethink. The Army needed well-trained and disciplined troops on the ground to gather intelligence. They turned to the SAS. B Squadron was taken out of the line. Over half the Squadron was officially debadged, posted out of the Regiment and into the new unit, which ultimately became 14 Intelligence Company, an intelligence-gathering unit completely separate from the SAS and known as the 'Det' (from 'Detachment'). The remainder of B Squadron began to train and select the members of the new unit to replace the SAS men posted to Ulster.

I was involved in the second-ever Det Course. Training was intense and although I passed I decided against going on the two-year unaccompanied tour to Ulster. I couldn't drive, which was a great disadvantage professionally. Army pay then was extremely poor, so few of us could afford a car, and the army driving courses were only for those who wanted to become part of Motor Transport Platoon. But the overriding reason was personal. I'd spent most of the last two years in Ulster, and Pat was giving me hell over the prospect of another unaccompanied tour as she wanted to start a family. My marriage was not going well. Pat had a volatile temper and the constant violent arguments reminiscent of my childhood were driving me to despair.

I returned to 2 Para, who were preparing to go on exercise to Turkey on Operation Deep Furrow. This would test the ability of three countries' Airborne Forces to reinforce the flanks of NATO in the event of a Soviet attack. It would be the largest airborne drop since Arnhem. We would join battalions from America and Turkey, and some two and a half thousand men would be in the air at the same time. We mounted the operation from RAF Lyneham and flew, mostly low-level, to Turkey. Military parachuting is anything but comfortable. The parachute weighs in excess of forty pounds and the equipment, which is attached to your chest by clips, weighs between seventy and a hundred pounds. You wear a steel helmet and are in a confined space with another sixty or so men.

Because of the weight Paras carry, dispatchers try to leave it till the last possible moment to get everybody standing and hooked up. Even so, the minutes you spend on your feet are agony, especially when the plane rocks backwards and forwards as it hedge-hops. The stink of sweat and vomit is overwhelming. There is never any thought of refusing to jump. Once the green light is on the sticks depart like a train at full speed. It is all the dispatchers can do to slow them down. Many years before an army psychologist had decided to conduct a study on the effects on paratroopers of the first man, an officer, refusing to jump. The doctor in question had dressed as a Para major and stood in the doorway. When the green light came on he was pushed straight out in the rush.

As we neared the drop site the dispatchers got us up to fit equipment, then to hook up. It seemed for ever before the green light came on. Two spaces in front of me was a new member of the Company called Barrett. As he neared the door he slipped. Before the dispatcher could retrieve him he plunged headlong through the exit. I hit the slipstream and found myself fighting for airspace. There were parachutes everywhere. Suddenly my chute collapsed and I was plummeting towards the ground. I hardly had time to scream. I felt the blessed relief of my chute opening again – then the ground hit me. I wasn't in position, but I was totally relaxed. It was the softest landing I ever made. I lay for several seconds looking up at the clear blue sky, filled with parachutes, and thanking whatever God there was for letting me off the hook.

When I stood up I realized that somebody near me was in trouble – bad trouble. A crowd was gathering around a still form on the ground. I discovered that it was Pete, the young Para who'd slipped. He was still alive, but barely. His platoon sergeant knelt next to him, his ear close to his mouth. As the field ambulances arrived I saw him give a shudder and he was gone. The operation had been expensive. Three Americans and two Turks also died in the drop.

The exercise itself was fairly uneventful, except for one memorable incident. We were told to assault and capture a hill defended by Turkish troops. We did so, but the Turks wouldn't move, saying they'd beaten off our attack. Tempers became a little frayed and a few fists and rifle butts were used. Then the Turks started to remove their magazines filled with blanks and fire live rounds. We decided to let them have the hill.

When we returned to Aldershot I decided to volunteer for C Patrol Company, the Battalion's reconnaissance platoon. I'd got off to a bad start but now I felt I wanted responsibility. It was difficult convincing many that I was capable of change and leadership. I'd made enemies as I'd not disguised the dislike I felt for some of my contemporaries. I was becoming too strong and streetwise for the continued bullying but certainly they could and did prevent my promotion. C Company ran its own selection process and with it the chance to start afresh.

My troop commander was Bob Dixon, a veteran of the Malaya, Aden and Borneo campaigns. He was a firm taskmaster and a great soldier with his own brand of humour. He classified all our enemies by what they ate or drank. Russians were 'vodka swillers', Chinese, 'rice gobblers', the Irish, 'potato bashers'. His experience was vast and I used to love listening to his stories about operations in Aden and Malaya.

Among Bob's anecdotes were absolute gems of military experience that would prove useful in later years, like the time his patrol had been travelling single file in the Malayan jungle and had hit a head-on contact. The undergrowth was so dense they couldn't deploy to either flank and broke the contact by peeling off from the front. Each man fired a few shots, or a burst of automatic fire, stepped to his right and ran like hell to the rear of the column. If done properly an almost constant weight of fire can be maintained and it is the best and safest way to break a contact in close country or at night.

Immediately after our selection course we were off to Malaya, the second time for me. As part of Patrol Company I was fortunate to undergo one of the last jungle warfare courses run by the SAS and the legendary Geordie Lillico. This was the man who'd been shot during a head-on contact with a company of Indonesian troops. Following the shoot-and-scoot tactics employed at the time, the unscathed members of the patrol made their way back to their emergency RV. Badly wounded and unable to walk, Geordie crawled out of the ambush area. He had a ground-to-air emergency beacon with him but when he tried to attract a passing helicopter he noticed the Indonesians setting up an ambush. He turned off the beacon and dragged himself through their lines, squirming through the jungle on his stomach for days. His leg became infected. He let the maggots eat the infection, then ate the maggots. After several near misses with searching Indonesian patrols he was eventually rescued and awarded the Military Medal.

It was an absolutely absorbing course with a very relaxed and informative atmosphere. Too relaxed for some of our officers. Our Company commander was an attached officer from the Canadian Army. He addressed the assembled ranks, telling us: 'You are not SAS soldiers. If I took the four best soldiers in this Company and trained them for six months, maybe then they would be near the standards set by the SAS.' I didn't know if I was one of the four best but that moment I decided that one day I would be if for no other reason than to spite him.

Our course completed, we were launched into the jungle in four-man patrols, with specific missions to perform. Not all of these were purely academic. My patrol had to recce an unmapped area and select a site for a future jungle camp. We had to navigate by dead reckoning so that we could direct any future patrol to the site we'd chosen. We found a great position with a freshwater supply and plenty of space for a helicopter pad, and mapped it extensively. We were on our own in the jungle for nearly three weeks. Training and exercises completed, we had two weeks R&R. My friends all wanted to go to a whore-house. I knew the very place.

Tokyo by Night had changed little in the years I'd been away. The décor had been altered and the furniture changed but it was essentially the same. Seated in the corner was the *mama-san*. She hadn't aged a day. I directed my compatriots to her to view the wares and negotiate prices and settled myself at the bar with a drink. A few minutes later the *mama-san* joined me. A nod of her head produced a chess board and we began to play. She fitted a black cigarette into a gold holder and blew foul-smelling smoke towards the ceiling as she considered her first move. Midway through the game, she gave an exasperated series of tuts and without looking up she said: 'Your game has improved a lot, Harry McCallion.'

I won two out of our three games. As I stood to leave a look of genuine disappointment spread over her face.

'You come back?'

I kissed her hand with all the gallantry I could muster. 'Nothing could stop me.'

Her huge smile made her appear suddenly much younger. I went back twice in the next two weeks, once with friends, the second time on my own. As I walked through the door the *mama-san* shooed away the girls who tried to grab my arm.

'He here to play chess, not jig-a-jig,' she announced with mock anger.

I promised as I left to come again the next time I was in the country. In 1984, on my final visit to Malaya, I kept my promise. Tokyo by Night was still there but the *mama-san* had gone. I imagine her in hell playing chess with the devil and winning two games out of three.

I landed in RAF Brize Norton to discover I was a father twice over. Pat had given birth to two bouncing boys. We christened them Harry and Christopher. Despite the birth of my children my marriage was by no means stable. Pat's Irish temper and my desire for adventure were incompatible. I tried to be a good father but I really didn't know how to be one.

A month later I was back in the New Lodge in Belfast. The area had changed greatly: the high-rise blocks of flats that dominated the area and had given us so much trouble in 1972, were now controlled by British Army observation posts sited on their roofs. The IRA were observing a ceasefire, although it didn't seem to be having much effect on the level of violence. People were dying every day or two. The Provos had their own 'advice centre' run by an IRA man called Seamus McCusker. We were told to go easy on them because of the ceasefire and not to harass them or spread-eagle them against the wall if stopped for a body search. To me this was madness, but I bit the bullet and did what I was told. I was now an NCO and second in command of a patrol. We soon learnt that the terrorists in the area were taking advantage of our more relaxed approach to move weapons about. A feud was brewing between the Officials and the Provisionals, and each side was arming.

When I wasn't on duty I spent many hours in the Intelligence

Room reading up on the local players and studying the recent contact reports. I happened to pick up an old copy of *An Phoblacht*, the IRA's newspaper, in which I read about the IRA execution of a man who'd confessed to setting up the ambush of James McGerrigan, the Official IRA man we'd shot. The shooting had been a total fluke; their killing of their own man totally unfounded. It was one less to worry about.

Three weeks into the tour, I was in command of one of the OPs on the flats when there was a report of shooting at the bottom of the New Lodge Road. My patrol commander, in charge of two Landrovers, responded and both vehicles careered around a corner into a civilian car. The commander was badly injured and as he lay unconscious somebody stole his rifle. The next morning I left the OP and took command of the patrol. Our OC, a very aggressive officer, gave all the patrols a new order: turn the heat up on the Provos until we recover the rifle. It was just what I wanted to hear. I hit the New Lodge like a tornado.

For an hour my two-vehicle patrol raced around the area, stopping known IRA men and spread-eagling them against the walls. We put the word out that things had changed. My patrol time had nearly finished when I spotted two youths just entering the area and before they realized it I'd turned my vehicles to intercept them. I was searching one when the man next to me said excitedly: 'Harry, this man's carrying a gun.'

I looked across. Inside the youth's pocket was a .45 Colt automatic. I'd struck pay dirt as they say in all good Westerns. Behind me a crowd had gathered out of nowhere. We got the two men into the Landrovers as fast as we could and I tried to drive through but couldn't make any headway. I called in for assistance but the patrols that could help were on foot and would take several minutes to reach me. Minutes I didn't have: my Landrovers were in danger of being mobbed. I had half my patrol dismount and cock weapons. When Paras do this nearly everybody in Ulster knows that the time for playing games is over.

We began to advance through the crowd. One man stepped forward, a piece of iron grating in his hands. He took a swipe at my head and missed me by inches. I felled him with a well-timed butt stroke. Then we were in the open and away. Minutes later I had both men held under arrest in the nearby North Queen Street

RUC station. Both got three years, but the man who was carrying the gun never learned his lesson. He was shot dead during a robbery on the Antrim Road only months after his release.

I relished the responsibility of my first patrol as a commander. I knew that I could lead and others would follow. I was still a driven man, believing the respect I so desperately craved from my peers could only be won by being more aggressive than my fellow-corporals. I looked forward to further action but the new 'get tough' order was short-lived and within days we were back to the old hands-off policy, despite the fact that the stolen rifle was moved up into the Ardoyne, and would be used by PIRA to kill four soldiers before it was recovered.

Sectarian murders were at an all-time high in the Province. Our area bordered the fiercely Loyalist Tigers Bay and on one patrol I stopped a well-known UVF man who had already served time for a sectarian killing, and asked him why his organization persisted in killing innocent Catholics and not Republicans or IRA men. His answer was brutally simple: 'Because they're easier to find.'

Two weeks later I was on duty at Templar House, which commands a view of the New Lodge Road. There was a sudden burst of shooting in the streets below. Looking through the sights of my rifle, fitted with a Trilux 'scope, I tried to seek out a target. I could actually see people being shot in the street, dropping like rag dolls as bullets drilled into them. But I couldn't see where the shots were coming from! A car suddenly sped round the corner towards Tigers Bay. It ran into one of our patrols and was stopped. The four UVF gunmen in it were captured and sent for trial. Seven people had been shot, two of whom died later.

We didn't expect any thanks for our capture of the gunmen from the IRA, and weren't disappointed. They exacted their revenge by shooting dead a Protestant watchman the same day.

Towards the end of the tour I stopped and had a long conversation with Seamus McCusker at his 'Incident Centre'. He was a solemn-faced man at the best of times, and much of his face was hidden by a full beard. He simply nodded in reply to my greeting.

'It's a nice day to be out keeping the peace,' I said.

'You're not here to keep the peace.'

'Oh, and why am I here, Mr McCusker?'

'To oppress the nationalist peoples of Ireland.'

'Really? Were my friends oppressing you when we arrested those UVF killers that shot so many of your people just a few weeks ago?'

'You only arrested them after they'd opened fire.'

'We could hardly have arrested them before.'

'You could if you sent them to shoot us in the first place.'

'Even you don't believe that.'

'Yes I do.'

The man was so full of hate and mistrust he could believe anything.

'You want to be thankful we're here. If we left, the Protestants would annihilate areas like the New Lodge.'

'We're prepared for that. When you leave, we'll all withdraw into west Belfast and wait for reinforcements from the south.'

'I doubt if even that would save you.'

'We'll take our chances. If we have to fight the Loyalists for another hundred years, eventually we'll reunite the country.'

'It's academic, we're not leaving anyway.'

'Yes you are, you'll all be gone in two or three years at the most.'

I looked him squarely in the eyes. 'I was told that by one of your contemporaries in 1972. No doubt somebody like you will be telling me the same thing in another five years.'

In October 1975 the feud between the Official and Provisional IRA that had been simmering for many months started to boil over. One of the victims was Seamus McCusker, shot to death, not by the British Army he had always claimed was sent to oppress him, but by a fellow Irish Republican.

I left the New Lodge in late July to undertake my Junior Infantry Section Commanders' Course at the Brecon Battle School. The course was difficult and at times exhausting, but always informative. I learnt things that would save my life in the very near future. One of the most instructive was from a major who'd just returned from a tour in Oman. I was to be able to put his lessons on booby-traps to good use.

The Battalion was training for an exercise in Germany. It was a disaster. The first wave, from the 10 Para TA, were dropped in the wrong place and landed in the Kiel Canal. Seven paratroopers died. The situation was made worse by the fact that the shipping had not been stopped. Vessels arrived in harbour for weeks afterwards with rigging lines from parachutes entangled in their props. I had a heavy landing in trees but escaped with only minor injuries and when I got to the platoon RV I found many men had suffered badly. We had thirty per cent casualties on the drop. Although the Army obviously never intended it to be so, it was some of the most realistic training for war we'd ever done.

The exercise culminated with an armoured assault by the German Army. Metal monsters bore down on us at speed, dust and mud spraying everywhere, and I wondered just what chance we'd have of stopping a full-scale attack by the Soviet Union. When it was over the German commander brought one of his tanks back for a closer demonstration and did a right turn on top of my trench, demolishing it completely. Anybody inside would have been crushed to death. As an infantry man I gave an involuntary shudder.

Then the German asked if we would like to inspect the Leopard at closer quarters and began an impromptu lesson on the tank's fighting qualities. He explained the engine, the gun and its method of firing, then pointed underneath.

'You will notice that the Leopard II has a very high axle.'

For just a second his voice lowered slightly and his eyes glazed, as he said with quiet intensity: 'This time when we go on to the Steppes we will not get bogged down in the snow.'

The officer quickly resumed his technical briefing.

The exercise over, we hit the high spots of Hamburg. I had a particularly nasty meeting with an Alsatian which was part of a cabaret act. He thought I was his lunch.

Once again I witnessed the ongoing efforts of the paratrooper abroad to master the native tongue and order hamburger and chips.

Paratrooper: 'Swei hamburgers, bitte.' So far so good.

Vendor: 'Mit pommes frites?'

Paratrooper: 'Ja, ein mit, and ein mitout.'

No problem.

I had been considering leaving the British Army and going abroad for several years and by the mid-1970s the urge to do so had become almost overwhelming. I'd been trained to fight and all that seemed to stretch ahead was endless tours in Ulster. I knew a hundred soldiers who could put their elbows on a bar and talk soldiering, but very few who could do so from experience so I decided to seek it abroad.

My enthusiasm was not shared by Pat. Our relationship was becoming increasingly stormy and I'd even walked out and lived in the barracks for a time. Pat was in every way a good woman and a devoted mother to our sons. But what I desperately needed was someone to tell me they believed in me. Someone who'd make me believe all the dreams I had could come true. Pat never gave me that. Yet I couldn't bring myself to desert her with two young children.

Added to the turmoil of my private life was my increasing frustration with my career. I believed I was a good soldier and I tried to show that I'd evolved from the difficulties of my teens and early twenties. Even so, the authorities were not looking at me as a potential senior rank. I felt the only way I could truly prove that I could lead and fight with the best of them was to do so on a battlefield, and that meant going abroad. The next problem was where. Rhodesia looked promising, but I wanted one day to return to the British Army. South Africa seemed to offer me everything I needed, including a major war on its border with Angola. I wrote to the South African Embassy and asked for details on immigration. They sent me heaps of forms to fill in, which I did, and I waited expectantly for their answer. It came back quite quickly: a resounding no. People could not emigrate to South Africa just to join their army. I would need a trade.

I was incensed. I had a trade, a good trade: I was a professional soldier with the best army in the world. I wrote back and told them in explicit detail about my training and my intention to join their army. A month later I received another letter. They sympathized with me, but theirs was a conscript army, not a professional army like the British, therefore soldiering was not a recognized trade. I wrote again. Surely they must have some regular units – could I not join one of these? It would be another two months before I got a reply.

In the meantime I was out on exercise on Salisbury Plain. For some reason we were not allowed to say that we were training for war against the Russians. Even the phrase 'red forces' was frowned on. Our enemy on exercise were the Phantasians.

The exercises always followed a set pattern. I could have written the scenario in my sleep. The Phantasians had invaded with a massed armoured assault. We would be dropped in and prepare to repulse their forward units. We always managed to repulse the first attack, then were told to withdraw to another defensive position. These exercises meant plenty of walking and plenty of digging. If every trench I had ever dug while I was in the Parachute Regiment was laid end to end it would have stretched from Aldershot to London. It was the middle of winter, and the ground was like granite and the weather atrocious. The Parachute Regiment had a uniform for summer, winter and tropical warfare. It was simplicity itself: we wore the same uniform.

To make matters worse, I had been promoted back into a rifle company as a section commander. My company had several new officers. It was a well-known fact the new second lieutenants in the British Army couldn't walk and talk at the same time. I was briefing my section on the night routine and ended by saying: 'This is only an exercise, and it's freezing cold. I don't mind if you keep the lower half of your body in the sleeping bag when you're on stag, but if you're going to grab a quick smoke don't let a bloody officer catch you.'

From the darkness behind me an angry voice announced: 'A bloody officer has caught you, Corporal McCallion. They will not lie in their sleeping bags and anybody caught smoking will be charged.'

I buried my head in exasperation.

On my return a letter awaited me. I'd been invited to the South African Embassy in London for an interview. The man I met was dressed in civilian clothes but was obviously a military man. He questioned me on my military background and experience, especially on my Ulster tours. Finally he lowered his chin so that it rested on the vee of his right thumb and index finger and observed me for several seconds without speaking.

'Are you a racialist?'

I laughed. 'I haven't a prejudiced bone in my body.'

'Why South Africa then?'

'I think the war you're fighting is just an extension of the Cold War. The ANC and SWAPO, who you're fighting in Angola, are financed directly by the Soviet Union.'

'So you don't believe in apartheid?'

'I don't know enough about it. One thing I'm sure of: there will have to be change in South Africa but now is not the time.'

He nodded, reflected on what I had said, then stood up and extended his hand. 'We'll let you know.'

On the train back to Aldershot I thought over what I'd said to my interviewer. I had mixed feelings. On the military side I was sure I'd acquitted myself well but on the political I was not so certain. I would just have to wait and see. Meanwhile another tour in Ulster loomed, this time in west Belfast. Already 2 Para had begun build-up training and my Company was due to undergo Northern Ireland training with the Army's Northern Ireland Training Advisory Team.

The day before we left I received a letter bearing the South African Embassy's stamp. I put it down on a table and looked at it for a few minutes, then made myself a cup of tea and looked at it for several more. For over a year I'd been trying to convince the embassy to admit me into their country and this letter contained their final word. Eventually I opened it and read: 'Your application has been given further consideration. It has been decided to allow your entry into the Republic of South Africa. An interview will be arranged with the South African Defence Force on your arrival. Your visas will be forwarded when you supply us with your leaving date.'

I was over the moon. But the euphoria was suddenly mixed with trepidation. People saved and planned to work abroad for years. I wanted to go straight after my next tour in Ulster. The first problem was money: I had none. I went to my friendly bank manager and explained my position. It must have been the most unusual request for a loan he'd ever received but he was not unsympathetic. However, he needed some security. It was a problem, but I had the answer. I would get two people as guarantors. Fearless and my brother Allan, now serving with the 3rd Battalion Parachute Regiment. Both agreed. I got my loan.

I returned from Northern Ireland training to confront the next big problem: my wife. Pat was adamant she wasn't going. The

Battalion was being posted to Berlin after our Ulster tour, which would have meant better housing and more money. Pat erupted like Mount Etna and even burnt her own and the twins' exit visas. For me South Africa was a dream come true. I watched dispassionately as the visas burned on our kitchen stove then put it straight on the line.

'I'm going to South Africa. You can come or you can stay, but I'm going.'

Neither screams nor threats, thrown pans or insults would budge me. Pat even asked the unit's padre to talk with me. With a week to go before I left Ulster she capitulated: she would come with me.

Within the Battalion and my Company in particular, nobody believed I would actually go. Many who'd known me for years thought it was only a ploy to get myself promoted. My relationships with most of my contemporaries of the time was, putting it mildly, strained. I had few real friends. I still had the potential to be extremely violent and was getting better at it all the time. Probably, because my peers really didn't know me, they found it hard to believe that I would take such a gamble with my life. The betting was two to one against me leaving and that's how it stood when I stepped off the ferry to begin my last tour in Belfast.

My Company had the Lower Falls and Divis Flats area to patrol, a hotbed of terrorist activity. If I'd had any doubts about leaving, this tour was to settle them for me. The Provos had resumed their murderous campaign with renewed fervour but the final briefing to all patrol commanders was that we were to treat them with kid gloves. We couldn't spread-eagle suspects against the wall, even if we caught them with a loaded gun. Far worse, we had direct orders not to fire on a car unless we could identify a weapon in it, even if the car had knocked down and killed or injured a member of a patrol. I, for one, decided not to observe any of it. I patrolled with the same aggression as I always did, which brought me into direct confrontation with my superiors on many occasions. I was undeterred.

There was a psychopath, a member of the INLA, who'd been particularly active in the Divis Flats area during my last tour. According to intelligence his main claim to fame had been the murder of a Protestant whom he'd lured to the flats and stabbed to death with a screwdriver. He was physically big with a reputation

70

as a bad man to tangle with in a fight. Before we arrived he'd even said he'd beat up a Para patrol commander. I met him in a dark alley.

'You're the man that wants to beat up a Para corporal?'

'That's right.'

'I'm a Para corporal.'

I handed my rifle to the man next to me and even as I did so he launched a hay maker at my head. It missed. Using the momentum of his swinging body I hit him with one of the best right crosses I'd ever thrown. He went down like a poleaxed cow.

'Do you know what your problem is?'

He stared back at me with glazed eyes.

I leaned forward and spoke slowly for his benefit.

'Your problem is that you let your ambitions outweigh your abilities.'

Having passed on my words of wisdom, I continued with my patrol. For the rest of the trip I made his life unendurable and hounded him until he left the area for his own peace of mind.

Only two weeks into the tour we got a kill. A hijacked car was driven through a roadblock. The patrol commander spotted a gun and opened fire, killing one man and injuring two others. The IRA shot up one of our patrols and injured a Para, though not seriously, in revenge. In the middle of the tour we had an extremely lucky escape when the Tail-end Charlie on a patrol escaped injury when a sniper's bullet passed through his flak-jacket as he was turning.

With three weeks to go before the end of the tour, I was in Leeson Street, near the junction with the Falls Road. I decided to check a well-known IRA club there. The entrance was up some old wooden stairs and as I neared the top I encountered a man leaving. He started to back-pedal so I grabbed him and thrust him down the stairs. 'Search that man.'

I heard a shout from the foot of the stairs.

'Harry, you'd better come and see this!'

My second in command had discovered a bundle of handwritten papers. The first one read: 'Since I have taken over as Intelligence officer of E Company I have noted the following cars using Springfield Road Police Barracks . . .'

A long list of cars followed. The other notes detailed the movements of men and weapons. It was an intelligence windfall.

71

I called for a mobile patrol to convey my prisoner to the RUC station.

'Why are you arresting him?' asked the duty watchkeeper, my platoon commander.

People were streaming out of the club and a crowd was starting to form around my four-man patrol. It was several seconds before I could answer.

'I can't give you details at this time. Request a mobile patrol and any other patrol in the area to give me urgent assistance.' There was no way I was going to explain the reason for the arrest over an open radio net, which I knew the PIRA monitored.

'If you don't give me a reason why you have arrested this man, I will not dispatch a vehicle for you!' came the response.

I was incensed. A crowd of nearly a hundred now surrounded me, my prisoner was struggling and I had an officer refusing to send me back up. First things first. I pulled the IRA man closer to me.

'If you try and run I'll kill you,' I shouted in his ear. Then I forced him on to the floor and stood on him.

'Patrol, cock weapons.' There was the sound of four rifles being cocked. The crowd moved back a little. I spoke once again on the radio to the watchkeeper.

'Now listen to me, I'm the commander on the ground and I have a good reason for arresting this man. I want a pick-up and I want it now!' My anger was plain for everyone to hear.

There was silence on the radio net, as if everybody was holding his breath. Then the watchkeeper came on, directing an armoured vehicle to my location. He ended by telling me to report directly to him as soon as I was finished with my present task.

'With pleasure,' I replied curtly.

My situation was still pretty bad. It would take the mobile patrol at least five minutes to get to me, five minutes I didn't think I had. The crowd were edging nearer. I took the decision to open fire if they encroached any further. I sighted at one particularly loud individual who seemed to be in control, aiming at his legs. Just as I was taking up the first pressure on the trigger, the crowd scattered, a patrol from D Company had arrived and charged into them from the rear. Before they could regroup, my armoured patrol arrived and I bundled in my prisoner. As I shut the door I threw my thanks to the D Company NCO.

He grinned back hugely.

'Always a pleasure. Glad of the fun.'

At HQ, Special Branch and the Battalion's intelligence cell nearly went crazy with delight at the information we'd brought. It saved many police officers' lives and helped to break up two IRA units. They even rang up my OC and asked him to pass on their congratulations. The watchkeeper's only remark was that I should have given him some hint of what was going on.

When the Battalion returned to Aldershot I was horrified to learn that I was to be placed on the rear party, which was responsible for guard duty. I had arranged to fly out to South Africa on 6 May and the Army would not release me until the day before. After six tours of Ulster I thought I deserved better.

Working an eight- to ten-hour day left little time for preparations. Most of our furniture belonged to the Army but there were decisions to make on what we could take with us and what we could discard. Pat was hoping I would change my mind about leaving right up until the moment we boarded the plane. In one way being on guard duty was a blessing as it prevented both of us from some soul-searching and the arguments that would follow. The night before my discharge we had a farewell dinner with Fearless, who was excited about the adventure I was about to embark on, and his wife Carol, who had been an Army nurse. She was probably glad to see me go. Chris had become very much a family man except when I took him out and got him into trouble. Carol summed up her feelings about me: 'Harry, you look like a thug, act like a thug and you are a thug.'

On 5 May I was officially discharged. I felt an almost physical sense of loss, for 2 Para had been the nearest thing I had to a family for over seven years and now I was turning my back on it, for reasons I still only half understood myself. I suddenly felt more alone and adrift than at any time in my life. I stopped and looked back at Browning Barracks, the depot of the Parachute Regiment, where I'd walked in a lifetime ago, poor and half starved. Then I took a deep breath and stepped into the future.

3

THE RECCES

'It's a dangerous thing we're going to do now, Jock.'
Sergeant-Major Deval De Beer, Caprivi Strip, 1977

I landed in Pretoria on 6 May 1977 and was taken to a hotel
and told that an interview with the South African Defence Force
had been scheduled for the next day. I made my way to Army
Headquarters bright and early, only to find that nobody knew
anything about me. I spent several frustrating hours trying to
convince a sceptical desk sergeant that I had only just arrived
from England. Finally, and I never found out exactly why, I was
taken to a separate building and introduced to a major in military
intelligence. I retold my story, then he asked me extensive questions
about my military background and my reasons for coming to South
Africa. Finally he said: 'Have you ever heard of a unit called
the Reconnaissance Commando?' I admitted that I had not. He
informed me that they were his country's equivalent of the SAS.
Would I consider undergoing Selection?

I tried not to appear too keen when I said yes.

There were three phases, the major explained. First, a series of
mental and physical tests (the same as SADF pilots undertook).
Second, Selection itself. Finally, continuation training, where we
would learn the necessary skills to carry out operations.

It was now late afternoon. The major told me a car would pick
me up at 9 o'clock the next morning, shook my hand and wished
me luck.

The car arrived promptly and took me to an army medical
facility where, for the next two hours, every piece of my anatomy
was inspected, prodded and explored. At the final examination

the doctor told me I was in excellent physical shape. As I was pedalling an exercise bike as fast as I could, my body festooned with wires and suction caps, and breathing into an oxygen mask, this came as quite a relief. I was even more pleased when I learnt later that one in every three applicants were rejected at this stage. I celebrated with a lunch in the canteen.

In the afternoon I was taken to a separate facility where I sat a series of mental and psychological tests which ended with a series of face-to-face interviews with three psychiatrists. The last two give me pleasure to this day. The first was conducted by an extremely attractive blonde, about whom I had several erotic fantasies during our interview. As her questions drew to a close she asked me: 'Have you ever shot anyone?'

'Yes,' I answered.

'Afterwards, what was the first thought that went through your mind?'

'What a good shot I am,' I said.

She noted my reply and then looked at me over her large spectacles. 'Did you see the person you had shot close up?'

'Yes,' I replied.

She fixed me with what she no doubt thought was an intimidating stare. She looked enchanting. 'What went through your mind then?'

I gazed into her lovely blue eyes. 'I thought to myself,' I replied softly, 'what a bloody good shot I am.' For just the briefest of seconds I got a smile and then she rose and walked out of my life for ever.

The final interview was with the senior doctor, a very distinguished man in his late forties. He hammered on at me about my reasons for being there, then dropped what he must have thought was his most testing question: 'Would you die for South Africa?'

'I don't intend to die for anybody,' I replied immediately, 'but I'm quite willing to risk my life for South Africa.'

Again I got a brief smile.

The interviews completed, I rejoined my driver. As he drove me back to my hotel he informed me I had another interview the following day with the head of Special Forces. The medical and psychological test results would be sent through in the morning, and I would be told if I was a suitable candidate for Selection. I would be picked up at 1.30.

That night I hardly slept. I had risked everything coming to South Africa and my fate was in the hands of people who had only a few brief hours to get my measure.

As the driver picked me up outside the hotel I was acutely aware that my future was in the balance. I knew my own physical capabilities but was totally unsure what these guys would make of me psychologically.

I was met again by the intelligence major who had conducted my initial interview. He greeted me with a smile and an extended hand. I took this as a good sign. I was, he said, going to meet the general.

I was taken along a corridor past a uniformed and armed guard, to a nondescript and unmarked door and ushered in without ceremony. Seated behind a desk was a man in his middle-to-late sixties with snow-white hair. When he looked up I was struck by the strength and character in his face. His grey-blue eyes seemed to stare right through me. This was General Loots, officially a retired officer in the SADF; unofficially head of all Special Forces operations.

Without prompting I came smartly to attention. He smiled and stood. He was roughly the same height as me, but slightly stooped so that he gave the appearance of being shorter. I extended my right hand as he extended his left. I realized his right arm was hanging useless by his side. I grasped his left hand awkwardly with my right. He nodded as if I had passed some kind of test. I was invited to sit facing the two officers. The major began the interview.

'You will be pleased to know that you have been assessed as being excellent Special Forces material,' he said. I tried not to let the relief show on my face. 'We now have to decide on what kind of offer we will make to you.'

The major looked at the general and continued: 'You are slightly older than most of the recruits for Special Forces and more experienced. Your psychological profile and test results are excellent, but I don't wish to give you a rank that would make it difficult for you to be accepted in the unit. We would like to make you full corporal. You could expect to make sergeant within two years.'

'That's fine with me,' I replied, trying to appear nonchalant. I had expected to start again as a private.

'Good. Now about Selection. You have two options: one starts on the 17th of this month and the next is four months after that. Which is it to be?'

'The 17th,' I replied.

The general beamed at the major.

'As I anticipated. Good. Now, it normally takes a man two weeks to go through the process of enlisting. You will do it in two days.' The major handed me a sheet of paper, typed in Afrikaans, with his personal signature and stamp on it. The young lance-corporal who had been my companion was called into the room and given an extended briefing, also in Afrikaans.

The next two days were heady stuff. My driver, in General Loots' staff car complete with two stars, raced from one location to another in the Pretoria military establishment. Faced with line after line of national servicemen waiting to be issued with equipment, we would walk to the front, produce the general's note and be issued with whatever was required. Only once did we run into difficulty, getting my identity documents. An overweight staff sergeant angrily announced that there was no way I could get them immediately. The lance-corporal argued with him while I looked on with some concern, then he asked to use the phone. After speaking into it for a couple of seconds he handed the receiver to the staff sergeant. The lance-corporal tried, with little success, to suppress a smile as the general gave the sergeant the appropriate instructions.

I had a full set of ID in two hours. As we walked to the car the lance-corporal answered my unspoken question by saying: 'The general asked the chief clerk what rank he presently held, then told him that if he did not want to be a private by the end of the day he had better make sure that you had your documents.'

Finally, on 12 May 1977, I was sworn in as a fully-fledged member of the SADF. The next day I was on a train bound for Durban, where the Special Forces were based. There, Pat, my twin boys, Harry and Christopher, and I were met by an army jeep and taken to an hotel. I was told that on the 17th a jeep would pick me up at 7 a.m. sharp and take me to the base. I barely had time to settle them in and get my equipment into some kind of order. As arranged, I was picked up and driven to the HQ of the Reconnaissance Commando, at the Bluff, Durban. As I was driven past the armed guards at the gate, it struck me that in a little over two weeks I had gone from being a patrol commander on the streets of Belfast in one army to being a non-commissioned officer starting Selection for the Special Forces in another.

The camp was swarming with people. In all 410, mostly national servicemen, were trying for Selection. My lack of Afrikaans proved to be a major stumbling block in making the instructors understand who I was and where I had come from, but eventually everything was sorted. I was informed that that day was the only administration day on the course and that at about midnight we would set off for the selection area in Zululand.

Everyone on the course had a pretty awful breakfast in the national servicemen's dining hall, then we spent the morning having our names and service numbers taken before being divided in squads. In the afternoon we were issued with our equipment: backpack, webbing, rifle and two 60mm mortar-bomb cases painted red and filled with concrete. These were to be carried with us at all times; failure to produce them meant being instantly thrown off the course. Together they weighed about 20lb. With full equipment I estimated each of us was carrying roughly 50lb, less food and water. All of us had R4 rifles, the South African adaptation of the Belgian FN rifle. Failure to keep this clean or within arm's length also meant being expelled from the course.

By 5 o'clock I had the unusual webbing and backpack in reasonable order and adjourned to the canteen for supper. I did not realize this would be my last substantial meal for a month. I met two other members of my squad, Dave Price and André Klopper, both of whom had served with the Rhodesian SAS. They were very likeable rogues and instantly I struck up a friendship with them. They kept all of us amused with their wild tales. Like the time the Rhodesian SAS had launched a raid deep into Mozambique. Sixty battle-hardened airborne warriors trudging down a dried river-bed towards a camp were suddenly confronted by a little mongrel, barking incessantly. Various methods were tried to silence the howling animal, including bribery, but to no avail. The barking roused the enemy camp and the SAS strike force had to withdraw. One of the toughest military units in the world, forced into inglorious retreat, by the smallest of enemies.

Another time they were given two prisoners to interrogate. They took both men up in a helicopter, bound hand and foot, and at an appropriate height they threw one out. The second terrorist nearly fainted with fear, looking from one to the other as if his head was on a swivel.

'Are you going to talk?' André demanded.

'Yes,' replied the terrorist, nodding vigorously.

'OK,' Dave put in. 'Who is your commanding officer?'

The terrorist looked from one man to the other, then at the helicopter's open doorway. 'You've just thrown him out of the helicopter.'

Shortly before midnight we were loaded into trucks for the long overnight drive to Zululand.

Like all Special Forces units, Recce Commando based Selection on their own operational experience. The unit had been formed in 1970 by Komandant Bradanbaght, a legendary figure in the South African Army, whose brother was a known ANC supporter.

Bradanbaght had selected one officer and five sergeants from the South African Parachute Battalion and set about training them, first putting them through Rhodesian SAS Selection, then taking them down to Mozambique to work operationally. Gradually the unit expanded. They were deployed mainly in Angola and Zambia against SWAPO terrorists, which required long periods in the bush, with little or no air support, pitted against an aggressive, well-armed and well-disciplined enemy. Such operations demanded men who were physically fit, able to carry heavy weights over long distances, who could survive in the bush on very little food and water and could operate in a small group without causing friction.

In addition, the unit's experience in the Angolan war had shown that if a small group of men, operating behind enemy lines, made contact with a larger force and acted aggressively with maximum firepower, it could often achieve results far out of proportion to its numbers. Aggression, therefore, was a trait much prized in the ranks of Recce Commando.

Phase one of Selection was basically a week of hell, designed to break those who weren't physically and mentally up to the job.

Phase two, lasting two weeks, tested endurance and team ability, to track, carry out specific tasks and navigate over long distances, while working in a six-man unit. Phase three was individual week. Survivors were transported to the Caprivi Strip in South West Africa, the operational base of Recce Commando, for a true test of one's ability to work, navigate and motivate oneself in solitude.

At daylight on 18 May 1977 we tumbled out of the back of our trucks and were told to leave anything we could not carry and form up in three ranks. Phase one was about to begin.

The instructors, about twenty in all, walked up and down, checking each man had his rifle, his pack and, of course, his two concrete-filled mortar-bomb cases for ballast. Satisfied each of us had everything in order, they dispatched the trucks. We were on a wide, hard, dirt road. Major Blauw, a senior operational officer, addressed us from the top of a Landrover with a loudspeaker. He pointed west. 'Walk,' he said, 'until we tell you to stop.' He climbed back into his vehicle and, accompanied by his staff, left us alone on the road.

I turned and began to walk west. I noted the reaction of my fellow Selection hopefuls with interest. They were all very young: some twenty, many just eighteen. The vast majority were national servicemen, used to being closely supervised. Many, robbed of this supervision, sat down to make a brew; some decided to rearrange their equipment. Perhaps three dozen actually began to walk.

At first the walk was extremely pleasant. The air was cool and I dropped into a familiar Para shuffle that covered the maximum amount of ground with the minimum effort. I was soon in front. As the morning wore on the heat increased. It sapped the energy from my legs and forced a slackening of pace. I kept plodding along. Occasionally a jeep full of 'Recces' would pass and some remark would be thrown at me in Afrikaans. I'd smile, nod and keep walking.

At midday I stopped at the top of a high hill for a break, made a brew and some 'Airborne' stew. I looked behind me along the road. Men were strung out for miles, most walking in groups of two or three, stretching back as far as the eye could see. After twenty minutes I repacked my kit and started to walk again. I was now starting to feel the effects of the heat very badly. I'd already drunk the contents of two of my three water bottles, and dehydration, followed by heat exhaustion, was a serious danger, I realized. So I rationed my remaining water to two sips every hour.

By later afternoon there was still no sign of the end. There were no checkpoints, no guides, just a seemingly endless road ahead of me. But at least the heat had abated. I was down to a quarter of a bottle of water and I still didn't know how far I had to go. At 6 o'clock I took another break. My feet were swelling uncomfortably in my new boots; the pack I was carrying had dug deep grooves into my shoulders; and I had friction burns on the inside of both my thighs. But most worrying was the fact that my water was all but gone. I made myself another meal: stew again, and took a final sip of water. I did not have enough for a brew. Shouldering my pack, I started to walk again. It was starting to get dark.

Before long I was stumbling along the road in total darkness, sometimes humming songs to myself. One in particular kept coming into my head: 'If My Friends Could See Me Now'. By 9 p.m. I had been walking for fourteen hours, almost three hours without water. The terrain was mostly flat, with occasional high hills. I was, as the Paras say, 'on my chin straps'. I ached in every bone of my body and my thighs burned so badly from the friction rubs I had to walk with my legs apart. My mouth felt like a Comanche's left moccasin. I decided I'd walk one more hour. Then, if I didn't find a checkpoint, I'd get some sleep.

Just after 10 o'clock, I began to hear the sound of the sea. For some reason this gave me hope. I rounded a corner and walked smack into a giant of a man in a Recce Commando T-shirt and shorts, standing in the middle of the road. He spoke to me in Afrikaans; I replied in English, telling him my name and rank. He looked at me closely then pointed along a small track leading off the main road. I followed it and found myself in a large, open space, bordered by two long tents. A magnificent figure of a man, about six foot tall, with a huge red beard and the shoulders and arms of a giant, came out to greet me. Once we had established that I could not speak or understand Afrikaans, I was told to fill one water bottle from the bowser at the edge of the clearing, and then to sit and wait for the rest of them. I did as ordered, stealing two huge gulps of water as I filled my bottle.

I sat for about five minutes before another instructor came over and asked: 'Have you any serious medical problems?'

I stood up and showed him the friction burns. He winced and called over several other instructors, who began an excited debate in Afrikaans. (I learnt later they were taking bets on how long I would last with my injuries.) The first instructor strapped up my thighs with medical adhesive tape and I found, much to my relief, that I could walk fairly normally again.

The long walk had taken its toll on me. I'd covered sixty miles in just over fifteen hours. Left alone, I fell into an exhausted sleep. I was awakened three hours later by a boot in the ribs. The clearing was full of trainees, some of whom had only just arrived. About a hundred of us were formed up into three ranks and berated as the worst, the absolute worst, bunch of candidates that had ever applied for Special Forces. After ten minutes' abuse, we were given forty minutes of rifle PT. We were then divided into teams of eight.

Major Blauw informed us that we really weren't up to the job we had applied for. Did anybody want to quit? Immediately twenty or so men said they did, and they were ordered aside. We were reformed again into eight-man teams and marched to the edge of the clearing. Stacked neatly there were about fifty logs, each the size of a telegraph pole. Each team was given one, then we followed the instructors back along the road at a fast trot. After about four hundred yards we stopped. In the darkness we could see a very large hill.

'Take the logs over the hill, turn left at the beach and you will get back into camp.' With these comforting words our guardians departed.

We turned and started to climb. The going was tough. It wasn't that the hill was steep, though it was, or that we were tired, though we were, or even that we were hampered by our packs and rifles, that made things so hard. It was the bush. The hill was covered with dense undergrowth. After an hour we were not even halfway up the bloody monster. Tempers were fraying; some teams just gave up. Then we had a stroke of luck. In the darkness we stumbled on to a small, but serviceable, path. Followed by the rest of the men, we were on the other side in just over an hour. We hit the beach and were back in camp by 4 a.m. We were given another forty minutes of rifle PT and told to get some sleep. I was so tired I barely had the energy to unwrap my sleeping bag, and the hard edges of my webbing felt like the softest pillow.

The shouts of the instructors woke us at eight. I had to check my watch twice. I would have sworn on a stack of bibles that I had only just got my head down. We were formed up in three ranks and asked who wanted to continue; another twenty or so departed. I estimated that there were about two hundred of us left, and we had only been going forty-eight hours. Over a hundred who had just not walked fast enough had been returned to their units. We were then told to get some breakfast and be ready at nine for PT, dressed in T-shirts, trousers, boots and webbing.

We were taken down to the beach and introduced to sandbag PT. Each of us filled a bag and for the next two hours ran them up and down the beach, in and out of the sea. At last we were told to stack the wretched things above the water-line, which led me to believe that I had not seen the last of them. We ran back to camp and the luxury of a forty-minute break.

We formed up again in T-shirts, boots and denims and were divided into groups of twenty or so. We set out on a run, which, after the horrors of sandbag PT, was a walk in the park. We soon relaxed into a loping stride and ran for about thirty minutes or so. The track wound way into the interior, the bush around us gradually getting thicker. Eventually we found ourselves by a large lake. Across one corner of it, spanning a distance of about a hundred yards or so, was a rope. I looked closely at the water. There were creatures in there, creatures with teeth. Crocodiles. On the list of things I most fear in the world, crocodiles are right up there at the top.

The instructors lined up on the bank and let fly with a variety of weapons. They didn't aim to hit anything, just scare away the local wildlife. Satisfied the water was clear, they set up armed sentries at both ends of the rope. We were told to strip to our shorts. The exercise was simple: you entered the water at point A and either swam or pulled yourself along the rope to point B, where you would find a track that brought you back to the start point. We were to continue this until told to stop.

Entering the water the first time was bad, although I was reassured by the presence of the armed guards. We continued the exercise for about an hour, then ran back to camp. When I got back to my equipment I found that it had been searched and all the food it contained removed. We were told that from now on the instructors would provide all we needed to eat. Looking at the smiles on their faces didn't convince me I'd be getting three square meals a day.

Lunch was a local version of sausages and mash. The afternoon was split between rifle PT and sandbag PT. After the evening meal we were given a lecture on snake bites by Sergeant Marius Fullun, the giant with the red beard, in English for my benefit. We were told that there were three kinds of snakes in the area: adders and vipers, whose venom attacked the blood and tissue; cobras and mambas, whose venom attacked the central nervous system; and tree snakes (*boomslang* in Afrikaans), whose venom prevented blood from clotting. So toxic was a tree snake's bite that a hospital in Johannesburg would fly the antidote to any part of Africa within hours of a confirmed strike. The tree snake's venom, although highly toxic, could only be delivered in small doses, giving a good chance of recovery if treated. A mamba bite, however, was almost always fatal. 'And the black mamba,' the sergeant told us drily, 'is a very aggressive snake.' Later I was to see for myself just how aggressive.

We had the luxury of a couple of hours off. I spent them trying to repair some of the damage to my body. My feet were pretty raw from running in wet boots, and my shoulders and chest were covered in sandbag- or rifle-inflicted bruises. Overall, after two days of almost constant physical torment, I was in reasonable shape. The friction rubs between my legs were giving me little trouble, thanks to the strapping.

As darkness fell we were told to be ready with full kit for a night march. I wondered what horrors awaited me in the hours ahead. If I'd known I might not have left the camp.

We formed into groups of ten. Each group was given a log to carry, as well as our packs, mortar-bomb cases and rifles. We then set out, accompanied by the instructors, on a cross-country march. After ten minutes there was not a muscle in my body that was not screaming in agony. Each minute stretched to eternity as we stumbled through the night. Every twenty minutes or so we would stop, put down our rifles and do log exercises: throwing the log above our heads from one shoulder to the other. Then it was pick up your rifle, log on shoulder, and off we would stumble, going God knows where.

I was unaware of exactly where we were when we stopped, except that I was in the centre of a world of pain. As I heaved huge gulps of air into my lungs I came slowly to the conclusion that we were back at the lake, the lake with creatures in it. The night was black. We were told to strip to our undershorts. The instructors opened up with their weapons again and posted sentries. I was terrified of what was to come. 'What the hell's the point of this?' I found myself saying aloud.

In we went. I was one of the first. I tried not to think of what might be in the water. I didn't even try to swim, but just grabbed the rope and pulled for dear life. I don't think I've ever covered a hundred yards of water faster. I was shaking when I got out and jogged back to the rest of the party. Thankfully we only had to do the exercise once. We put on our packs, shouldered our logs and jogged to the main camp.

On arrival I discovered that more than twenty candidates had refused to go into the water. I was about to go to my sleeping bag when I felt a tap on my shoulder. Turning, I found myself confronted by an instructor, a huge, good-looking man with raven-black hair.

'You wanted to know why we make you swim the lake in darkness?'

I started to protest that I had not intended any criticism.

He raised his hand. 'It's a natural question from a professional soldier, Corporal. During the Angolan war we were being chased by a large group of Cubans and MPLA regulars. We were trying to get back to our own lines. Our way was blocked by a river. There were ten of us. Two flatly refused to get into the darkened river and swim to the other side. We were lucky: a scout found a narrow stretch we could ford and we managed to get the two of them across there. But it was all very near to being a disaster. That's why we let you see the crocs in daylight and make you swim at night.'

I nodded. 'Thanks for taking the time to explain things to me, Staff.'

He gave me a smile of genuine warmth. 'Anytime. Now go get some sleep.'

We were woken at roughly three-hourly intervals throughout the night for spells of rifle and sandbag PT. Once, when we were standing in three lines after a particularly strenuous session, I found myself resting my head on the shoulder of the man on my right. In seconds I was asleep.

I was shaken awake by one of the instructors. 'Do you want to carry on?'

'Yes,' I replied.

His eyes twinkled in the dark and his face broke into a wide grin. 'You'll probably make this course. You know when to sleep.'

The rest of 'hell week' was more of the same: rifle PT, sandbag PT, log PT, night runs. At the end of the week our numbers were down to about a hundred. It was time to begin phase two.

We were split into six-man teams, the normal operational unit of Recce Commando. We had to operate fully blacked, face and hands covered in camouflage cream. We were given co-ordinates of the first of a series of checkpoints, sixty kilometres away, and told to get there as fast as possible. Those who arrived before it closed would receive rations; those who didn't wouldn't. Over the next week we'd be given just enough food to allow us to keep going and no more.

Although I can't say I enjoyed any part of Selection, phase two was the closest I came. My group was a mixed bag of pirates and ruffians, Dave Price and André Klopper (the two ex-Rhodesian SAS men); Major Peter Schofield, a forty-year-old ex-British Army Parachute Regiment major, who was doing this part of Selection before running the Recce Commando free-fall training; and Janni Smit and Danny Villiers, two members of the South African Paras. Each of us had talents and strengths that would prove useful to the group. Major Schofield was a natural leader and excellent navigator. Dave and André knew the bush and were terrific scroungers, often conjuring up food from nowhere. Janni was a great cook, making meals out of practically anything. Danny was a natural athlete; he'd run ahead to checkpoints, in the hope of arriving there before they closed. I could judge distance, a skill I had developed years ago in the wilds of the Welsh mountains and on Salisbury Plain. By a combination of pacing and judgement I could tell how far we'd travelled on a single day, an essential skill in featureless country. I could also wake at any time I chose, so it was left to me to get everyone up in the morning – sometimes no easy task given how tired we were.

We'd be up just after dawn. If we had any food we'd eat, but more often than not we'd make do with a communal brew. Then we'd walk. Our walks had no set pattern. We'd walk until one of us needed a rest, take a break, then continue. At midday we'd have another brew, and at night whenever possible, a meal. We never tried to walk in the dark; navigation was impossible. We'd collect huge amounts of wood and make a big fire, sit round it and swap stories. The major told us of his exploits in the Radfan Campaign in Aden, I talked about Ulster, and Dave and André, natural raconteurs, provided the most enjoyment with their swashbuckling tales of Rhodesia and elsewhere.

We once almost lost André in mid-anecdote. As he leant across to shift a log on the fire, Janni shouted 'stop' and switched on his torch. Sitting on the log, inches from André's hand, was the biggest scorpion I had ever seen. How Janni saw it in the dark I will never know.

When phase two finished, we were down to about sixty men. We had lost Dave and André, who had apparently left the Rhodesian SAS without permission. It seems they had been on leave in South Africa when a major operation had been launched in Angola, and, fearing their country was about to become embroiled in another major war, they had approached South Africa's Special Forces and offered their services.

They had made no secret of the fact that they were on leave and the Army, desperate for experienced soldiers, had accepted them. Unfortunately this had resulted in a major rift with the Rhodesian SAS, who immediately classed them as deserters and threatened to arrest them if they ever re-entered Rhodesia. They were told that they would have to return to Rhodesia and obtain a formal discharge before they could undertake Selection again. As far as I know, neither man did. The major too went his own way. Ahead of me was perhaps the most difficult part of Selection.

For phase three, the individual stage, we were transported by aircraft to the Caprivi Strip in South West Africa, the operational base of Recce Commando. There was one major river in the area; the rest of the country was semi-desert bush, and the heat was oppressive. For the first time we were given deadlines. If you were not at the checkpoint on time you were off the course, no excuses. Water was a critical factor. Once away from the river, if you ran out of water you couldn't hope to make your checkpoint.

There was also a terrorist threat from SWAPO terrorists based in Zambia. We all carried four magazines for our R4 rifles. (Shortly after our Selection ended, four members of the South African Airforce were ambushed and killed just south of where we were training.)

We were forced to move in the heat of the day. I was often close to collapse, and my dehydration was made worse by chronic gippo guts from drinking unpurified water. I staggered from one checkpoint to the next, just making the timings but getting ever more tired. Sometimes I risked moving after dark on a compass bearing. One night, as I approached the river, I heard the sound of a large animal. Out of the dark loomed a huge hippo; we stared at each other for several seconds, then, rather contemptuously I thought, he turned and shuffled off. I had never faced such hazards fighting the Phantasians on Salisbury Plain.

On my sixth day alone, I found myself at a checkpoint by the river. I was near total exhaustion. Even the weight of my water bottles, on which I depended so much, seemed to me to be too great. I decided I could make it to the next checkpoint and back on one. As I stood to leave I found my instructor beside me. 'If I was you,' he said conversationally, 'I would fill both my water bottles.'

I didn't need to be warned twice. I reached the next checkpoint by mid-afternoon. Instead of being sent back towards the river I was sent deeper into the desert. I went nowhere near the river for the rest of the day.

I had to be at base by dawn the following morning. I staggered through the night, more asleep than awake. I made the checkpoint just before first light.

I was met with a ferocious assault from the three instructors. I was without doubt the very worst example of a soldier they'd ever seen. I was subjected to a ten-minute bout of rifle PT before being given my next checkpoint, a kilometre away. I was told I might very well be thrown off the course when I got there. I wasn't even allowed to go to the river to refill my water bottles. Didn't I want to give up now?

I turned and started to plod up the hill. That kilometre was the hardest and longest I've ever walked. The hill seemed like a mountain; my pack bore down on me like the weight of the world. If I could have cried, I would have.

Gradually the trees got bigger and I found myself in shade. As I shuffled along I saw the outlines of buildings on my left and right. A shout went up: 'Here's one!' Men poured out of the buildings, mostly wearing the Recce Commando beret and black T-shirt. They formed two lines. As I walked through them they began to clap and cheer. At the end of the line stood Major Blauw, magnificent in full uniform. He offered me his hand. As I shook it he said: 'Congratulations, Corporal McCallion, you have passed Recce Commando Selection.' He handed me my maroon beret. I still have it to this day.

The assembled Recces gave a cheer. Never before had I felt so proud. A beer was pushed into my hand; as I was led away the major shouted after me: 'Your next RV is the bar.'

Of the 410 hopefuls who had started Selection, thirty-nine completed phase three. I'd lost 20lb and made friends that would last me a lifetime. After I'd showered and shaved off my four-week growth of beard, I had a huge steak dinner, which I constantly interrupted to go and greet another member of Selection as he staggered in. That night we assembled in the unit's bar, a beautiful oasis in the desert, where we all got drunk. For those of us who'd been through Selection that took about two beers.

We had a few days off before we began our Special Forces training. This started with two weeks' weapons training; we had to familiarize ourselves with a huge variety of small arms. The Recces worked almost exclusively outside South Africa. In the main, we dressed and carried the weapons of the opposition in the country in which we operated. In the basic Recce Commando team of six men, five would carry AK47 assault rifles (the finest close-combat rifle I've ever used), one RPD light machine-gun, one RPG 7 rocket launcher and 60mm Portuguese commando mortar. If the job was a 'straight' raid many of the commandos preferred to carry the Para version of the R4, which had a folding butt, because of its harder hitting power.

Next we did a two-week demolition course concentrating on

the use of claymore mines (the Rhodesian mini-claymore was the favoured weapon) and sabotage techniques.

Each Recce carried Soviet-type chest webbing for the AK47 magazines. This consisted of five long pouches. Instead of a magazine in the middle pouch each man carried a mini-claymore, with twelve inches of safety fuse and a detonator and friction striker. In an emergency, if your team wanted to break a contact, you'd plant your mine, hit the striker and then run. Roughly thirty seconds later the claymore would explode. The enemy had been known to run through the first, and then the second line of claymores. Nobody had ever run through a third.

Bushcraft, tracking and survival were next, back in the Caprivi Strip. The course leader was a legend in the South African Defence Force, Sergeant-Major Deval De Beer. He had once spent six months living with the Bushmen of the South West African Veldt, with only a rifle and a bag of salt, surviving on only what he caught and found to eat. He was one of the very few whites ever to have mastered the complex language of the Bushmen and they looked on him as something of a god. Reputed to be the best tracker in Africa, he was the only person who ever got a Grade A on the Selous Scouts tracking course.

He had once tracked a SWAPO incursion party that had murdered a family in South West Africa, from the front of a fast-moving Landrover. The Recces had caught up with the terrorists and eliminated them. For a man who was in every sense a living legend, he was unexpectedly small, one of the very few men in the unit smaller than me. Yet his awesome knowledge of the bush, coupled with a physical stamina that enabled him to outrun or outmarch any man in the unit, demanded the respect of everybody who met him. Before we went to the bush camp he introduced himself to each man personally. He observed me coolly. I returned his gaze unflinchingly. His weather-hardened features were creased white at the corners of his eyes and mouth. This was a man who liked to smile and laugh a lot.

'What's your name, Corporal?'

'McCallion, Sergeant-Major.'

'Ah, the paratrooper from England. What's an Englishman doing coming to fight for the Boer?'

'I'm Scots,' I replied, a little indignantly.

'Scots are good fighters, I hear. Play good rugby. Do you play?'

'Yes. Hooker.'

'Good, good. What do your friends call you?'

'Jock.'

'Then I'll call you Jock too.' He slapped me hard on the shoulder, nearly bowling me over.

On our first night in the bush, as the sun began to set, a mournful cry drifted across the still river to our camp. Every man stopped what he was doing to listen. The cry went on, hauntingly beautiful and infinitely sad. I looked questioningly at De Beer.

'It's a fish eagle, Jock.'

'It sounds so sad.'

He nodded. 'It is. They mate for life and if their mate dies they never take another. That's the sound they make when they've lost their mate.'

It was something I will never forget. Even now, years later, when I watch the sun go down, I still hear it, an echo from my past.

For the first three weeks we were given no food, apart from a cup of coffee in the morning and at night. We survived on what we caught ourselves. There were lions in the area. Whatever we did, De Beer said, we were not, repeat not, to go near one after a kill. The R4 rifles we carried were probably not enough to stop a charging lion.

After about five days, two stalwarts stumbled out of the bush and almost tripped over a lion which was busy consuming a large kudu. They screamed and jumped back, expecting the big cat to charge them. Instead, it took off as fast as it could in the opposite direction. Thinking themselves lucky to be alive, and not wanting to look a gift kudu in the mouth, they hoisted their prize and made their way back to camp. As they told their story our mouths watered at the prospect of an unexpected meal. Deval De Beer was sceptical. They had been lucky, he warned them, but allowed them to prepare the kudu for the pot.

Four days later they chased a second lion from its kill. On this occasion the sergeant-major was not so charitable. We were refused permission to cook it and warned any such future adventures would result in dismissal.

An ex-Green Beret Special Force soldier and Vietnam veteran

had joined the course as a fully-fledged Recce. He'd already been on an operation. He'd missed the survival stage of his training, due to some administrative problem concerning his Selection, so knew where the survival camp would be based. He, and another candidate, took advantage of the fact to dig in a cache of food. How either of them expected to get away with it was hard to imagine, for in addition to the redoubtable Deval De Beer, the entire area was patrolled by a half platoon of Bushmen – probably the finest trackers in the world. Once they had seen your footprints they could recognize your track, even if you swapped shoes. In a dramatic fireside confrontation De Beer banished the two men from the course.

The rest of us continued training and it was exhilarating stuff, culminating in a night hare hunt. Powerful searchlights were mounted on the Mercedes Unimog all-terrain vehicles and we travelled at breakneck speed through the darkened bush until a hare was picked up in the beam. The hare, mesmerized by the light, would either freeze or run in circles pursued by those on foot. Over thirty hares were brought back and skinned, our first real meal for three weeks.

The next phase was the tracking course itself. Having spent most of my life in a city, I hadn't the faintest grasp of these skills. It was at this stage that I first came to be impressed by and then to marvel at the wisdom of Deval De Beer and his Bushmen assistants. The ground for them was a story-book – each little indentation or crushed blade of grass providing an endless source of information.

I would often sit down at a track junction and listen engrossed as Deval, or one of the Bushmen, would reveal in great detail the men and animals that had passed over that patch of ground over the past few days. Driving out of the camp one day Deval suddenly yelled, 'Stop', and leapt from his vehicle. He landed in the bush and grabbed a handful of twigs and a long, thin stick. Telling everyone not to move, he walked slowly around his vehicle and stopped barely ten feet from us. Watching from the back of the truck, I saw him shake the loose bundle of twigs. Suddenly a snake struck the bundle with lightning speed. Deval let it continue striking until it grew tired, then trapped its tail with the stick, which he slowly slid up its body to its head. He then grabbed the eight-foot monster by the back of the head and held it up for us to see.

'This,' he informed us, 'is a black mamba. If this snake was to bite you, you would be taken back to camp but be dead long before you got there.'

As the camp was only five minutes' drive away this concentrated the mind wonderfully.

'Look at it,' he continued, 'and remember it. If you're walking in the bush and you get in its way it will kill you.'

I studied the snake with the fascination that most humans feel for reptiles. Its body was more grey than black, quite thick in the middle but tapering to a long, sleek head. Deval threw it from him. As he did so the five Bushmen who were with us screamed and ran behind our truck. Deval immediately brought his rifle up to his shoulder. The snake landed and reared up at least five feet from the ground, so fast it was hard to follow. It dropped down again to the bush floor and actually advanced on Deval, who was staring at it fixedly over his gunsight. Man and snake watched one another from a distance of less than ten feet before the snake retired to the safety of the bush, rearing up every so often to make sure we were not following.

Later Deval stopped at a water-hole. It was the dry season and the muddy edges were covered with animal tracks. Deval called me forward and pointed to one particular set. 'What made those, Jock?'

'Kudu,' I offered, with more hope than conviction.

'Good. Male or female?'

I hadn't a clue. Seeing my distress, he continued: 'It's female. See here, it urinated, you can tell by the way it spread its feet.'

I nodded.

'Now follow them, see how the stride pattern suddenly lengthens, something scared it, it started to run.' He followed the antelope's footprints, then stopped.

'It almost made it, but was too slow. See?'

Running from the opposite end of the water-hole were a set of deep pug marks. I looked up at Deval.

'Lion?'

'Yes, Jock. Male or female?'

'Female. A male's would be much heavier.'

'You're right, even a small male would leave a bigger imprint. They have wider paws than the female.'

There were signs of a disturbance at the edge of the dried-up mud bank that surrounded the hole. Even my untrained eye could tell that the two animals had collided and rolled over.

'Is this where the lioness made its kill? There's no blood.'

'Yes, they don't usually tear their prey – mostly they suffocate it by putting their jaws over its mouth and nose. See?' He pointed to the ground. 'You can make out where she lifted it up after it was dead and dragged it away.'

It was all there, if you could read it, all the drama of the African bush, just waiting to be unlocked. Deval nudged me in the ribs.

'We'll make a tracker out of you yet.'

Despite Deval's confidence I just picked up the rudiments and only managed to pass the tracking stage with a little assistance from a Bushman sergeant who seemed to have taken a shine to me. When following my allotted trail I completely lost the track and was searching vainly for any sign. I had forgotten the first lesson in tracking: don't look at the ground, but for possible routes the quarry might have taken, and only glance occasionally down for confirmation of the trail. I happened to notice that my Bushman commander's eyes kept flicking behind me. I did a 180-degree turn and was able to pick up the track again and complete my assignment. Whether Deval and his instructors noticed my extra help I have no way of knowing. Nothing was ever said, though when Deval congratulated me on passing the course he said he would never trust me to track anything at any time.

This was the most enjoyable three weeks of my stay in Africa. The nights were spent round a large fire after a hearty meal, drinking coffee and listening to Deval as he told story after story about the African bush and the Bushmen he so dearly loved. He told of the blood feud between the Bushmen and our present opponents in Angola and South West Africa, SWAPO. Bushmen had always been hunted and oppressed by their black neighbours, who coveted their women with their exquisite, slightly oriental features and diminutive size. To the lasting shame of the white man the oppression of the Bushman had continued right up until the twentieth century. As late as the early thirties there were still organized Bushman hunts. Nevertheless, with the advent of the war in South West Africa the Army was not slow to capitalize on their tracking and fighting skills. They were used first as trackers, then later organized into a fighting force, 31 Battalion, which performed heroically in the Angolan war.

As Deval told it, in the early stages of the confrontation with SWAPO a Bushman patrol had found an ambush position. They reported it to a white officer, who checked the position and decided it was an old one. Two days later a Bushman patrol was sent out to have a look at this 'old' position. Seven men were ambushed and annihilated. For a race of only two to three thousand this loss of seven young males was a catastrophe. The various bands of Bushmen formed together, sent their women into hiding and headed *en masse* for the border to exact revenge. They were prevented from crossing the border by the South African Army and police. After negotiations during which some of the old chiefs were taken into custody and their rifles confiscated, they eventually gave an oath not to cross the border unless ordered to do so, but they swore eternal vengeance on any member of SWAPO who fell into their clutches.

Towards the end of the course, as we sat round our camp-fire, we were told that two buffalo had to be killed to feed the Bushmen. Traditionally a member of the Selection course shot one. I was chosen. Deval said: 'Here you see a great white hunter, all the way from Scotland. Tomorrow he is going to hunt the most dangerous animal in Africa armed with the weapon least suitable for the job! I want you all to wish him well.'

My companions gave a round of applause. I grinned from ear to ear and felt elation and anticipation well up inside me.

At daybreak Deval gave us a lecture on the African bull buffalo and how to hunt it with an FN 7.62 rifle. 'A bull weighs well over a ton. It can, and will, charge at speeds of up to forty-five miles an hour. If you don't stop this beast it will kill you. Its skull is solid bone, nearly an inch thick; its horns are over four inches in diameter. When it charges it cannot be killed with a head shot with an Express .50-calibre elephant gun, let alone an FN 7.62. Your only hope is to shoot it in the spine. When it's coming straight at you, your target area is two inches wide by about a foot long.'

My comrades, who had been rather envious on the previous night, were showing distinct signs of relief that it was me and not them who had been chosen for the hunt. Deval could see my unease. His face broke into a broad smile. 'Don't worry, Jock, you're going to shoot your buffalo from the back of one of our Unimogs, not on foot. Hunting on foot is a job for professional hunters, who are fresh and have the correct weapons and a back-up, not for a tired recruit with only an FN.' He paused. 'This is, of course, if you get a clean kill. It it's only wounded you'll have to track it and kill it on foot.' Deval's grey-blue eyes bored into mine. His voice, normally cheerful, had become ice-cold and emotionless. 'The most dangerous animal in the world is a wounded bull buffalo. It will dog-leg into thick bush, where we can't take the vehicles, and wait. Its eyesight is poor, so it normally charges at about fifty metres. You only have four to five seconds at the most before it kills you. If it comes to that, remember, aim for the spine. Nothing else will stop it.'

There was total silence. All eyes were on me. My mouth was dry, and anyway I couldn't trust myself to speak, so I simply nodded. Then Deval gave a great laugh and slapped me hard on the shoulder. 'But I'm sure you'll get him first shot, Jock.' Everyone laughed.

We mounted two Unimogs and set off. I was on the back of the first vehicle, just behind Deval. Our driver was Fabes, a sandy-haired, swashbuckling Afrikaner with a physique most body-builders would give a year's supply of steroids to possess. The morning was beautiful, the air so dry and clean it made you feel you'd live for ever. Barely fifteen minutes from the camp we sighted the herd, two to three hundred strong. A hundred yards or so from them, Deval called us to a halt.

'Remember, Jock, only a bull, and aim for the spine. Are you ready?'

I checked my FN; it was cocked and had a full mag. Deval looked at Fabes. 'Let's go.'

In seconds we were among the stampeding herd. Out of the mêlée, a magnificent bull came straight at us. Fabes swerved as its lowered horns grazed the front offside of the Unimog. Then it was beside us.

Above the thunder of hoofs Deval shouted: 'Shoot, Jock, shoot!'

I raised the FN. The barrel was shaking terribly. I couldn't get a sight on the animal's back. For a split second I had one, and my finger caressed the trigger. As I fired the Unimog hit a bump. I knew instinctively I'd missed my target and almost in desperation I fired twice more. The huge beast veered off. We came to an abrupt stop. I raised my rifle again but Deval's hand came up.

'Don't! You can't get a killing shot from this angle.'

He dropped lightly to the ground. Fabes stood up, nervously scanning the bush. Deval walked several yards behind us then dropped to his knee. He touched the bush floor with his hand, then his nose. Looking at me, he said: 'You've hit him, Jock. Bad, but not bad enough. You'd better get down.'

I walked slowly over to Deval, whose face was chalk white.

'It's a dangerous thing we're going to do now, Jock.'

Years later I was to read how the son of the great wartime commando leader, Lord Lovat, was killed doing exactly what I was about to do and remembered Deval's words.

He pointed to a patch of bush some seventy yards away. 'I think it's in there. We're going to walk slowly towards it. Never take your eyes off it. When it charges . . .'

'I know, the spine.'

The bush was thick – small trees and clumps of dense scrub and thorn-bushes. I kept my eyes fixed on where Deval had indicated but for the life of me I couldn't see anything. How could something as large as a buffalo just disappear? We were thirty yards into the bush when I heard a noise like a low, gruff cough. We froze. It was hard to tell where the sound came from, but it sounded awfully close. I was about to step forward again when Deval's left hand grasped my shoulder. He pointed slightly to the left of the bush we were heading towards. I saw a greyish-brown shape. I was raising my rifle when there was a thunderous bellow: a mixture of pain, anger and defiance. The bull emerged, head down, charging us at full speed.

It seemed to fill my entire world, like an express train coming out of a tunnel. I sighted along the barrel and fired. A puff of dust erupted from the creature's horns. Too low. I fired again. This time the shot was high on its left shoulder. For just a second panic threatened to overwhelm me. Was it stoppable? I gritted my teeth, my eyes fixed on the target. ('The spine, Jock, the spine.') In a microsecond the first lesson on marksmanship I ever learnt in the

Paras came back to me: don't jerk the trigger, squeeze it. Slowly, I did. The bull suddenly did a forward somersault and lay with its left leg twitching. I later measured the distance from where it fell to our position. It was exactly fourteen metres.

Deval had his rifle resting nonchalantly on his shoulder.

'You didn't fire?'

He shook his head. 'No, it's your kill. Besides' – he turned and smiled – 'I always knew you could stop it.'

Those words meant a lot to me. I walked over to the buffalo. Its back was broken but it still tried to get to its feet. Suddenly I felt like crying. It had a heart as big as Africa. Even though it was mortally wounded, it wanted to fight me with its dying breath. I turned away, unable to watch as Deval gave it the *coup de grâce*. I was aware of him standing beside me, a sad, ironic look on his face.

'I know what you're feeling, Jock. It was the same with my first buffalo. But always remember, we shot it not for sport but to feed others. That's the way of Africa.'

One of the instructors shot a second buffalo from the back of the Unimog, showing us how it should have been done. We loaded both carcasses and drove to the Bushmen's camp some five miles away. There were very few men there; most were employed by or actually serving with the SADF. We unloaded the two buffalo and the women set about butchering them immediately, showing a skill many a high-street butcher would have envied. I noticed our own Bushmen mixing with old friends and talking excitedly in their high-pitched, clicking tongue. 'They're telling of your hunt,' Deval said. 'They say you're a great hunter from across a great river, who risked his life to bring them food. You're part of their history now, Jock. The Bushmen don't have a written language, they keep their history alive by storytelling. As long as this band lives the story of your hunt will live.'

That night the instructors gave us a superb meal and afterwards I moved to sit beside the slowly winding river. It was pleasantly warm, the sky still lit by the sinking sun. The wind was filled with the calls of late hunting birds, grunting hippos and the occasional snorting of a cat. It was a timeless moment of awe-inspiring beauty. I wished I could sit there for ever. My reverie was interrupted by a loud shout. Deval emerged out of the darkness, a radio in one hand, a bottle of brandy in the other, followed by Fabes and two instructors.

'Jock, do you know which is the best rugby team in South Africa?'

I shook my head, smiling.

'Northern Transvaal. Do you know where I'm from?'

'Northern Transvaal?' I ventured.

'That's right.' He poked a finger playfully in my chest. 'Now do you know which team has won the Inter-Provincial Championship?'

'Northern Transvaal?'

'Right again. Now, Jock, you're going to have a drink with us to celebrate.'

A mug filled with a generous measure of brandy was pressed into my hand. We raised our improvised glasses in a toast and knocked back a slug. I nearly gagged. I hadn't eaten properly in six weeks and my stomach threatened to rebel against this sudden assault by alcohol. Fabes slapped me on the back and refilled my mug. For two hours we sat toasting Northern Transvaal and swapping stories, mine about Ulster, theirs about the Angolan war, and we all became gloriously drunk.

Suddenly Deval ordered us to be quiet. At first I heard nothing, then in the distance the sound of a small outboard motor.

'Do you know what that is?' He didn't wait for an answer. 'Poachers coming across from Botswana to shoot hippo. Bastards. I hate poachers.' Without warning he jumped up, lifted his rifle and fired in the direction of the river. In seconds the instructors were on their feet firing bursts with AK47s and FNs. Every now and again they would pause and we could hear quite clearly the sound of the boat circling. Then they would open fire again. Eventually the boat took off at high speed towards Botswana. Highly satisfied, we adjourned to bed.

I woke at first light with a monumental hangover and staggered to the main camp-site. No sooner had I arrived than a patrol from the South African Border Police turned up. Deval, looking much the worse for wear, went to greet them.

'Two fishermen from Botswana were fired on during the night.'

'You mean poachers,' Deval said.

The burly police officer shrugged and smiled. Both men had been hit, one in the leg, the other in the arm.

'Were you firing last night?'

'Yes, indeed we were,' Deval said. 'We had a live firing exercise.'

The police officer looked at Deval, then at us, shrugged again, said he would have to report to his superiors, and left. We heard no more about it.

After packing up we drove back to Fort Doppies to clean up and have an end-of-course party. The bar in the operational camp was colourfully decorated with captured weapons and trophies. Everything had a story behind it, even the solid oak bar. Marius Fallun, the giant with the red beard, had wandered into the South African Border Police local for a drink, during the course of which the police had boasted that their bar was the heaviest in South West Africa. Even four Recces couldn't carry it outside. If they could, they could have it. Marius surveyed the bar. He couldn't carry it outside on his own, but if he could pick it up could he have it? Certainly, his hosts had replied. To their astonishment he did so. It weighed over three hundred pounds. The next day Marius arrived with a truck and four other Recces. The bar was in Fort Doppies that night.

Fabes told me the story. As we drank more I felt I should repay him and decided to teach him the Irish drinking song 'I've Been a Wild Rover'. Fabes loved the song, making me repeat it over and over again until he could remember every word. Its story, of an unreformed drinker, fighter and wanderer, exactly mirrored his own life. From then on he would break into song at the earliest opportunity, banging out the chorus on the bar with his big fists. As Fabes was to singing what Adolf Hitler was to race relations, not everybody was happy I taught him.

By midnight I was merrily drunk, leaning against the bar and soaking up the stories of all the other trophies. People began to drift away from me. I turned to find out why. Behind me was the former Green Beret who had been caught stashing food on the course. He ordered a drink and after a little preamble began a tirade about how badly he had been treated. I let him ramble on. Then he started to insult Deval De Beer. I told him, in quite colourful language, that he was not fit to mention the man's name.

He threw a drink over me. I suggested we step outside. He was over six foot tall and muscular and stood in a classic karate pose: feet well spread, left fist forward, right turned upwards to strike. I thought, Harry, you might have bitten off more than you can chew. The American launched a beautiful roundhouse kick to my head. It missed by a mile.

I began to walk round him, smiling, my eyes never leaving his hands. I never look at a man's eyes, always his hands. Nobody ever hit me with their eyes. I spoke to my adversary, keeping my voice low and calm.

'I don't know any karate, but let me show you how we fight in Glasgow.' Leaping up, I head-butted him, breaking his nose, and as his head came forward on the rebound I bit off the top of his ear. All thoughts of karate deserted him as he scratched my face like a demented woman. We fell to the floor and by the time we were pulled apart he was in a terrible mess.

Very little was said about the fight. Deval gave us a talking-to then sent the American off to get stitched up. I went back to the party. On his return to Durban, the American was put on admin duties and then invited to leave the unit. The only real flak I got was from one of his friends. As the party started to disperse he came up to me and pointed his rifle at my head.

'I don't like the way you fight,' he muttered drunkenly.

He was ushered away by his friends. Funnily enough, and quite by accident, I shot him twice in the leg during some live contact drills six weeks later. After that I never saw him again.

We returned to Durban for a well-earned break and on my first day back I was involved in my second and last fist-fight in South Africa. The most popular programme on children's TV there was a puppet show featuring a gigantic dragon called the Cry Monster who was continually trying to eat the other puppets. In the unit we had a man nicknamed the Cry Monster. He was a Boer to his bootstraps; brought up to believe that everything English was the work of the Devil and that the English had tried to exterminate the Boer women in concentration camps by feeding them broken glass.

All this was unknown to me. I walked into the unit's bar for a quick beer before going home and became aware of a large head turning to observe me.

'Hey, Englishman, where have you come from?' said a guttural, drunken voice.

Even sitting the Cry Monster looked huge. I gave him the benefit of a cold stare. 'I'm not English, I'm a Scot.'

He stood up. It was like watching a volcano getting ready to erupt. He lumbered slowly towards me and bent down so that his face was close to mine. A finger like a large sausage poked me in the chest. 'If I say you're an Englishman, you're an Englishman.'

I poked him back. 'No I'm not.'

He hit me; a short, vicious jab just below the heart. I felt as if my chest had caved in. Desperately, I stabbed out with my right thumb, driving it into the big man's eye. He roared with anger, throwing his head back. I punched him in the throat with my left fist. Another hammer blow hit me in my right side. I distinctly heard a rib break. My back was against the wall. A titanic blow, that would surely have removed my head, thundered into the wooden panelling, leaving a vast hole. More blows hit me as I began to slide towards the floor, punching furiously at my adversary. His body was like iron; I might as well have thrown snowballs at him. From beyond my vision I heard a shout. Everything stopped. The unit RSM stepped into sight; he was a man nobody argued with. He spoke in a low voice, first in Afrikaans. The Cry Monster stood to attention.

Then, in English, the RSM said: 'You're a disgrace to the unit, fighting in the NCOs' bar. Be in my office in five minutes.'

With great difficulty, I stood to attention. We had the most intense tongue-lashing I've ever had, in two languages. The fight cost me a week's pay, and two broken ribs. Eight months later, after returning from operations, I walked into the same bar. There sat the Cry Monster. I stood beside him. From across the room a Recce asked: 'Hey, Englishman, are you just back?'

The Cry Monster threw a huge arm round my shoulder. 'He's not an Englishman, he's a Scot.' He looked across at me. Sitting down made us almost the same height. 'What will you drink, Jock?'

After a five-day break, we went back to the Caprivi Strip to finish our training with an eight-week tactics course. Rising at first light and finishing at 2200 we learnt and practised every skill we would need to operate in the unit. We fired thousands of rounds of live ammunition. Three members of the course were shot during live firing exercises – about par for the course. The officer in charge was Lieutenant Kocky de Toit, a tall man with a lean, teak-hard body. His swarthy features were dominated by a hooked nose that gave him the appearance of a bird of prey. His opening talk showed his devotion to his chosen profession.

'This next course will decide which of you will go forward on to operations. Soldiering is not a part-time profession. I am never off duty. When I drive my car I observe the countryside around me and think how I would cross it if there was an enemy patrolling it. When I'm walking and see a hill, I wonder how I would attack it if it was an enemy position. Within a few short weeks, those who pass this course will be in combat. After that you will come to realize that you can never let your mind become dulled. Not if you want to live and not if you want to be a Recce.'

One afternoon I was given the task of clearing out the unit's armoury. It was a gun freak's heaven. Explosives, ammunition and weapons of every shape and design were scattered about. I found a small pack of Australian detonators, half the size of normal ones. I kept these; I had a use for them.

The course finished with stiff written and practical examinations. We were also 'buddy-rated'. Each man gave his fellow students a rating of between ten and zero, for as we'd lived, worked and sweated together for nearly six months it was an excellent way for the instructors to find out just what we thought of each other. I came third. One of my final tests was a TEWT, Tactical Exercise Without Troops, with Kocky de Toit. He sat in the shade of a low tree, clipboard in hand, and fired questions at me. What patrol formation would I use to cross that stream? Where would I lay an ambush on the river? What are the unit's ambush drills? What method of initiation would I use to set off the ambush? The questions came thick and fast. Suddenly Kocky stopped and observed me over the top of his clipboard.

'Why are you here, Jock?'

The question took me completely by surprise. I said the first thing that came into my mind. 'I'm trying to pass this tactics course.'

Kocky smiled. 'That's not what I meant. Why are you in South Africa? Why are you trying to get into the Recces?'

I started to give him what had become my standard reply to such questions: South Africa was the last bastion of democracy against communist aggression in Africa and I thought it was my duty to help defend it etc. Kocky listened patiently then sighed.

'Don't try to bullshit me, Jock. I'm going to be leading you in action very soon. What's your real reason for being here?'

I looked him squarely in the eyes. 'I want to fight. The British Army has spent a fortune training me, only to send me to Ulster against an enemy they won't allow me to fight. I want to find out if I can do it for real.'

'I thought so. It's as good a reason as any. For me, of course, it's different, I'm a Boer. Do you know what that means?'

'Farmer.'

'It means more than that. To us it means the land itself and the freedom to rule ourselves, to be our own people. Even the blacks call us the white tribe of Africa. To me that's something worth fighting for.'

'What about the blacks? Don't they have the same rights?'

He grimaced. 'Of course, Jock, only a madman could resist change for ever. But now is not the time, not with the communists pulling the ANC's strings. If the rest of the world will just give us time we will find our own solution, an African solution.' He paused for a second to collect his thoughts before continuing: 'Now, Jock, you have twenty men, two 60mm mortars and three light machine-guns. Tell me how you would deploy them to attack a three-man enemy observation post on that hill . . .'

Our training was nearly finished. Of the 410 men who started only twelve remained. We were allowed the luxury of a drinking party, secure in the knowledge that there would be no training the next day. It was a marathon session where we started on beer but ended up drinking vast quantities of rum. At some time in the early hours of the morning I was called upon to partner Kocky in a game of darts. I was very drunk.

'Here's the darts, Jock.'

'Right, boss. Where's the throwing line?'

Kocky guided me to a chalked mark on the wooden floor. 'Got it, boss. Now where's the board?'

'Underneath that light, Jock.' He pointed an outstretched arm. Seeing a dim light in the distance, I took careful aim and threw. My dart punctured the light.

The next morning we all took time to surface. When I woke

my head was pounding and my mouth felt like the inside of Gandhi's left flip-flop. When we'd recovered sufficiently Kocky called us into the briefing room. He looked around our twelve bleary-eyed faces.

'It is normal at the end of training for the Selection Course to undertake an operation.'

All thoughts of my hangover disappeared.

Kocky surveyed us and smiled.

'We have one for you.'

4

OPERATIONS

'Gentlemen, we are going to change history.'
Commandant K, from the briefing for Operation Milk
Float

Our first operation, code-named First Blood, was to destroy a temporary base in Zambia belonging to SWAPO, the guerrilla group fighting for the independence of South West Africa (now Namibia). The base was a small transit camp, situated less than ten kilometres over the border. It had been recced by Lieutenant de Toit and the support group, who knew the ground well and estimated there were no more than thirty terrorists there. Like all good military operations the plan was simple. We would be lifted by helicopter to within five kilometres of our target and walk the rest of the way. South African helicopters had been deliberately flying over the area for several weeks, so their distant sound would not unduly worry the camp's inhabitants.

Once in the area, we would split into an assault group, led by Kocky de Toit, and a fire-support group, under the command of a senior sergeant who had flown up from Durban. The assault group would be divided into two teams of six. I had command of one. Kocky would be in the centre with his radio operator. The fire-support team would lay a string of claymore mines along the side of the enemy camp, then proceed to a flanking position. They would be armed with three RPD light machine-guns, two commando mortars and an RPG rocket launcher. At H hour Kocky would fire a green flare, the mines would be detonated and the camp raked with fire for exactly thirty seconds, then switched to a secondary arc of fire on the camp's perimeter. Anybody breaking over this line would be shot. Kocky would then fire a red flare and we would advance into the killing zone, killing any enemy we encountered and driving others into the path of the waiting support machine-guns.

After months of Selection and training we were going to see action. Despite the fact that this time we were doing it for real, nothing seemed different. We rehearsed everything in minute detail: boarding the helicopter, the patrol formation to the target area, the setting up of the assault and finally the assault itself. Two hours were given to prepare kit and test weapons for an inspection at 5 p.m. Then supper followed by an enforced rest until 10 o'clock, when a final inspection would be made. I always found sleep difficult before an operation but the idea of an enforced rest is a good one, giving each man the opportunity to relax his body, if not his mind. The three companions who shared my room spent most of the time reading the Bible. The Afrikaner soldier is a deeply religious man. They are fond of saying they fight all wars with a rifle in one hand and the Bible in the other. I didn't believe in organized religion, but on the assumption that I could be wrong, I always tried to make peace with God before a battle. I would simply ask Him to look on the good things I had done and if I had forgotten Him, to please not forget me.

At 10 a.m. the next morning we paraded. I was armed with an AK47 with a double magazine, two thirty-round mags welded together, with five thirty-round mags in my chest webbing. In addition, I carried a Beretta 9mm pistol with a fifteen-round mag, two fragmentation grenades, a white-phosphorus grenade and two red smoke grenades, food and water to last me twenty-four hours, a map, compass and kit, the fighting battle order of a combat Recce soldier. We had a final inspection; weapons were checked, each soldier jumped up and down to check for any excess noise, then we moved off on foot in single file to RV with the helicopters in open ground to the west of the camp.

Thirty minutes later the helicopters landed at our own LZ and we embarked. We flew in a circular route to the drop-off point, in case any SWAPO patrols or agents had detected our departure. Then we were out of the helicopters and in enemy territory. We fanned out into our patrol formation, in single file with two lead scouts and a flanking scout on each side. Not for the first time did

I marvel at the silence with which my fellow Recces moved. Most had been born and raised on farms and had been hunting since they were big enough to hold a rifle. They glided through the bush like ghosts.

We took our time reaching the target area, stopping frequently to listen. Every forty minutes we would have a five-minute stop and change our scouts. Hardly a whisper was exchanged. Two and a half hours later we reached the outskirts of the enemy camp. Even a poor tracker could begin to see the tell-tale signs of footprints in the soft sand of the surrounding bush. The countryside was mostly sparse with occasional large clumps of low trees. The enemy's camp was in one such clump which surrounded a small water-hole.

Lieutenant de Toit deployed the assault force, making sure each man knew where the enemy was. Kocky was so cool and professional you'd have thought he was out for a stroll in the park. The fire-support group moved off. It would take them most of the night to lay their long line of claymores and if they were discovered we would have to do an immediate assault in darkness. I checked my watch: 0100, about four and a half hours until dawn. We were lying within arm's length of each other and one man would rest for thirty minutes while his buddy kept watch. The night passed slowly. I felt a gentle shake on my shoulder. I must have dozed off. I checked my watch: 0530. The sun was just beginning to rise; a bird began to sing. I looked to my left to see Kocky getting to his feet. It was H hour.

Kocky lifted his pencil flare gun and fired a green flare. Almost immediately there was the deafening concussion of the claymores being fired. I don't know what it did to the enemy but it shook me. For a second, I felt as if all the air had been sucked out of my lungs. Then the machine-guns opened up, and the air was filled with hundreds of speeding red bees – boy, did they sting! Smaller explosions erupted in the camp as the RPGs and mortars found their mark. It seemed to be going on for ever. Above the din I heard Kocky shouting in Afrikaans for us to get to our feet. We stood in our assault line, all of us straining like sprinters waiting for the starter's gun for the word to advance.

Then there was silence. It was so sudden it caught me by surprise. I heard a drawn-out, coughing whine. Although I didn't realize what it was then, the noise was to become all too familiar to me. It was the sound a dying man gives as the air escapes from his body.

'*Advance!*'

I was so keen I ran forward two or three paces.

'Steady there, Jock,' Kocky shouted. I fell back into the assault line and we advanced into the killing zone.

What amazed me most was that no fire was directed at us. We simply walked in. I was aware of several running uniformed figures. I pointed my weapon at one and hesitated. After all those tours in Ulster I thought I should be giving a warning. Then the man on my right opened fire and the figure collapsed. I saw a second figure, naked to the waist, an AKS assault rifle in his hand. I fired, and cursed. I'd meant to fire two well-aimed shots but my AK was on auto. I'd hit him with about five rounds. As I went to step over him he groaned and moved. I fired again, this time a single, well-aimed shot. His face dissolved. I moved on now, firing at the fleeting targets around me. I saw a movement in a bush slightly to my right and a splash of red where no red should be. I fired two shots and a terrorist reared up, an AK47 in his hands. He was close enough for me to see the terror in his eyes. I fired twice more and he flipped over backwards and disappeared.

The sound of machine-gun fire halted me. We were at our limit of exploitation. Kocky held up his hand and we did an about-turn, moving back through the killing zone. There was the occasional shot as a wounded terrorist was dispatched. Recces seldom took prisoners unless specifically ordered to do so. Our second sweep completed, we thoroughly searched the bodies and collected all weapons and documents. Twenty-nine were accounted for in the camp and another five outside. Thirty-four, so our intelligence had been almost perfect. We booby-trapped several of the bodies with white-phosphorus grenades in the hope of catching some of the rescue party.

We did a quick head count. Everybody was there, none of us had a scratch. Kocky surveyed the carnage around us with grim satisfaction. I was so excited I could hardly breathe. He smiled down at me from his great height.

'Reminds me of my first op, Jock.'

'Really?'

'Yes, there we were, four against four hundred.'

My jaw dropped open; I was hanging on his every word. Then suddenly his darkened face broke into a broad grin.

'Toughest four we ever fought.'

He gave me a playful punch in the chest.

'Got you.'

I burst out laughing: it was just what was needed to bring us all back to reality. After gathering all the enemy weapons that were serviceable and laying a few anti-personnel mines under the ones that were not, we moved off quickly in our patrol formation, travelling faster now it was daylight. We covered the return distance in less than half the time and treated ourselves to a quick brew before the helicopters arrived. In less than three hours after the attack began we were back in Fort Doppies.

'Well done. You are all now members of the best special forces unit in the world and don't ever forget that,' Kocky roared. We gave a mighty cheer. 'Now go get a shower. The next RV is the bar.'

This custom was to characterize all future operations I undertook. After the action, good or bad, we would adjourn to the bar and everybody would have his say over a drink. The patrol commander would write up his report and circulate a copy among the men. Anyone was then free to voice his views to the commander or go direct to the CO. To some this might seem like anarchy but it had its roots in the first Boer Commandos and generally ensured that there were no hidden grievances that could destroy the cohesion of a small fighting unit. Our first operation had been an almost textbook success. We were on a high, and it was a very merry bunch of Recces that got drunk that night. I suppose I should have realized that it couldn't last.

For some time rumours had been circulating in the unit that a major strike was planned against SWAPO in Angola. Instead of going back to Durban after 'First Blood', we joined the preparations for what was to be the largest operation ever carried out by Recce Commando. The target was the main SWAPO supply base in Angola, code-named 'Camp Moscow'. It was just ten kilometres across the South West African border. They called it Operation Yeti.

The plan was simple. Two Hercules C130 transport planes would take just about every operational member of the unit, 120 in all, just to the north of the target. We would drop at night, walk the short distance to the camp and deploy and assault at first light. The camp was built in the shape of a huge vee, facing south. By attacking from the north we hoped to avoid the heavy 14.5mm and 12.5mm anti-aircraft guns dug in for ground defence. These were formidable weapons, capable of piercing armour. Behind them it was estimated there would be about 500 terrorists. But with surprise on our side, we didn't anticipate too many problems.

We practised for two weeks. The assault force, over a hundred strong, was to be divided into two wings. Fire support came from ten commando mortars. It was decided that they would fire the heavier South African Army sixty-millimetre mortar round instead of the Portuguese round it was designed for. This was to have disastrous consequences. After the attack 32 Battalion, a mercenary Battalion comprised mainly of ex-Portuguese commandos and paratroopers, would be flown in to cover our retreat.

As H hour drew near we made our final preparations. Each man was carrying very heavy personal ammunition and extra mortar and machine-gun rounds. As we expected to be in and out in less than six hours most of us carried only two water bottles.

After embarking at the main air base in South West Africa, the Assault Group flew north. Almost immediately things started to go wrong. Flying time should have been about an hour but two hours later we were still airborne. The pilot was hopelessly lost, in the flat, almost featureless terrain of southern Angola. Eventually, ninety minutes behind schedule, we parachuted into the night and made our RV. There had been no casualties during the drop. We set off south.

Daylight found us still walking. We stopped to try and find our bearings but this proved impossible. It was decided to ask for a spotter plane to fly us out. Two hours later it found us and relayed our position to us. It was not good news: we were not only seventeen kilometres from the target, but on the south side, the most heavily defended quarter. Nevertheless our commander, Major B, decided to continue.

We began to walk northwards. Our meagre supply of water was no match for the oppressive heat, and stops were frequent in the face of increasing dehydration. By mid-afternoon we were beginning to detect signs of enemy activity; vehicle noises quite close by and heavy boot imprints in the numerous small tracks we were crossing. We lay up and Major B made communication with the overall army commander, a general back in South West Africa. The major wanted to lie up and attack at first light as originally planned. His orders from the general were clear: he could attack now or withdraw.

Major B decided to attack. (I later asked him why. His answer was enlightening. There were many in the high command who distrusted the very concept of Special Forces; not to have attacked might have given them an excuse to disband the young unit.) We strung out in battle formation, our fire-support group on our left, and headed towards where we believed the enemy to be. At almost 1600, the enemy found us. A 14.5mm machine-gun opened up on our right flank, spitting death into our ranks. We turned to face the threat. The weight of fire was incredible, our whole attack faltered and disaster on a gigantic scale threatened to overwhelm us.

Then, quite unexpectedly, there was a lull. It was all we needed. With a collective roar we began to advance, firing magazine after magazine. Each man fought his own private battle whilst zigzagging forwards. In such circumstances the only thing that matters is to keep moving, and to get out of the enemy's killing zone. This calls for speed of thought and action, guts and aggression, the desire to close with the enemy and kill him. The intensive training and selection Recces go through now paid dividends. Slowly, but with a growing momentum, the tide turned, as the best fighting force in Africa attacked with a ferocity that was awe-inspiring to watch. Our mortars were going crazy but because they were using the heavier bomb some of the rounds dropped short, killing and wounding our people.

Then we were inside. There was only the briefest of fire-fights before the enemy withdrew. In fact we had captured only half the camp, the southern arm of the vee. The enemy still occupied the northern arm. They kept up a long-range contact with us but showed no inclination to counter-attack. It was time to take stock. We collected the enemy dead, sixty-six in all. But we had paid a price. The left flank had been caught in the deadly crossfire of the camp's vee formation. There were seven dead and fifteen wounded. Two gallantry decorations were won by men going out under fire to collect our dead and wounded.

Major B called for 32 Battalion to come in. While we waited our wounded were cared for and all the enemy weapons centralized. We also managed to locate a source of water and refilled our bottles. Then 32 Battalion, a piratical-looking bunch of rogues, arrived in a swarm of Puma helicopters. Our first priority was to evacuate our wounded. As they were being loaded Major B took their commander aside. With our combined forces we could attack the other half of the camp, he suggested. The reply was an emphatic no. The other commander had been told we were to evacuate, not continue the attack. This was a bitter blow: Recces dead and the job only half done.

After loading the dead, injured and all the terrorist weapons on to the helicopters, we turned and walked south. The march was exhausting; most of us were asleep on our feet. Eventually we crossed the border. A convoy of trucks emerged from the darkness and took us back to the main air base from where we had launched the assault. Although not a complete success, the bravery of the unit in such circumstances was awesome. I believed then, and still believe now, that few fighting units in the world could have done as well and none could have done better. Almost a year to the day after Operation Yeti, Camp Moscow was completely destroyed in a parachute assault by two battalions of the SADF.

Back in Durban everybody was preparing for Christmas. I was given a welcome three weeks' leave, the first real break I had enjoyed since leaving England. I settled my wife and family into our comfortable flat. The unit arranged credit for me so that we could buy furniture. The kids were enjoying the sunshine but Pat was very unhappy. She missed her friends in the UK and matters were made worse by the fact that she was seeing very little of me. We spent most of the time simply getting to know Durban, a lovely city with long, golden beaches. While on leave I bumped into other Recces and as ever in such circles rumours abounded. The most persistent was that my group, under Major B, were going to be sent on extended operations. Exactly where was unclear, but southern Angola or Zambia were the favourite bets.

On 2 January the rumours were confirmed. Major B, Lieutenant Kocky de Toit and Lieutenant D would be taking us on an extended phase of operations in southern Angola. This was top secret and nobody outside the unit was to know. Of course every married man told his wife, and every single man his girlfriends, and forty-eight hours later half of Durban knew. We were to leave on the 17th and spend two weeks in build-up training. This was very gentle compared with what had gone before: mostly shooting, mine laying and ambush drills.

On the final day of training we had a gigantic party. We would spend the following day with our families and leave at noon the day after. At 0200 most of our group had sought the sanctuary of their sleeping bags. I found myself alone in the bar with Kocky. He suddenly looked round and asked: 'Where have they all gone, Jock?'

I shrugged.

'They shouldn't have done that, Jock. Do you know why? Because, Jock, we're not all coming back from this job.'

I laughed. 'Well, just as long as both of us do.' We toasted each other.

On 17 January we paraded at 0800. There was an excited buzz around the camp. We were told to draw our special kit at 0900. At the unit's stores we were each given a three-foot oblong box. Opening it, I found four sets of uniforms: two dark green and two in Rhodesian camouflage. I turned to the man next to me and said: 'Somehow, I don't think we're going to Angola.'

With heightened expectation we headed for the briefing room.

The CO surveyed our assembled ranks. 'Men, you are going to do the job you want to do. You are going to Rhodesia to help our brothers-in-arms, the Rhodesian SAS. Never forget who you are and where you came from. You go with our hopes and blessings and take the honour of the unit with you.' It was a stirring speech, and looking at my fellow Recces I knew it had the desired effect. On their faces I read determination, commitment and anticipation.

Our intelligence officer (we would get a detailed brief once in the country) gave us the overall picture. It was not exactly rosy. In simple terms, the Rhodesians were losing their war. No matter how fast they destroyed guerrilla groups, new ones sprang up to take their place. The Rhodesian Special Forces were strained almost to the limit and had been for some time. Our job would be to relieve them in a key area – the Gaza province of Mozambique – and disrupt the main infiltration route for Robert Mugabe's ZANU guerrillas. The area was heavily patrolled by regular

FRELIMO troops (the Mozambique Liberation Front, founded in 1962 and victorious in their war against the Portuguese) who were well armed and trained by the North Koreans. The Rhodesian Army had a nickname for the area we were to work in: the 'Russian Front'.

Flown out by Dakota (the South African Airforce would not risk a Hercules), we landed in Rhodesia some three hours later and were driven in convoy to our new home at Buffalo Range, in the Triangle Region. Our neighbours were the famed Selous Scouts, commanded by the legendary Lieutenant Colonel Ron Read Daly. We took over our tented encampment from the departing members of the unit and had time to swap a few stories before they departed. The first news was not encouraging. Three members of the Rhodesian SAS had been killed in an accidental explosion the previous night while laying a mine. We were using the same type.

At first we laid simple pressure-detonated mines, with an anti-lift switch. The enemy countered by sweeping for these with Russian-designed, Korean-supplied mine-detectors. These gave off a high-pitched signal, similar to a sonar beep, when a mine was located. Our scientists countered this by designing a device which worked like a tuning fork. When the detector 'beeped' this device vibrated, setting off the mine and killing the operator. One up for us. It took a long time to train a mine-clearance operator. The FRELIMO reverted to the tried-and-tested method of prodding for the mines with long, thin metal rods. We lost several mines to the opposition in this manner. An equalizer for FRELIMO. We countered by encasing our mines with three thin sheets of polystyrene, between which were two sheets of metal wire. When the rods pierced the two sets of wire, forming a circuit, the mine exploded. The opposition lost several men before they realized what was happening. Two-one to us. No matter how well a mine was dug in, after a time there was always some sand subsidence, and FRELIMO would walk along tracks looking for these slight depressions. They became quite adept at spotting them, clearing away the sand, and if there was a mine, detonating it. Another one for FRELIMO. To prevent them doing this we incorporated a light-sensitive electronic switch on the top of the mine which detonated it when exposed to sunlight. If things carried on like this the mines would eventually jump up and chase the clearance parties.

For the present we settled in and were briefed on the area by our Rhodesian SAS colleagues. We would be working about 150–200 kilometres over the border in Gaza. This was an exceptionally arid area, and water was the main problem for extended patrolling. As ours would last for over three weeks, we were advised that each man should carry at least seven litres of water. Along with food, ammunition, spare mortar ammunition, mines, grenades, radios, cooking utensils and so on, this meant that each man was carrying in excess of eighty pounds.

Our main target, the ZANU terrorists, were held in little regard by our Rhodesian allies, but the FRELIMO regulars, especially the Z Force troops, trained in counter-insurgency by the North Koreans, were a very different matter. They would counter-attack in large numbers. These troops had killed two Recces just before Christmas 1977.

The FRELIMO X Companies operated in strengths of up to a hundred, using heavy mortar support and usually the Soviet 82mm mortar, which they man-packed. Once they were on your trail, they were difficult to shake, their main aim being to stay in loose contact and thus prevent completion of the mission: laying mines and ambushing ZANU guerrillas. If pursued, we had two alternatives: either be picked up by helicopter and redeploy or move east into a range of low hills which was excellent ambush country and FRELIMO had never followed a patrol there. If things became really bad we could count on immediate fire support from two Rhodesian Airforce Hawker Hunter jet fighters.

Casualty evacuation was a problem. The only helicopter then available to the Rhodesians was the South African-supplied, French-built Alouette. It didn't have the range to reach our operating area without refuelling in the bush from a fuel drop made by a Dakota midway between us and the border. The Alouette would land in the bush, refuel, fly on to us, pick up the casualty, fly back, refuel again and then return to Rhodesia. It was difficult, time-consuming and dangerous but the only way we could get our casualties out. We knew that if we took a casualty we would have to hold the position for at least two hours. Our briefings completed, we prepared for our first deployment on 26 January 1978. It was my twenty-fifth birthday.

We would be in two twenty-three-man groups comprising three six-man teams and a five-man HQ element operating roughly ten kilometres apart. I was under the command of Lieutenant D. Lieutenant Kocky de Toit commanded the second group. Much to my surprise I was given command of a six-man team. This was my first combat command and I felt honoured.

The day before our insertion, I prepared my own surprise for our enemy. I'd always been fascinated by booby-traps and on my Junior Infantry Course in Brecon several years before, a major who had served in the war in Oman had told me of an interesting device. I wanted to see if it worked. I took one of the Australian booby-trap detonators I had found while arranging the ammunition store back at Fort Doppies in the Caprivi Strip. I emptied a 7.62mm AK47 round and inserted the detonator into it, then tamped round it with a small amount of plastic explosive and resealed the round. The theory was simple: when the round was inserted into a rifle and fired, its .22 percussion cap would explode the detonator, which in turn would ignite the plastic explosives. I had been assured that this would have disastrous results for whoever fired the rifle.

In the early morning of the 26th, we gathered at the airfield, a short drive from our tented camp. Quite unexpectedly, a crate of beer was produced and my comrades all toasted my birthday. Then we enplaned on to a darkened Dakota and within seconds were airborne. The plane flew a zigzag pattern towards our drop zone and carried out dummy drops both before and after we jumped. At 0350 we stood up and hooked up. At 0400 precisely, we dropped into a darkened Mozambique night from a height of four hundred feet.

I was the last to jump and a sudden gust of wind separated me from my comrades. On the ground I rolled up my chute, threw my pack on my back and, carrying my chute, set off to find them. Being alone in hostile territory at night is a very unpleasant experience. Every few minutes, I would stop and listen, then give a short, low whistle, hoping my comrades would hear it and terrified that someone else might. Eventually, much to my relief, I found them. We greeted each other like we hadn't seen each other for years instead of twenty minutes. The drop had been a complete success with no casualties. We centralized and camouflaged the chutes, moved off a short distance and laid up for the remainder of the night. At first light we stood-to for ten minutes, had breakfast and began to patrol towards the Beira railway line.

Our days rapidly fell into a well-organized routine. One hour before last light we would dog-leg so that we would lie facing our tracks, able to ambush any terrorist group that followed them. Then we would set up camp, have our evening meal and settle in for the night. Movement at night was impossible as a large body of men made too much noise and the risk of ambush was too great. In the morning, after standing-to, we would move off for about half an hour and then have breakfast. We'd then patrol until 1300, when the heat made any movement almost unendurable. We would dog-leg again and lie up until it was cool enough to continue to patrol, usually about 1700, then move off again until just before last light.

Three days after our drop we hit the railway line. It was a single track with a hard sand road on either side. A steep embankment, about three feet high, bordered the bush on either side of the track. We crossed, stepping on sleeping bags so that footprints wouldn't betray our presence. We reorganized into our fighting formation on the other side. Lieutenant D decided to go on a short recce. Dropping his pack, he took his binoculars and made his way up the embankment for a quick sweep up and down the track. He was back in seconds.

'There's a civvy coming down the track. We'll grab him and ask whether there are any terrs in the area.'

Immediately Fabes volunteered for the job. He stripped off his equipment and produced a wicked-looking fighting knife. Corporal Taffy P (Taffy was a nickname given to blasters in South African gold mines) went with him, armed with an AK47 to provide close cover. The rest of us waited in the bush. In the few seconds before our victim appeared, we crouched like schoolchildren playing a prank. All around me I could see eager, grinning faces and I felt an almost overwhelming desire to burst out laughing.

Down the track came a man in dark-green uniform, a long-barrelled AK47 resting on his shoulder. Behind him was a second uniformed figure with an RPG rocket launcher. The smiles vanished from our faces. In one movement twenty-one weapons came to bear on the two men. In front of us Fabes, unaware of his danger, gathered himself to spring. He raised himself, saw his quarry was armed, and threw himself flat. The men swung towards the movement. Taffy engaged both of them at close quarters. In a rush the rest of the group swarmed on to the embankment to support our friends. We'd been lucky there were only two. Taffy had shot both to doll rags, but if they had been scouts for a larger group we might very well have taken casualties. We had learnt a valuable lesson.

The RPG, a much-prized weapon, had been holed and was therefore useless. We booby-trapped it by digging a small hole in the ground and inserting a phosphorus grenade. We then laid the damaged RPG on top of the grenade and pulled the pin. The weight of the rocket launcher held the ignition lever down and we camouflaged the area with twigs and leaves. This booby-trap killed a FRELIMO engineer who foolishly picked up the damaged launcher. The AK47 was still serviceable, so we seized it. Its magazine had been holed by two of Taffy's rounds. Before we withdrew I inserted my booby-trapped 7.62 round into the damaged magazine and discarded it. I hoped the FRELIMO clearance team would find it. They were always short of ammunition and I hoped they would empty the damaged magazine of its ammunition and insert it into another weapon. Late that evening we made comms with our base and told of our first contact.

Kocky's group had also had a contact. They had been dog-legging into their morning LUP when a FRELIMO patrol had bumped into them. In the battle eight FRELIMO soldiers had been killed and they lost a member of their patrol, Corporal Manny Ganou, an ex-Portuguese Commando and my next-door neighbour in Durban. He had been one of my instructors during Selection and had shown me many kindnesses since. His loss had a quieting effect on us all.

For the next three weeks we rampaged over our little patch of Mozambique, laying mines and ambushes, and on one occasion we drew our enemy into our killing zone by detonating a small explosive device. Some ten minutes later several locals drove a herd of cattle along the railway line across our front. Suspicious about the explosion, the enemy wanted to use them as bait for an ambush. We held our fire and waited. To my right I heard voices.

Several armed men appeared and checked the building into which we had thrown the device. Still we waited, wanting to draw as many as possible into the killing area.

Then I heard a sound I had never heard before: a high-pitched squeaking. Slowly along the track came a hand-propelled trolley, just like the ones in Westerns, with two men pumping its double handle. Seated on top of a pile of mealy bags was a FRELIMO officer and walking along behind him was a line of armed men. I raised my AK47. Just as the ambush was to be initiated the officer turned and looked directly into my eyes. He knew he was about to die. Fear, surprise and horror registered on his face as I opened fire. The group opened up with everything we had. There were no survivors. The man I shot was a local FRELIMO paymaster carrying a satchel stuffed with 30,000 Mozambique escudos. We were rich. We talked about how we would spend our windfall. The discussions proved purely academic. We were met at the airfield on our return by an officer from Rhodesian Intelligence who'd heard through radio intercepts that we had killed the paymaster.

'I believe you were lucky enough to have intercepted a paymaster.' His voice was upper-class English. 'Would you be so good as to hand it over? I have the necessary written orders from your OC.' He handed us a typed sheet of paper and we surrendered the money.

'This will help to pay some of our informers inside Mozambique. Thank you very much.'

C'est la guerre, I thought, and found out later that 30,000 Mozambique escudos were worth a little under £500. Tax exile would have to wait. We were debriefed by Major B, who listened intently as we described our first operation and then stood to address us.

'Well done. On your first mission, both the enemy and I have been impressed.'

'The enemy?' Lieutenant D enquired.

'From our radio intercepts we have discovered that FRELIMO are aware that some new formation is working in Gaza province. They intend to counter with the best they have.'

'X Companies?'

'Exactly. This is going to get a lot tougher in the coming months. Don't get complacent.'

We had two days to rest up, then were reinserted, this time by helicopter, to lay another ambush on the Beira line. Waiting in an ambush is a nerve-racking time for any soldier. Unable to move, you are afraid your very breathing will be heard by the enemy. When they do arrive your heart beats so loud and fast, you wonder why they can't hear it. You never stare at the enemy, fearing that to do so may draw his eyes to yours. Then, mayhem. The terror on the enemy faces before they die. In seconds it's over. You search their bodies, destroy their weapons and booby-trap the area. It becomes almost routine. After the initial elation, a wave of bone-deep weariness floods over you as the adrenalin eats up your reserves of energy. The overwhelming emotion that lingers in my memory of that time is tiredness – tiredness and fear. Fear is a good emotion to cultivate; it keeps you alert. Without it few survive.

We did not have long to wait in our ambush position, less than an hour, then a party of ZANU terrorists walked into it. We could hear them coming a mile off, laughing and joking with each other as if they were on a Sunday afternoon stroll. We killed seven of them in the opening burst and two others who ran into one of our cut-offs. As we were clearing the ambush site we came under long-range mortar fire and withdrew for a pick-up.

Insertions became almost routine and our successes mounted. There was only one worrying development. We had been followed twice by FRELIMO Regulars. In one case, we had been lying in the blistering heat of the afternoon. I had just made a brew and was reaching for it when I quite clearly heard the sound of a mortar bomb being slid down a tube and fired. I froze, staring directly into the eyes of the man opposite me. The enemy was very, very close. The bomb was in the air and we didn't know if it would come down on top of us. Those few brief seconds, as we waited for it to land and explode, seemed to stretch into hours. I became aware of the minutest detail: a drop of sweat on the lip of the man opposite me; his dark-brown eyes wide with fear and anticipation; the slow, lazy curl of the steam from my tea; my own heart banging against my chest. The bomb exploded harmlessly in the bush at least fifty metres from us. In seconds, we had packed up and slipped quietly away.

It seemed only a matter of time before we hit a major contact with these well-trained soldiers, especially as we were planning for an extended period in the field. The group was to be split into three groups, two of ten men and a larger one of twenty-four. The smaller groups were to lay mines over a large system of tracks that ZANU and FRELIMO were using instead of the road which ran alongside the Beira line. The twenty-four-man group, under Kocky, was to carry out aggressive ambushes and patrol to our south, hopefully drawing all the FRELIMO attention and giving us a relatively free hand to lay our mines.

The mine-laying parties were commanded by two senior sergeants, Danny V and Louis K. Danny, who was in charge of my group, was a thickset, dour man who'd been a professional soldier since he was eighteen. If you got more than three words out of him in a day, you thought he was making a speech. Louis was exactly the opposite. He was as thin as a rake, with an amazingly long, drooping moustache. He could have played Dickens's Fagin to a tee, but his looks were deceptive. He was exceptionally aggressive and a natural killer.

We were again inserted by two helicopters, the pilots undertaking various dummy landings in the hope of confusing both the locals and FRELIMO. We moved to a safe distance from our landing site and began laying mines that night. The next afternoon we heard the sound of heavy firing about a kilometre to our south in Louis' patrol area. We set up our radio and made comms with base, telling them that we thought our other mine-laying group had hit a contact. They tried to contact them; all they got was silence. We feared the worst, then I heard a faint crackle on the radio net and tuned in.

'Hello, Alpha 2, this is Alpha 1, can you receive me? Over . . .'

There was a distorted, garbled reply that I could hardly understand and almost immediately the signaller at base tried to cut in.

'Alpha 2, this is Base, come in. Over . . .'

'Base, this is Alpha 1. Don't interrupt, Alpha 2 has a damaged set. I'm going to try and relay . . .'

'Alpha 2, don't try and speak, just depress your switch – one for yes, twice for no. Understand?' I waited breathlessly for the reply.

'Click.'

Relief flooded through me. 'Good, I roger your yes. Have you hit a contact?'

'Click.'

'Roger your yes. Have you casualties?'

'Click.'

'Roger your yes. Is your set damaged?'

'Click.'

'Roger that. Are you still in contact with the enemy?'

'Click, click.'

'Roger your no.' I thought quickly back to our briefing. After the drop-off Louis was to move north, laying mines as he went. We'd moved nearly ten kilometres during the time we had been inserted.

'Alpha 2, have you moved north from your drop-off point?'

'Click.'

'Roger that, Alpha 2. Have you moved more than ten Ks?'

'Click, click.'

'Roger your no, Alpha 2. I'm going to arrange a pick-up, wait out to you. Hello, Base, this is Alpha 1. Alpha 2 has had a contact, has casualties and requires immediate extraction. He's less than ten Ks north of his original pick-up.'

'Roger, Alpha 1, we're already on our way. Tell Alpha 2 to throw red smoke when he hears the 'copter. Over.'

'Roger, Base, out to you. Alpha 2 from Base, throw red smoke when you hear the 'copter. Over.'

'Click.'

'Roger your yes, Alpha 2. We'll stay on listening watch until you're picked up. Out.'

I put down the handset with a sigh. I looked across at Danny V, who'd been listening intently. His mouth pursed and then he nodded.

'That was very well done, Jock.' A speech indeed.

Louis' group was picked up four hours later. We later found that a FRELIMO group had followed them up. Louis had detonated the defence claymores and opened fire, killing at least five of the attackers. His group had then come under sustained machine-gun fire, the first burst hitting the radio operator and damaging his radio. Louis had extracted his force under heavy fire and inflicted more casualties, finally laying down several banks of claymores to discourage any follow-up. His radio handset had been badly damaged, forcing him to make comms by holding two pieces of wire together. Louis was later awarded the Honour Cross in silver for his bravery during this action.

Our mission was now of even more importance and for the next three weeks we laid mines with renewed intensity, getting resupplied by airdrop when necessary. To our south, Kocky's group was hitting contact after contact, drawing FRELIMO to them like iron filings to a magnet. On our twenty-second night in the bush we heard the worst possible news. I was making comms at last light when I received a flash message to stand by for a signal in code. I got the code book out and recorded the letters and figures but as I deciphered it tears started to well up in my eyes. It read simply: 'Sunray call sign one is dead.' Our sister group had been lying up at midday when an X Company of some 100 FRELIMO Regulars had followed them. The sentry had spotted their lead scouts and detonated the defence claymores. Kocky marshalled his forces for a sweep through the contact area. An undetected, wounded man shot and killed him as he led his men forward. The group had then come under sustained close-range fire but had fought their way out using mini-claymores to give themselves some breathing space.

The loss of Kocky was a hammer blow. He was liked and respected; his humour and love of life had touched each of us. He was the best officer I'd served with in any army.

We were told to await a second message. A few minutes later it came: at first light move deep into the bush and await pick-up helicopter. We assumed that because of the loss of Kocky they were taking us out for a rest, to rebuild our morale. We were wrong.

After landing back at Buffalo Range we were given an hour to wash and change before being called into the main briefing tent. We received a rundown on the other patrol's activities. Whereas we'd been in and out of the field regularly, they'd spent two long periods in the field with a large break between them. They'd lost Manny Ganou on the first insertion and on their second they'd been harried continually by a strong and persistent X Company before Kocky was nailed too. This much we knew or had guessed. When the helicopter had come in to retrieve Kocky's body, three members of my Selection had got on to it and, despite pleas from the group's second in command, resigned in the field. The redoubtable Major B told us that we were all volunteers and could resign when we liked, but there was a time and place for everything. If any of us had the slightest doubt that we could continue to serve as Special Forces soldiers, now was the chance to say something. Nobody moved or spoke. Major B nodded, and carried on with our debrief.

We were back in action within days. For the next four months we harried the ZANU guerrillas mercilessly. We all collected trophies of one kind or another. I still have a plain silver arm band from the first man I killed in Mozambique. Others took more personal trophies. One, Jan, cut the ear off his first kill and kept it in a leather pouch round his neck. On a break from operations he joined me at the breakfast table. He was sandy-haired, and with clear, baby-blue eyes and the sort of boyish good looks that drew many an admiring glance from passing females in Durban.

'Morning, Jan.'

'Morning, Jock.' He began to write furiously on a typed sheet of paper.

'What's that, Jan?'

He looked up. 'My resignation.'

I was taken aback. Jan was a well-respected member of the unit.

'Why are you leaving?'

'I'm thinking of getting married. This is no life for a married man.'

I had to agree. I'd hardly seen my wife since my arrival and my kids were calling me Uncle Daddy.

'What are you going to do in civilian life?'

'Become a preacher.'

That really shocked me. I looked at the leather bag. 'What are you going to do with the ear?'

He looked down. 'Oh, I'm going to keep that.'

True to his word, he left the unit after the tour to become a preacher. I wondered what his congregation would say if they knew what he kept in the leather pouch around his neck.

My booby-trapped round proved a success: radio intercepts confirmed a ZANU terrorist dead in the area from an exploding rifle. I used the same trick three times in all. The ZANU terrorists were as bad as the Rhodesians had told us. Often when in a contact they would throw their weapons over their shoulder and fire backwards as they were running away. One Recce wit remarked that it wasn't the bullet with his name on he was scared of, but the one addressed 'to whom it may concern'.

Losing Kocky de Toit made us a little mad. We'd always booby-trapped the bodies of our kills. The opposition had become very adept at finding the grenades and anti-personnel mines we left for them. After one ambush in which we killed six ZANU guerrillas, we decided on a new ploy. We cut off the head of one of the dead and planted it in the soft sand. It looked like the man had been buried alive. Next we wrote messages in the sand: 'Death Commandos, Strike!' and so on. We booby-trapped the remaining bodies as usual, with one added refinement: we buried a vehicle mine under the corpse of the beheaded terrorist. The trick worked to perfection. The FRELIMO engineers, clearing the ambush site, found all the anti-personnel booby-traps, but completely missed the vehicle mine until they loaded the dead terrorists on to a truck and drove straight over it.

Towards the end of the tour we hit a contact on the railway line, just south of Mapai. Having stumbled across six armed terrorists we downed four very quickly; the other two ran for their lives. I suppose we were getting a little overconfident; we chased them and ran straight into a larger group. I exchanged shots with a shadowy figure some thirty metres in front of me and failed to see a nearer man. He fired from less than three metres. As he did so I spotted him and hit him twice in the chest. He rolled on to his back screaming. I tried to move and found I couldn't. Looking down, I saw blood seeping from my thigh. My first reaction was blind anger. Putting my AK47 on auto, I emptied half a mag into the man responsible and then hopped to a nearby thorn tree. Using it for support, I began to move my leg backwards and forwards. I had been lucky, the bullet just went through the muscle. It was painful and messy but it would still hold my weight.

I ran to the officer in charge of us, a newly arrived captain from Durban. 'I've been hit, boss, I've been hit.'

He looked more scared than me. 'Fuck off, Jock, don't be stupid.'

I pointed down at my thigh, now oozing thick, dark-red blood. 'I'm not kidding.'

'Get across the railway line. We'll cover you.' He raised his voice. 'Jock's been hit. Give him cover.'

The firing around me intensified as I hobbled to the relative safety of the opposite side of the track. I was given some very quick first aid, but we were still in contact so had to move out fast. I spent the next two days running with a hole in my thigh, unable to get a casevac because of the constant attention of an X Company. Finally two Hunters were brought in with an air strike to cover my escape. As the helicopter took off with me aboard I saw mortar bombs raining on my friends below. I felt like a deserter.

I was out of action for three weeks and returned in time for what was supposed to have been our grand finale. Operation Hammer was an assault on a concentration of guerrillas just south of the main Mozambique town of Mapai. We would provide a stopping group for an assault force from the crack Rhodesian 2nd Commando Light Infantry.

We went in using Alouette helicopters, behind two Hawker Hunter jets carrying 1000lb bombs. In front of these was a Canberra bomber carrying 500lb bombs. The Canberra dropped its load, the six explosions throwing a wave of destruction in front of us, then the two Hawker Hunters loosed theirs. Our small helicopters bucked and reared. As the dust began to settle, we landed and a Dakota flew overhead dropping 2 Commando.

War sometimes has a compelling, if awful, beauty. At such moments the sheer joy of being part of all of this was almost overwhelming.

Our main priority was to act as stopper groups for 2 Commando, who would flush the enemy in the camp into our killing embrace. My group was commanded by a particularly aggressive Afrikaner sergeant, Davie K. We were no sooner on the ground than he spotted movement to our front.

'Terrs, Jock. Follow me.'

I raced after him, along the small path we had to prevent the enemy from using. We left our machine-gunner and his number two behind to cover us. The bush was almost clear up to the edge of the enemy camp. Suddenly, in the tree line, I saw movement. Davie saw it too. His R4 rifle came up in a fluid, sweeping movement and he opened fire. I dropped to one knee and fired twice at the black figure outlined against the trees' lighter green. It fell, and almost immediately I saw a shock of blond hair.

Jumping up I pulled Davie's arm down as he was about to deliver a killing burst.

'Don't. I think he's one of ours.'

A burst of heavy automatic fire split the earth next to me. We both dived for cover. In front of us we could hear English voices calling to each other. I rolled over and made contact with a helicopter flying overhead and with his aid I managed to make comms with the group in front of us. Warily we approached each other. They were Rhodesian engineers who'd been set down right smack in the middle of the camp by mistake. The man I'd shot was an American, tall and lean, his blackened face contorted with pain. Both my shots had hit him, one through the side, the other through his elbow. He held his ruined arm as the helicopter landed to casevac him. I felt awful.

'I'm sorry.' Even to me it didn't sound adequate.

The American's pained features broke into a grin. 'It wasn't your fault, buddy. We were in the wrong place.'

His arm might never be the same again. 'That's a heavy price to pay for being dropped in the wrong place.'

He patted my shoulder with his good hand. 'Fortunes of war, buddy. Fortunes of war.' He stepped on to the helicopter and threw us all a final thumbs up before being taken away. We resumed our cut-off position. Although 2 Commando were in the centre of the camp, we could hear only sporadic single shots, not the full-scale battle we'd expected.

In fact, although technically superb, Operation Hammer had been a fiasco. The hundreds of guerrillas who were in the location just two days before had moved on. In all, only ten were killed, leading some to describe it as the 'Six Million Dollar Cock-Up'.

Our tour had come to an end. In five months we had totally disrupted the enemy supply routes into southern Rhodesia and in doing so saved many settlers' lives. Although we had lost two valuable members of the unit, we had killed 154 enemy by body count, with another twenty-five confirmed by radio intercept. This in what was regarded by all as the most difficult theatre of operations in Africa. We had faced the Russian Front and come out of it intact. We were replaced by 5 Recce Commando. Our Rhodesian SAS comrades, among the finest soldiers I ever saw, showed us their gratitude; they couldn't give us medals but each of us was presented with an official Rhodesian SAS plaque. Mine still hangs above my head as I write.

Back in Durban we received a hero's welcome from the unit's senior officers and three weeks' leave, during which I had an unexpected visit from a major in the unit. A new commando was being formed, specializing in seaborne operations. They needed junior NCOs. Was I interested? My initial reaction was guarded, for I was not a strong swimmer. The major played his trump card. There were some spectacular operations being planned, larger and more important than anything yet attempted by Recce Commando. He would not be drawn further, but I was intrigued enough to agree to join the new commando.

4 Recce Commando were to be based at Saldanha Bay, just outside Fredenburg, in Cape province. In order to join the unit, I was chosen to crew the unit yacht, the *Compass Rose*, from Durban to our new base in the Cape. We sailed out of Durban on a calm, warm night. It did not last long: barely eight hours out of Durban we were hit from our stern by a force eight gale. The waves around us became a heaving mass, gigantic foaming monsters that seemed intent on smashing us to pieces.

There is something infinitely terrifying about being in a small boat at night in a storm. Looking astern you saw each angry wave as it thundered towards you, and wondered how your tiny craft would survive its impact. One second you would be in a deep trough, looking up at a wall of water, the next high up on its crest, being tossed like some hidden giant's plaything. To make things infinitely worse, I was suffering badly from seasickness. Of this there are two stages: when you are scared you are going to die, and when you are scared you are not going to. Sleep was impossible off watch and even rest had its perils. Stumbling into a narrow bunk, wet through to the skin, I tried to turn on to my side, my turning coincided with a particularly violent lurch of the boat that threw me halfway across the small rest room. On watch I always tied myself to the boat, terrified that I would be thrown into the sea, as I knew that to fall overboard in such circumstances would almost certainly prove fatal.

As we neared East London the weather suddenly changed; the sea became as flat and tranquil as an English village pond. Approaching the harbour, we enjoyed the company of a school of dolphins. With a full moon reflecting off the water and phosphorescence cascading from their bodies, they seemed encased in sheets of silver. For a time these beautiful creatures played chicken with the bow of the yacht, whistling to us all the while. It was one of those moments that are for ever etched in the mind.

Saldanha Bay, an old abandoned whaling station situated on an island, was an excellent base for a seaborne commando. We had security and privacy to train and prepare for our forthcoming operations. All new members took a diving course, then small-boat training. Finally the entire commando set about finalizing the unit's drills, from landing raiding parties to contacts both on shore and at sea. Within four months we were a tightly knit fighting unit which owed much to the charismatic leadership of Commandant K, the unit's CO. He was well over six foot, thin and slightly stooping, with ginger hair and a magnificent full beard. He'd served on attachment with the Israeli Seaborne Commandos, and the development of 4 Recce owed much to that experience. He combined good leadership with a dry, caustic humour. His driving ambition was to create a seaborne commando to rival any in the world, and in pursuit of that ambition he was entirely ruthless.

As in all small units rumours about impending jobs were almost constant. We had all noted the attachment to the unit of a certain English-born lieutenant from the South African Navy, who spoke English with no trace of an accent. He was frequently absent for periods of two to three weeks, and it was obvious he was engaged in reconnaissance but where and against whom we didn't know.

As 1978 drew to a close, I was one of fifteen members of 4 Recce called into the unit's briefing room. On the large blackboard was written the legend 'Operation Milk Float'. Commandant K glanced around at our expectant faces and announced: 'Gentlemen, we are going to change history.'

The government in Pretoria were extremely worried that Robert Mugabe's ZANU guerrillas would seize power, installing a black, hostile, Marxist state on its western border. This would give the ANC, at that time perceived as a tool of Moscow, a safe base from which to train and launch attacks against South Africa itself.

Pretoria's options were limited. Direct military intervention was out of the question: it would alienate the few friends the government still had in the world, most notable of whom was

Britain, who had steadfastly resisted the international call for sanctions. Covert support by our own Recce Commando had helped, but increasing casualties had resulted in our unit being withdrawn towards the end of 1978.

On the ground in Rhodesia the military situation was bleak. Magnificent though it was, the army was tired and overstretched. There seemed no way to stem the flood of ZANU guerrillas infiltrating the country. Whites were leaving in a steadily increasing flow, further draining both resources and morale. It was against this backdrop that Operation Milk Float was conceived: a strike at the very heart of the black opposition. There were to be three stages. First, the assassination of Robert Mugabe, who was living in exile in Maputo, the capital of Mozambique. Second, the assassination of Joshua Nkomo, the leader of ZIPRA, the smaller Matabele tribe of Rhodesia. Nkomo was a hated figure following the downing of a Rhodesian civilian aircraft and the machine-gunning of the survivors by his terrorists. Third, the destruction of the Mozambique oil terminal at Beira, thereby crippling the economy of the poverty-stricken front-line state. If everything went to plan, there could eventually be all-race elections, in which a moderate black government could be installed.

The operation was breathtaking in its scope and audacity. To undertake phase one, 4 Recce Commando would insert an eight-man raiding force of Rhodesian SAS inside the harbour at Maputo. This was the deepest infiltration ever attempted in the Rhodesian war. Recce Commando would have the responsibility for transport in and out of the harbour, and the assassination would be carried out by the Rhodesians. Even so, we risked the real chance of capture as the South African Navy had orders to abandon us rather than risk a confrontation with Mozambican forces. Our cover story, in case of capture, would be that we were attempting to kill Mugabe for a $250,000 bounty deposited in a South African bank as the operation was officially 'deniable'. The cover story was a half-hearted affair to which none of us paid that much attention. If we were caught the very least we could hope for was a life sentence in a Mozambican jail but more likely execution. We all decided that come what may, we were not going to be captured.

Despite the deniable status of the operation, we were told that it had been sanctioned at the very highest level. Any resources we thought necessary would be put at our disposal. We were to begin preparations for a deployment in six weeks, early January 1979.

Getting to the mouth of Maputo harbour was not a problem as we had the South African Navy at our disposal. To deploy the large raiding force from a mother ship in neutral waters on to a hostile shore, our first thoughts were to use a submarine, but getting from sub to shore was something else. The largest inflatable boat we had at that time was the French-built Mark II Zodiac, which could carry a maximum of five. In addition, we wanted some kind of protection in case we ran into a patrol boat. Within four days we had been supplied with the much larger Mark IV Zodiac, capable of transporting twelve, to which we fitted twin fifty-horsepower Sea Horse outboard motors linked to a simple console by which the coxswain could control the speed with two throttles and steer with a small wheel. Next to him sat the navigator and commander armed with an RPG rocket launcher. In the front an RPD light machine-gun was mounted on a bolted swivel mount, to give immediate fire support. The raiding party sat, back to back, facing outwards, on a low double seat running fore and aft. It took less than six weeks from conception to get the boats in the water.

The raiding party of Rhodesian SAS came down to practise with us in late January. We believed that only one Zodiac would be needed, but our first attempt, made from a submarine, was a fiasco: in heavy seas the Zodiac's floor buckled under the weight of troops and their equipment, after moving only a few hundred metres from the mother boat. With red faces, we paddled our way back, unable to use the engines in case we were swamped.

We rethought our initial plan. A submarine's deck was too cramped for us to assemble more than one Zodiac and we realized we would need at least one other boat. We decided to use one of the navy's fast patrol boats. These provided an excellent platform to work from and were extremely fast and well armed. The major drawback was that we would have to deploy farther out to sea, to ensure we were not spotted from the shore. Our first trial was highly successful.

In the meantime the Rhodesian SAS raiding party had had second thoughts about their strength. They wanted to increase it to twelve men, which meant using three boats. We tried to assemble three Zodiacs on the patrol boat but in the limited space available and with the time restrictions imposed we would have only an hour in which to assemble and launch. We soon found it could not be done from a single boat and decided to use two: one-third of the entire South African Navy's combat strength.

Our group would be under the command of Commandant K. Lieutenant Taffy P commanded our boat. He was not the Taffy P I'd served with earlier, but a roguish Recce officer who had risen rapidly through the ranks. He was about five foot ten inches tall, with a stocky, muscular frame, and his craggy features were hidden behind an unkempt full beard. Taffy's sense of humour was renowned. He loved a joke even if it was at his own expense. At the very first briefing he spoke earnestly to me.

'Timing is going to be all-important, Jock. I've even bought a new watch.'

He thrust a chunky, shiny watch in my face.

'It's a Rolex, best timekeeping watch in the world.'

I nodded seriously. 'Friend of mine had one of those – dustproof, shockproof and waterproof.'

'Yes, they're great watches.'

I nodded and smiled. 'Not really. His caught fire.'

Taffy paused, got the joke, burst into a bout of uncontrollable laughter and ran off to tell it to someone else before I had a chance to.

The raiding party was commanded by Lieutenant Colonel Graham W of the Rhodesian SAS. The most highly decorated soldier in the Rhodesian Army, he was one of only two awarded the Rhodesian Grand Cross of Valour. He looked more like a schoolteacher – tall, slim and slightly bent over, and never without his dark-rimmed spectacles – than one of the finest fighting men Africa ever produced.

By mid-February we were ready to go. We were told the Rhodesian CIA had infiltrated several agents into the Maputo area. They would contact us directly by radio to inform us if the target was in. There was an added twist: we would be taking a TT, a turned terrorist. He believed his job was to act as a front man in case the raiding party encountered any patrols or civilians. In reality the Rhodesians intended to kill him and dump his body at the scene. On it would be incriminating documents, implicating in his assassination Mugabe's military chief of staff, the legendary guerrilla fighter Tongerrera. Commandant K briefed us on this new twist.

'It's important that the TT at no time realizes that he is expendable, for obvious reasons. The Rhodesian who is to kill him has instructions never to let him out of his sight. Are there any questions?'

'I don't like the idea of this man being armed. If he realizes what's in store for him, he may try to take some of us out,' I said.

'The Rhodesians have thought of that. The AK he's carrying has been specially doctored so it can't be fired. It will be swapped when the body's left for another untraceable weapon.'

'Canned goods,' I murmured, more to myself than to anybody in particular.

'What's that, Jock?'

'Canned goods, sir. That's what the Nazis called dead Poles they dumped over the German border to give them an excuse to invade Poland. It started the Second World War.'

Commandant K scratched his head. 'Yes. I remember the story. This is a little different as he's a convicted terrorist. Don't think of him as canned goods, more as a disposable item.'

Because of the sensitivity of the operation the Rhodesians were under strict instructions that, no matter what the outcome of the job, the TT was not to return. When he stepped on to the fast patrol boat he was a dead man. He had been captured after a raid in which a white family had been massacred. He should, and would have been, sentenced to death. He thought that by agreeing to accompany the Rhodesians he would win a reprieve. All he had was a stay of execution.

On a bright, sunny afternoon two days later we embarked on the fast patrol boats from Saldanha Bay. It would take us a day to get to our destination. A large, fair-haired Rhodesian called Jake, designated to kill the TT, never left his side and often laughed and joked with him throughout our journey. Most of the time he would sit, an arm cradled around the unfortunate man's shoulder, the other hand always within easy reach of a specially adapted AK47 with an extended silencer: the chosen instrument of the man's death. Once, while his charge went to the toilet and he was briefly alone with the rest of us, he glanced around and gave a broad smile. I want him to trust me, he explained. There is something perverse about watching a man eat, rest and laugh when you know he is going to die. Yet I could feel no real pity. He had chosen to play a big boys' game, first taking up arms and then turning on his own kind. Big boys' games are played by big boys' rules.

In the late evening of the following day we rode at anchor just over the horizon from Maputo, waiting for the radio message from the Rhodesian agents on shore. Taffy P gave us our final briefing. 'When the raiding party come back they'll probably have half the Mozambique Army chasing them, firing everything that can kill. There is a good chance we will have to go ashore under fire to evacuate the raiding party. We run the risk of losing men, and maybe even a boat, but I know each of you, and I know that I can depend on you.' At 1800 precisely we heard our target was at home.

As night fell the patrol boats took us as close inshore as they dared, about five kilometres from the Maputo harbour beach. Working with the precision that spoke of long hours of practice we began to assemble our raiding boats. Thankfully the sea was quite calm and within forty-five minutes, a new record for us, we had the inflatables ready. Then we launched. The sea was as flat as a pool table, the sky as black as a widow's shawl. Our muffled engines hardly disturbed the silence as we sped towards the coastline. My boat was in the lead, and behind me and slightly to my right and left were the two other boats in a loose arrowhead formation, their camouflaged sides almost impossible to see in the darkness. Only the occasional splash of white, as water cascaded over their bows, betrayed their presence.

The mysterious, English-speaking lieutenant who had been attached to the unit had recced the harbour by joining a legitimate cargo ship as its first officer. From him we learnt that both machine-guns and cannon emplacements were at the harbour mouth and that the harbour itself was patrolled by thirty-foot armoured launches with .50-calibre machine-guns. Their standard of alertness was assessed as 'poor', but we were going to have an interesting time if we ran into one of them. Alert or not, a .50-calibre machine-gun would chew one of our boats to bits.

Just before 2100 we slid to a halt about a hundred metres from the beach.

Maputo was well lit but strangely quiet for a capital city. We checked the beach with our starlight night 'scopes. It looked like Brighton on a warm summer's night. Satisfied there was no immediate danger, we paddled to the shore. As we neared the beach the sound of the waves softly breaking on the sand was mixed with the sound of faint music; someone was playing a radio not far away. There was a soft bump as the Zodiac's hull grated on to the sand. I swung the RDP light machine-gun round in an arc, searching the night for any danger. Behind me I heard a soft rustling, then, like phantoms, the raiding party slipped ashore. We waited until they were out of sight, ready to give fire support should they hit a contact, then, satisfied they were safely on their way, we paddled back out a hundred metres to wait for them.

This was the most dangerous time for us, for we had to stay reasonably close to the shore in case our comrades needed to make a fighting retreat after the assassination. Our three light machine-guns and RPG rocket launchers could provide vital close-range support. But we were vulnerable. A single, well-placed round would put a boat out of action. Sitting in the quiet darkness, I steeled myself for the action that must surely come.

As well as the evacuation, there was also the danger from the Mozambican Navy. If a patrol boat caught us with our backs to the well-lit beach and blocked our escape to the open sea, it would be good night Irene for all of us. Our only hope lay in remaining undetected.

The minutes slipped slowly by. The night was warm and pleasant, and you had to keep reminding yourself that you were on a dangerous mission. Voices. Along the beach, in extended line, clearly etched against the harbour lights, an army patrol appeared. I counted them as I covered them with the RPD: five, six, seven, eight. I could see their faces clearly and noted their weapons: six AK47s, one RPG and a light machine-gun. They stopped just in front of our position, and the sound of their laughter floated across the sea to us. Sweat rolled down the back of my neck. One man, probably the commander, was talking into a radio in Portuguese. Was this just a routine patrol or had somebody seen something and reported it to the local militia? For what seemed like eternity, they stood in a loose group in front of us. Surely one of them must spot us? Then, with agonizing slowness, they moved off. I realized I had been holding my breath and let out a sigh of relief.

Staff Sergeant B, my boat commander, moved down the length of the Zodiac to join me.

'Do you think they saw anything, Jock?' he breathed into my ear.

I shook my head.

'Keep alert. I think somebody may have seen the raiding party get ashore. We may get a patrol boat next. Remember, don't fire unless you're absolutely sure you've been spotted.'

I nodded again, and checked my watch. It was 2200. The raiding party should be on their target by now. At any moment, I expected to hear the sound of firing as they attacked. If there was a patrol boat out there, it might very well come closer inshore to investigate the noise. Suddenly my heart lurched inside my chest. From behind and to my left I heard the low cough of a boat's engine.

I swung my machine-gun round. About two hundred metres out to sea we could see the silhouette of the patrol boat, its searchlight sweeping the sea as it chugged past. If the light caught one of our boats, or the raiding party attacked now, we were in a deadly killing zone. Around me I was aware of my fellow Recces making ready. Every weapon on the Zodiac was pointed towards the launch. My lips peeled back across my teeth in a silent snarl of defiance. If that bundle of rusted nuts and bolts came this way it was in for a shock. It didn't alter course. The sound of its engines gradually became fainter and then died away completely. The danger had passed. I swung the gun round to cover the beach again.

Time dragged on; 2300 came and went, then midnight. By midnight time was becoming critical. We had only three hours of complete darkness left. If the raiding party didn't come soon, we faced the prospect of being caught in daylight at the harbour entrance. Suddenly, on the shore, three green lights blinked, followed by three red, then three green. It was the pick-up signal. As we beached I saw several men coming towards me. In the lead was the TT, and behind him was Jake. I saw Jake lift the silenced AK47 he was carrying. I leant to one side as two dull cracks rang out and the TT slumped across the bow of my boat. Jake picked up the fallen man's legs and dumped him unceremoniously in the bottom of the vessel.

We paddled out a hundred metres, started our engines and raced towards the open sea at top speed. I glanced at the night sky. Already the faint horizon was tinged with grey as the first fingers of morning reached into the night sky. It was going to be tight. At the harbour mouth Staff Sergeant B brought us to a halt.

'Get rid of the body,' he ordered.

Jake and another man began to weight the body swiftly with AK47 magazines. I scanned the nearby coastline. I could clearly see the outlines of buildings. If I could see them, they could see me. There was a soft splash as the TT was dropped into the water. The body went down several feet then reappeared. Jake cursed, leant over the boat and grabbed it. From the top of his boot he produced a double-edged fighting knife and plunged it into the corpse, slashing the stomach wide open. The body sank without a trace.

Jake glanced at me. 'Too much air in the body,' he said simply.

It was obvious he'd done this sort of thing before.

It was now broad daylight. We were clear of the harbour, but still visible from the shore. Commandant K, risking all, brought one of the fast patrol boats closer inshore, and we disembarked the raiding party. He handed me a paper on which was written a compass bearing.

'Tell your skipper to keep on that bearing until he finds us.'

The fast patrol boat disappeared. Freed from the weight of the raiding party we could make better time but had only gone a short distance before Lieutenant Taffy P's boat came to a grinding halt. Its planks had buckled. We were still clearly visible from the shore, a bare three kilometres away. Taffy stood up in the boat and called me over. As we closed I could see that beneath a thick coat of black camouflage cream, his face was strained. 'I'll have to sink the blasted thing. Remove the guns,' he shouted to his crew and watched as they jumped on to our boat. He pulled a double-edged diving knife from the top of his boot and holding it in two hands, plunged it into the side of the Zodiac. There was an immediate explosion as the compressed air erupted through the puncture. Its violence surprised us all, especially Taffy. Bowled over by the force of the blast, he sat in the bottom of the sinking boat, his hair and beard standing rigid. Despite the danger we were in, we all collapsed in laughter. Taffy looked like a character from a Bugs Bunny cartoon who'd had a bomb go off in his hands. With difficulty we controlled ourselves and helped the still stunned commander on to our boat. He watched as his vessel slowly sank.

'I hope the commandant understands. Each one of those engines cost 5000 rand,' he said in a dull voice. I burst out laughing again. At any moment the entire Mozambican Navy could appear and the lieutenant was worried about a couple of engines.

'Don't worry, boss. If worst comes to worst we'll have a whip-round for you,' I offered. He looked dully at me, then broke into a grin. Shaking off the effects of the exploding inflatable, he ordered us to proceed on our bearing. Two hours later, over the horizon, we RVd again with our mother ships and disembarked. Twenty-four hours later we were back in Saldanha Bay.

At the debrief Lieutenant Colonel W explained that his force had got right up to Mugabe's house, where they had quickly established no one was home. They had staked out the place for several hours, pushing their luck to the limit, but their target had not appeared.

Some four weeks later the Rhodesian SAS had a crack at phase two of Operation Milk Float. In broad daylight twenty men attacked the home of Joshua Nkomo in Zambia. He was warned (the rumour was by British MI6) only minutes before the attack began and escaped by the skin of his teeth.

Three weeks after the attempt on Nkomo, our commando landed a force of twenty Rhodesian SAS next to the oil refinery in Beira. They destroyed it with rocket-propelled grenades, causing a fire so severe that it burned for several days. Eventually it was put out by fire engines sent, ironically, from South Africa. And thus ended Operation Milk Float. History would not be changed.

My contract with the SADF expired shortly after the Beira raid, but I had time for one last operation: reconnaissance of an oil refinery in Angola. On a moonless night, three Mark II Zodiacs, under the command of Staff Sergeant B, were launched from a submarine off the Angolan coast. Our intention was to recce the refinery for a sabotage mission. As we approached the shore, in a loose arrowhead formation, Staff Sergeant B in the front boat suddenly raised his hand and all three boats glided to a halt. He picked up an IWS night viewing aid and surveyed the shore. As I was sitting slightly behind him I saw him stiffen. He handed me the viewing aid, and as I looked through it my stomach turned over. The beach was swarming with troops, and more were arriving every minute from trucks drawn up on the hill above. Cubans. And armed with heavy weapons. They'd installed a new radar detection station in the area and had picked us up leaving the submarine. We made the best possible speed back to the sub and dived. We didn't even take the time to dismantle the boats. We sank them and only just in time: our own radar was picking up boats speeding towards us. It was a nerve-racking two hours before we were back in international waters. The operation had a tragic conclusion, for just under two years later it was attempted again and this time the raiding party was surprised on shore. Two Recces were killed and their officer taken prisoner.

I desperately wanted to stay for another year because of the talk of similar seaborne operations against targets in Angola, but as a foreign national that would have meant committing myself to a three-year contract. Of course I could have resigned from the Recces but would still have been with the SADF. With great sadness, I decided to return to the United Kingdom. Africa had changed me physically. I was a lot stronger, my endurance and stamina having been tested under the most extreme conditions. Mentally too I had undergone a metamorphosis. Although still in my early twenties I felt much older and more confident, able to face whatever the world could throw at me. My comrades arranged a big farewell party for me, and Recces came from as far away as Durban to bid me goodbye. Recce Commando was an outstanding fighting unit. In the two years I had been operational they had lost seventeen men in action but had destroyed over 2000 enemy. Their bravery in action was awesome, and their friendship and loyalty to me, a stranger in their land, matched it.

5

THE SAS

'Were you at the Embassy Siege?'
'No, but I know 2000 men who were.'
Lofty Wiseman, author, ex-Sergeant-Major, 22 SAS

Within five days of landing in the UK towards the end of 1979 I was back in the Army. I had spent over a month in contact with the Records Branch, preparing for my return. There had been some resistance to my going straight into SAS Selection, but my persistence had eventually paid off. Military Intelligence thoroughly debriefed me on my activities in Africa. I went to Aldershot for a day to get outfitted and then on to Hereford to prepare for Selection. Although physically fit I needed some hill work before this started. I had some four weeks to get ready.

Selection for 22 SAS takes place in stages. The first involves a three-week build-up followed by 'test week': six marches in mountainous terrain (mainly the Brecon Beacons in Wales) carrying progressively heavier loads. Recruits who survive this are then officially on 'continuation' training. The next major hurdle is jungle training and finally, recruits join members of the rest of the Army for the All Arms Combat Survival Course, which ends with aspirants facing the specialist inquisitors in a resistance-to-interrogation exercise.

The Brecon Beacons were a formidable place in which to train. The weather was always foul. On the Selection before mine, one of the Regiment's heroes, Major Mike Kealy (who won a DSO at the battle of Mirbat) had died of exposure while out with a Selection group. I talked to the last man to see him alive. He had seen that Kealy was in trouble with exposure, but the officer had refused all offers of help. 'Put yourself in my position, Harry. There was I doing Selection and a Sabre Squadron commander tells me to leave him alone. What would you have done?' The death of such an experienced officer was a sobering lesson on the dangers we faced in the Welsh hills.

On the first day the entire course was taken into the Regimental Briefing Room, known as the Blue Room. We were told that in the weeks ahead we would climb the equivalent of Mount Everest, carrying weights, starting at 45lb and increasing to 65lb, not counting our rifles, food and water. At this point, one man packed his kit and left.

The first week was designed as a gentle introduction. We were given simple map-reading exercises to ensure we would not get lost in the hills. At the end of it we had our first real physical test, the 'Fan Dance': twice over Pen y Fan, the highest mountain in the Brecon Beacons. It was a timed march, designed to cull any who were not physically up to the course. Navigation was not a problem – the damned monster could be seen for miles. The difficulty was to get inside the cut-off time, which, although we were never told, was estimated to be around four hours.

We left Hereford at 0700 and drove the forty or so miles to the exercise area. The weather was absolutely atrocious, even by Welsh standards. The wind threatened to knock us over, even though we were carrying in excess of 45lb. Rain, mixed with driving sleet, stung any exposed part of your body.

The course had been divided in two: one started from the Storey Arms side of the mountain, the other from Torpanty railway station on the opposite side. Somewhere in the middle we would cross. I started my climb from the Storey Arms and within minutes found myself alone, fighting to keep climbing and moving against the driving wind and rain. Each step was a personal victory. Inch by inch, foot by foot, I slowly made my way to the top, covering the last few hundred yards on my hands and knees.

Going over the top of the Fan was perilous; there were steep slopes on all sides. A single slip would mean disaster. I decided to slide down on my backside, an uncomfortable way to cover ground, but the safest and fastest. The going became slightly easier. We were in a natural hollow and the wind was not so bad. I hit the old Roman road and jogged down to the turnaround point, grabbed a drink of water and gulped down a Mars bar, the staple food of most Selection recruits, and began the climb back.

I made reasonable time until I hit the base of Pen y Fan again. If anything the weather had worsened. Waterfalls ended in mid-air as the water was thrown back up on itself by the ferocity of the wind. The next twenty minutes were desperate. Crawling on hands and knees, rifle in one hand, I edged my way back up the steep slope, over loose shale and jagged rocks. It was exhausting and soul-destroying, but eventually I reached the top once again and had a fairly easy run down to the RV back at the Storey Arms.

I found one of the instructors sitting in the front of a Landrover and reported in. He sipped a hot brew of tea and struck my name off the list. Then he glanced at the sky and said: 'Nice day for it.'

I gave a humourless laugh and found myself a place on the back of a three-tonner. I had completed my run in three hours fifty-five minutes and was the fourth man in. Behind me the rest were spread out for miles. Once the truck was reasonably full we were dispatched back to base. I sat down to my evening meal with a certain amount of satisfaction.

These feelings were almost immediately dashed. Instructors were moving round the room, checking heads. We were told to assemble in the Blue Room after tea. There Lofty Wiseman, the sergeant-major in charge of Selection, told us that one man was unaccounted for. He asked for volunteers for an immediate search and as a man the entire course stepped forward. Twenty were chosen and the rest of us were split into two groups; one would go out at first light, the second would relieve them at midday if the missing man had not been found.

At midnight I was woken by the return of the search party. One of them simply said: 'He's still missing.'

Outside, I could hear the wind howling and the rain smashing against the basha's thin wooden walls. I pulled the bedclothes tighter around me. 'God help him,' I whispered softly.

I had an early breakfast at 0600 and reported to Lofty outside the Training Wing office. It was now assumed the missing man was injured, perhaps unconscious. We would go back to the Storey Arms, make our way to the top of the Fan, and begin a circular search.

As a group we began the slow climb up the dark mountain

towards the trig point at the top. This would be the centre of our search. As we topped the rise we saw through the gloom a figure seated with his back to the white triangular stone. One of the search party called out to him but heard no answer. The missing soldier would never answer anyone again. He sat, his pack still on his back, resting against the stone, his rifle still in his hands. By his feet we could see scuff marks where he had tried in vain to get back onto his feet.

We could only guess what had happened, but it was likely that he had turned with the force of the driving wind and found himself on the northern side of the mountain, the Cwm Goody side. Then, realizing his mistake, he had battled back up the mountain in the darkness to find the rest of us gone. Tired, he had sat down for a brief rest, and the icy fingers of exposure had clamped around him, sending him into a sleep from which he never awoke. The scuff marks at his feet were testimony that he had realized what was happening and had tried to get up, perhaps already in that deathly sleep, but he had not made it. Nobody had thought about looking for him on the Cwm Goody side of the mountain. The slopes forming Pen y Fan are all steep but to have fought his way up that side, against fierce wind and driving rain, must have taken a horrendous effort. In silence we gathered round the dead man. Few could remember him amongst our dozens, yet each of us felt a sense of loss.

One of us asked Lofty: 'Well, what happens now, sir?'

Lofty took a couple of seconds to reply. He looked at the fallen man and then at us.

'Well, he's failed Selection for a start,' he said. It broke the spell. In minutes we had rolled up the stiff body in a poncho and carried it down to the waiting trucks.

SAS Selection grinds you down. As we slogged our way through the next two weeks our bodies became a mass of sores, caused by the friction of our heavy bergens. No matter how well we padded our shoulder straps, ugly, deep red welts appeared on our shoulders and lower backs. Once you had your bergen on, it wasn't too bad; the pain was just defused by all the other pains you were suffering. But getting it on in the morning and off at night was no fun at all.

Soon the course was down to less than half its original strength.

Our first march, code-named Pipe Line, was thirty kilometres in the rocky terrain of Wales's Black Mountains, carrying 45lb. Unlike any other selection I was ever involved in, you got no encouragement. Recruits were told the time to parade the next morning – never if they are doing badly or well. But each of us knew that in order to pass we would have to average at least four kilometres an hour. This meant finishing in about four and a half hours. To do this we had been given simple advice by our instructors in the build-up to test week: one, gain height as fast as you can; two, stay on the high ground as long as you can; three, jog on even ground and down the hills; four, don't get lost.

We had paraded at 0600. The three-tonner swayed in the blasting wind and some fifteen of us huddled in our sleeping bags could hear the slap of sleet and rain against thin canvas. The course was divided between six trucks which went to separate jump-off points. This prevented recruits following one another as you never knew if the man in front of you was going to the same checkpoint as you were. From the front cabin the Directing Staff (DS) would tell you the order of leaving. You would wait until the man before you was called, then get out of your sleeping bag, pack it on top of your bergen, get out of the truck into the driving rain and snow and wait to be called forward. The DS gave you your first location, checked you had plotted it correctly on your map, entered the time you started and off you went. From then on you moved from checkpoint to checkpoint, always trying to keep going at a reasonable speed. I was so hyped up on my first march, the DS who watched said I ran the first half mile uphill. At the final RV, I checked my watch: four hours dead – a reasonable time.

As soon as the truck was half full for the return journey, you were on your way back to Hereford, and a warm shower and dry clothes. After clearing your rifle and preparing kit for the next day, it was time for the evening meal. Food plays an important part during Selection. We consumed mountains of it, loading our plates then coming back for seconds. At breakfast it was the same: three or four eggs, sausages, bacon – as much as you could eat as during the day there was little time to stop. Most of us kept going on chocolate bars. I ate so many Mars bars I still can't touch the things.

The next two days were more of the same. We were becoming fewer. Injuries took their toll, as did a growing list of those throwing the towel in. After day three, the instructors began to cut those who were not making the necessary timings. You were never told the night before a march but paraded the next day and simply told not to get on the truck but to report to training wing office at 0830 instead. It was a heart-wrenching moment. By day four, we were down to about thirty-five men. The next three marches were the toughest: Point to Point, Sketch Map and finally, Endurance.

Point to Point is a fearsome march taking in the highest mountain points in the Brecon Beacons, among them the dreaded hill 642, so steep we crawled most of the way up it on hands and knees. Our bergen weight was increased to 55lb and the weather was worsening all the time.

There were only four people in my three-tonner. The first left when he was called, while I lay in the warmth of my sleeping bag listening to the howling rain, desperate to stay warm for as long as possible. The next man out was a guardsman. He unzipped his sleeping bag a couple of inches, said in a low voice he was throwing his hand in, and rezipped the bag. The next, a paratrooper from my old battalion, walked to the end of the vehicle, looked at the driving snow and rain and got swiftly back into his bag.

I could hear the DS's impatient voice calling for the next man. I scrambled from my sleeping bag fast and with it trailing from my bergen made my way forward and told him the others were not coming. He gave me the grid reference of my first RV, noted the time, rolled the window up and went to sleep. I moved off a hundred metres, packed my bergen properly and began to slog my way towards Pen y Fan, my first checkpoint. Every man who passes Selection will tell you the same thing: there comes a time when you are at your lowest ebb, a time when you must dig deep into your soul to find the strength to keep going. My moment came on Point to Point.

The snowstorm was so thick, if I shoved my compass out at arm's length I couldn't see it. I was sweating with exertion despite the fact that I had lost contact with my feet hours before. They were just lumps of ice. I felt light-headed and was probably suffering from exposure. I stopped and forced myself to eat a Mars bar; my hands were so cold I couldn't unwrap it properly and just ate the paper as well. It would be so easy to drop off the high ground, find a road and a truck to take me back to where I could sleep for a month. I shook my head. In my mind's eye I saw a succession of leering faces from my past. I saw every bully I had ever known. I started to get angry and the anger warmed me. Into the unheeding wind and snow I screamed my defiance. 'I won't let you beat me, you bastards.' I made the rest of the checkpoints. Getting into the three-tonner, I checked my watch. Six hours: not brilliant, but good enough. I was so cold I couldn't get out of my wet clothes and two lads, who were there ahead of me, helped. As soon as I was in my sleeping bag I was out.

Somebody woke me when I got back to Hereford. I was stiff, weak and sore, and hobbled to my basha like an old man of eighty. Even in the warmth of the building I couldn't stop shaking. I'd enough medical training to know that I had nearly gone down with exposure. I daren't tell anybody, for fear of being taken off the course. I ate as large a supper as I could and drank as much warm liquid as I could force down, then went to bed. Parade the next morning was at 0530. I had nine hours to recover. I woke at 0430 and began my morning ritual: I dressed my feet with an elastic bandage to prevent blisters and to give some protection to my ankles. Then I put on two pairs of socks and my still wet boots, washed, shaved, ate breakfast, drew weapons and paraded. By the time we boarded the trucks there were only twenty-nine of us left.

Sketch Map was next: navigation by means of a small, hand-drawn map. Recruits are given normal maps, sealed in plastic, but to use one means to fail the march. As I waited to start, I was a worried man. The day before had been a nightmare, and I was unsure what toll had been taken on my strength, but moving up the first hill I began to feel good. When I got to the top I felt terrific. Athletes have since told me that, in any strenuous activity, they go through a 'dying' stage. Once out the other side the body releases extra reserves of energy and most important, the mind is strengthened. After checking my compass bearing, I set off at a trot. I could hardly wait to be told my next grid reference before moving on again. At the top of the last hill I looked down to see a truck and knew this was the last RV. I threw back my head in the snow and rain. I was invincible. My time, under four and a half hours, was a record for the Sketch Map march.

We were at base at 1700. At 0100 we paraded for the final hurdle on test week, the fearsome Endurance march. It was nearly eighty kilometres, to be completed in less than twenty hours, across the length of the Brecon Beacons, carrying 65lb. Only two trucks were needed to take us to the start point as we were down to twenty-three men. Unlike the other marches, we all started from the same point. We huddled together outside our trucks waiting to be dispatched. At 0300 Lofty wound down the window of his Landrover and shouted 'Go!' We all looked at each other stupidly, then set off at a run like lemmings to a cliff edge. Within ten minutes we were strung out over a hundred metres along the steep sides of the mountain. The initial panic over, we all settled into an even pace and when daylight broke some four hours later I was already over Pen y Fan and heading down for the first RV at the Storey Arms.

I kept up a steady pace throughout the day. The weather was better than at any time since the start of Selection. By the halfway point I was fourth but as night began to fall the weather suddenly worsened: driving sleet and rain. As I reached the second-to-last RV, I was cold and wracked with pain. I felt a weariness such as I had never felt before but as I pushed my legs on through the snow, each step in its own way a victory, I knew I had to keep moving. If I stopped I might not be able to start again. I remembered the body at the trig point, and Lofty's words.

We had come round in a huge circle and would finish back where we'd started, at Talybont reservoir. I knew that the final RV was close but the last few hundred metres were agony. I stopped and tried to eat a Mars bar but it was frozen solid and my fingers were so numb I couldn't even prise it out of my pocket. I gave up the attempt. Of the last stretch I have only the vaguest of memories. I was in a wood, stumbling from tree to tree through the snow. Then I was on a road. I wasn't allowed to walk on roads. I looked up. It was Lofty. 'Next RV, Staff?' I croaked.

'This is the final RV, Harry. Get into one of the trucks. You've passed test week.'

Inside the truck, I took my boots off and my feet swelled like balloons. The pain was excruciating. But I'd passed. I'd finished fourth in a time of seventeen hours exactly. The man who'd finished first, in a staggering time of fourteen hours, was Lance-Corporal 'Doc' Pollock, a qualified doctor and formerly a major in the TA Parachute Regiment. In his early thirties he had wanted to join the SAS so badly that he had resigned his commission to attempt Selection, knowing that if he had accepted a regular commission he would have been too old to try for Selection by the time he had completed training. Prematurely bald and slightly built, he was nevertheless one of the fittest men I've ever met.

As soon as the first six were back, we returned to camp. I wanted nothing more than a hot shower and a warm bed. Doc had other ideas. He wanted to go into town. Throwing me in a shower, he practically dressed me and helped me hobble to his car. After a couple of pints, Doc decided that a Chinese meal would put me back on my feet. I managed a single mouthful before my head fell forwards into a plate of chicken curry. Luckily, Doc saved me from drowning. I woke up the next morning with most of it still in my hair.

All twenty-three who had started Endurance had completed it and all of us, with the exception of Doc, looked dreadful. Far from looking like super-fit SAS recruits, we shuffled about like old men. The next three weeks were quite pleasant as we undertook weapons training and tactics in preparation for our next major hurdle: the jungle.

We did fitness training every day. Often it was just a run but sometimes we would go into the gym for circuit training, which always ended with a game of 'murder ball'. Each of us wore a pair of boxing gloves and we were divided into two teams: skins and shirts. Lofty explained the game. 'The aim is to move this ball on to your opponents' mat.' He pointed to two mats placed at opposite ends of the gym. 'There is only one rule: if you have the ball, you can get punched.' He looked at an officer. 'Do you understand, boss?'

The officer gave a sardonic grin. During Selection all candidates, officers included, take orders from SAS NCOs, acting in their capacity as Directing Staff. 'Even my tiny little brain can comprehend that, Sergeant-Major.'

Lofty nodded while handing the officer the ball and as he took it hit him squarely in the face. Within seconds the officer was engulfed in a mêlée of bodies.

Our jungle training took place in the sweltering heat of Belize. We had two days to become acclimatized before we were inserted into the prepared jungle camp. We were divided into four-man patrols. In my patrol was an Army Physical Training Instructor, Phil D, an intelligent and thoughtful man but completely lacking in soldiering skills. A stocky, fair-haired man from the SAS Signal Squadron, Frank K, was extremely outspoken and sometimes almost abrasive. He had been attached to the SAS for some time as a signaller and had views on everything. His manner put my teeth on edge many times and on more than one occasion it was with great self-restraint that I didn't strangle him. Our last member was an engineer, John H, a fellow Scot and a laid-back comedian who did much to soothe our frayed tempers over the next few weeks with his dry sardonic wit. He was keen and a quick learner. We all took a liking to him – it was hard not to. We had the first day to make our bashas and settle in. The SAS's love affair with the jungle, stemming from its many jungle campaigns, is reflected in the fact that every structure, from their own homes to the camp barracks are called bashas. None of my compatriots had been in the jungle before, so it fell on my shoulders to educate them in the art of making themselves comfortable in their new surroundings.

Unlike most other special forces in the world, the SAS does not undertake any psychological studies of potential recruits. It doesn't have to: the jungle asks all the necessary questions. Working arduous hours, in stifling heat, always wet, being stung and bitten continually by insects is bad enough. But the jungle has much more up its sleeve. Every tree has a hook or thorn to catch your clothes. If you fight it when you get snagged, you rip your clothes and skin to pieces. Dirt and debris from overhead branches always finds its way down your neck and on to your back, making you feel like you're being attacked by ants. You take two steps back for every three forward. In such circumstances tempers easily became frayed. The smallest things seem to have an importance out of all proportion. A chance remark, a lost letter, even a borrowed brew, can make normally placid men fly off the handle. The DS, always present, watch for any signs of anger or frustration. Someone once wrote that the jungle was neutral but he was wrong. The jungle is an enemy; it could finish your SAS career before it started, or even kill you. And the jungle in Belize was the worst and the filthiest I had ever seen.

The DS occupied the centre of the camp. Scattered around them in a loose circle were our various patrols in our own little camps. Our days soon settled into a routine. We rose just before first light to stand-to. It wasn't difficult to get up in the morning, as half an hour before first light every bird and insect that could do would break into song. The first thing you did was to change from your dry sleeping clothes into your wet day clothes, never a pleasant experience. After stand-to, we had half an hour for breakfast, then we made our way to the central camp for morning 'prayers' (all SAS briefings are called prayers) to be told what the day had in store. Every Sunday was a 'fresh day', a day off when the admin helicopter would bring us in fresh rations; a few potatoes, some vegetables, meat and the mail. It was always a glorious day.

Our training consisted of contact drills and patrols. The first were to test our reactions to contact with the enemy, while the second were simply the routes we went when moving through the jungle. The SAS still based all their contact drills on the four-man patrols they had used in the Malaysian and Borneo campaigns of the late 1950s and early 1960s. I believed that this was a dated system that needed to be drastically overhauled. My experiences in Africa had convinced me that patrols needed to be at least six-strong, with a heavy concentration of firepower, including at least one light machine-gun and a mortar. The SAS contact drills relied on the 'shoot-and-scoot' tactics of their earlier jungle wars. If one man was injured, two men were needed to evacuate him, leaving only one man to hold the enemy off. When I was training in jungle warfare, Special Forces patrols were pitted against aggressive, heavily armed enemies, and one man's firepower would not hold them at bay for very long. Their main advantages were their superior aggresssion and training and, most importantly, surprise. Special Forces patrols popped up where the enemy least expected to find them, behind their own lines. In a contact, the South Africans had used the element of surprise to its maximum effect, attempting in the first vital seconds of a contact to scatter their enemies and cause mayhem and confusion. This often convinced the enemy that they were facing a much larger force. The SAS tactic of a quick fighting retreat, 'shoot and scoot', just handed the initiative to the enemy. In many ways the SAS has been a very innovative organization, but at that time it was in some ways extremely slow to change and seemed to be training to fight the last war rather than looking forward to the tactics needed to survive in the next. It was only six years later, in 1985, that they began to adopt the more aggressive and larger patrols I knew were needed for modern Special Forces.

The secondary jungle was almost impossible to move through. Most of the larger trees had been logged and giant ferns grew in abundance. The only way to get through was for the point man to fall forwards the length of his body, then push on and repeat the process. It was exhausting work. Moving in this fashion was also dangerous. You were often spiked by broken branches which caused deep cuts, and you couldn't see where you were going, or where you were falling. Three men from one patrol fell one after the other over a small cliff. Fatalities were only avoided because they landed in water and not on rocks, but even so two were so badly hurt that they were unable to continue training for several days.

One patrol of only four kilometres took us nearly twelve hours. When our patrol had to put in a cache, which another would lift, it took us fourteen hours of back-breaking toil. Darkness found us still outside the jungle camp and we had to walk chest-deep up the river that ran through the camp to get back. One of the DS told me that we wouldn't be doing this in Africa. I didn't have the heart to tell him I'd done this in Africa. Even though there were no crocodiles, the river was infested with snakes and leeches. I had twenty-four attached to me after the march.

At the end of the training we were launched out on our own, with a specific series of tasks to perform: collect a cache, recce an enemy camp, then RV with other patrols to undertake a troop ambush. On one stop we were lying up, ready to make our midday communications, when we heard a rustling very close by. We all carried live ammunition for protection and as one we reached for our mags. Before we could fit them, a gigantic wild boar with enormous, razor-sharp tusks charged through the camp, overturning the radio and crashing headlong back into the jungle. I fitted my mag and sighted my rifle, but there was nothing to shoot at. For several seconds we all looked after it, John rubbed his stomach and made a gesture as if frying bacon. We all laughed silently, then carried on with our tasks. These were hard routine patrols: no talking, no cooking. We became almost like one person, knowing instinctively what every gesture and sign meant.

We RVd with the rest of the course for the troop ambush.

Unlike the Recces, the SAS cached their bergens before an ambush, something I still do not agree with. In Africa we had dug our bergens into the ground in front of us, giving us easy access to more ammunition and providing extra cover. If there was a counter-attack by the enemy we could grab them and run. The last thing I wanted to do if we were being chased was to start looking for my bergen, especially if it was dark. We ambushed the staff with blank ammunition as they walked down a river. They replied by firing live ammunition over our heads. We followed procedure by bugging out and at the emergency RV were hit again and lost our bergens. We then had to make our way back to camp, which necessitated an overnight stop without our equipment. We slept on the jungle floor, which is alive with things that want to make a meal of you. It was a very uncomfortable night.

This was the final exercise of the jungle phase, of six weeks of purgatory. We shaved for the first time and went back to base, where we had three days to get a quick suntan before going back home.

Unfortunately tragedy struck again. On his first night out of the jungle, a young Commando Engineer from my course got drunk in a pub just outside the camp. No one ever found out exactly what happened but the gate sentry heard a squeal of brakes and a departing car, followed by a groan. The young lad was found unconscious with his back broken. He would never walk again. Most likely he was hit by a speeding taxi on the unlit dirt road and dumped by the driver at the camp's entrance. The next day Phil D and I were queuing for lunch when we overheard a conversation. In front of us, two young soldiers from the Irish Rangers who were with the 2nd Battalion in Belize were talking about their forthcoming home leave. One expressed his doubt about being able to get on an aircraft the next day. Why? he was asked.

'Because of all the injuries. They're shifting one bloke back who's a stretcher case.' He paused to look around him then lowered his voice in a conspiratorial whisper. 'He was SAS, you know. Crawled ten miles with a broken back.' Thus are legends born.

We flew back to England, none of us knowing who had passed and who had failed. We ate our supper in silence, each of us wondering what the outcome would be. It was difficult to assess your own performance. The jungle is as much a test of character as fitness. Twenty-two of us waited for Lofty to come into the room. He entered, a single sheet of paper in his hand.

'The following will report to the Training Officer for RTU.' He began to read out the names slowly. As each name was called the man left the room. Our group became smaller and smaller. When he had finished, there were twelve of us left. 'Congratulations to the rest of you. You've passed your training. You're on leave for a week. Those who need travel passes see the squadron clerk.' He turned and left. For a second we were all silent, then as one we let out a mighty cheer and congratulated each other. My entire patrol had passed. I felt good.

I joined Pat and the boys, now living in Bath, on leave. The first three days were very pleasant; I just loafed around. But on the fourth day I had a bad fever. The local doctor gave me some antibiotic to get me on to my feet and told me to report to the doctor in camp. I did so after leave but apart from feeling weak the fever seemed to have passed. We were doing some pistol work, an introduction to one of the Regiment's specialities, close quarter combat. I was thoroughly enjoying myself when the headaches began, a nagging pain at first, then gradually worsening until they became so bad that I collapsed in the basha. The doctor was called; the fever was back. I was rushed to the general hospital and 'barrier-nursed'. This meant that all medical staff treated me in a sterile environment, achieved by separating me from them and the other patients and maintaining a strictly sterile 'barrier'. Blood tests failed to determine what I was suffering from so they did a lumbar puncture. I had a strain of viral meningitis. A day or so later getting to hospital and it would have been curtains for me. The next two weeks were a nightmare but gradually, thanks to the excellent nursing, I fought off the effects of the disease. Even so I had lost pounds and was extremely weak.

The final phase of Selection, Combat Survival, was to start on the following Sunday. On the Saturday I was still in hospital but I finally convinced the doctor I was well enough to leave.

'You're not going to do anything strenuous, are you?' he asked as I left.

'No, of course not,' I protested.

On the Sunday I paraded with twelve remaining candidates on the All Arms Combat Survival Course. In the Blue Room was

Recce Commando selection, 1977. Candidates were made to swim across a crocodile-infested lake: it was worse at night.

Author shooting buffalo, north-west Africa (left); it was killed within fifteen feet of the author.

Outrigged for parachute training in South Africa, 1977.

The author (front row, far right) on a SAS Recce Commando diving course in Cape Province, South Africa, 1978.

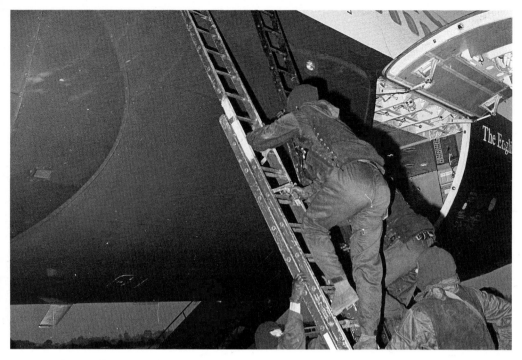

SAS anti-hijack drills, London, 1981. The author is the last man on the ladder.

The author (centre, back row) with his squad of Quatri rangers, 1984. The unit went on to excel in the Gulf war.

SAS anti-ambush drills, Northern Ireland, 1983 – live ammunition was used.

Jungle training in Malaya, 1984. Note the M203 rifle with its underslung grenade launcher – SAS standard weaponry.

A hearts and minds campaign in Malaya, 1984: the SAS bring medical relief to the isolated villages. The SAS man on the left later became an army padre.

Harry McCallion meets Prime Minister Margaret Thatcher, Carrickmore RUC station, Northern Ireland, 1988. The IRA blew up the station a couple of weeks later.

The author and squad on parade for Margaret Thatcher.

Plaques of the four units where the author served. From left to right: 2 Para, Recce Commando, RUC and 22 SAS.

assembled the cream of the British Army's sergeants and officers. Lofty called the role. My name was not on it. I stuck up my hand, and Lofty looked down at me.

'Harry, I thought you were dead!'

'Not yet, Lofty.' He wrote down my name.

On the first night of the course we undertook a short navigational night exercise. Normally this would be a piece of cake for anyone undergoing Selection. Phil D and I were buddied up and dropped off. Phil set off at a brisk trot. I managed four or five paces then stopped, gasping for breath. Phil came back apparently very concerned and asked if I was OK. I nodded, hardly able to breathe: it felt like some giant hand had my chest in a vice. I knew I just needed a couple of days to get my strength back. Phil helped me round that night; without him I don't think I could have made it. We arrived second from last, raising more than one DS eyebrow. We were just inside the cut-off time. Phil had taken the real risk of failing the course to stay with me – something for which I have always been grateful. But I was right, over the next two weeks my full strength returned. At the end of the week I was feeling as good as I ever had.

While we were on a three-day survival exercise, building our own makeshift bashas and surviving on what we could catch I was interrupted by a voice from the past.

'Long time no see, Jock.'

I turned sharply. Graham W, who had led operation Milk Float, stood there in all his glory. I leapt over the bushes and we clasped hands like long-lost brothers, much to the surprise of the regimental adjutant who was accompanying him.

Graham, now a colonel in charge of the Rhodesian SAS, was handing over the Regimental Silver to 22 SAS for safe keeping. We went out for a drink after the exercise. He told me, sadly, that the war was lost. He was going to leave Rhodesia and farm in South Africa. We got drunk and talked of mutual friends, some of whom had died since I'd left. At the end of the night as we parted he said: 'Ah, Jock, they were great days. His strong, almost studious face broke into a sad, ironic smile. 'Just think what might have been.'

As I watched him disappear into the night a wave of depression swept over me. He had lost his war, his regiment and his country.

Selection's final hurdle was resistance to interrogation. We paraded at 0900 the next day, were thoroughly searched and issued with Second World War greatcoats and uniforms. Everyone was taken to a holding centre and handed over to the tender mercies of the Hunter Force, the Gurkhas. For the next twelve hours we were processed by our captors. They had been told to give us a hard time and, obedient as ever, they didn't spare the rod. We were continually harassed, made to do press-ups in puddles, lean for hours against frozen walls or sit cross-legged on the concrete floor, our hands clasped behind our heads. The Hunter Force was always among us, prodding with rifle butt or baton, screaming obscenities in Gurkhali.

Then there was an almighty explosion and rapid shooting. Men dressed in paramilitary uniform burst. in, shouting: 'We are the resistance. Follow us!'

In seconds a hooded man was among us, a shaded torch in his hands.

'Right, lads, we've broken you out, but there are roadblocks between here and the border. I'm going to issue you with sketch maps and you'll be dropped off in pairs. You'll be passed along a pipeline of agents to the border and we'll meet you there and drive you to safety. Choose your partners and be prepared to begin dropping off in twenty minutes.'

As the cattle truck sped at breakneck speed through the night it was impossible not to be caught up in the realism and excitement of it all. Phil D and I teamed up. In minutes we were out in the darkness, given the grid reference of our first contact in a hurried, conspiratorial whisper and raced through the darkened woodland and over hills. Once clear of the drop-off point Phil and I stopped for a quick conference, having by now become quite good friends.

'Just my luck to get buddied up with an invalid,' Phil said.

I grinned in the darkness and whispered back: 'I know, the weight of this oxygen tent I'm carrying is killing me'.

Phil leaned over and placed his lips close to my ears as he warned me: 'Don't bloody lose it — we both might need oxygen by the time this course is over.' We took a quick bearing, finding the North Star at the end of the Plough, and trotted off north to our first RV.

During the next seven days we were constantly hounded by the relentless Hunter Force. We moved only at night, lying up during the day and surviving on the occasional piece of bread, handed quickly to us by our contacts at our RVs. The nights were cold and we huddled together for warmth under our greatcoats. The locals, briefed by the Army, were hostile, reporting any sighting to the Gurkhas. Finally, cold, tired and hungry, we arrived at our last RV, were given two slices of bread and ushered once again on to the cattle truck. Again a hooded figure moved among us.

'Well done, lads, to get this far. We'll soon have you over the border to safety, I'm . . .' His words were interrupted by a squeal of breaks, shouting and shots in the night. The back of the lorry was lowered. Twenty Gurkhas, armed with rifles, trained a searchlight on us. We had been captured. In seconds we were handcuffed and hooded. From now on each of us was on his own.

We were transported to the interrogation centre, where we were stripped and verbally abused and then issued with overalls and hooded once again. For the next forty-eight hours, when not actually being interrogated we were held in a softening-up room. White noise, so loud it must have shaken the foundations of the building, was played constantly. Inside our hoods the noise seemed to vibrate into the very lining of our skulls. We were kept in stress positions, either spread-eagled on our fingertips against a wall, or sitting bolt upright, our hands clasped behind our necks. Both postures were excruciatingly painful after just a few minutes. Any attempt to relieve the pain, by relaxing your fingers so that your palms rested against the wall, or leaning forward when you were sitting, resulted in a swift, violent blow from a Gurkha guard.

The rules of the interrogation sessions were simple: you were allowed to repeat the big five: name, rank, serial number, date of birth and blood group. Any deviation, a single 'yes', 'no', or even a nod in reply to a question, would result in failure. Each interrogator had a different approach, from the comedian who tried to make you laugh to the hard man who tried to make you cry. Sometimes the two worked together: the Mutt and Jeff approach – one hard, one soft. Perhaps the most persuasive, and for us most dangerous, were two girls who pleaded with you to sign a piece of paper otherwise they would get into trouble.

When you are still reasonably fresh, the interrogations are fairly easy to resist. Some even seem funny. But after hours of softening up, the continuous exposure to white noise, the pain of the stress exercises and, perhaps most important, the lack of sleep, they became distinctly less so. In the end each of us was hanging on to his sense of reality by the skin of his teeth. More than forty-eight hours after I had been captured I was taken into a room and introduced to a lieutenant colonel who told me the exercise was over. I refused to believe him until a member of the Selection staff came in and told me that I could relax and answer questions. The officer debriefed me on what I thought of the exercise and told me my performance under interrogation had been graded excellent. Then I was led out to the dining room for my first hot meal in nine days. Never have eggs, bacon and sausages tasted so good. I was ecstatic.

Seated at my table was John H, looking anything but happy. I asked him what was wrong. He looked up glumly.

'The bloody girls managed to persuade me to sign a chitty.' He looked down again. 'I've failed interrogation.' There was more bad news. Another member of my jungle patrol, Frank K, the signaller, had also failed. Using the knowledge gained from being attached to the signal squadron, he had smuggled a compass on to the training area, but had been captured and the compass discovered. Frank and me had simply never got on. To me he was a big-mouthed REMF (Rear Echelon Mother Fucker). All through Selection there had been friction between us. Yet to have come this far only to fail at the last hurdle was a bitter blow to swallow and I would not have wished it on anybody. Frank was already off the course. Someone called John's name and he stood up and extended his hand, saying: 'See you, Harry.' I watched him walk out, one of the saddest figures I have ever seen. A year later John was allowed to take Selection again, starting from scratch. This time he passed everything and was posted to A Squadron. He won the Military Medal for bravery in an Ulster gun battle in the late 1980s.

I was left alone at the table with my thoughts. A few minutes later the squadron clerk sat next to me. There was more bad news. Doc Pollock, who had set the outstanding time on Endurance, would not be badged. His family had spent some time in Eastern Europe and the Intelligence Corps would not countenance his inclusion in the ranks of the SAS. Of the 120 or so who had started Selection, we were down to only eight. The clerk fixed me with an unswerving stare.

'Can you take a joke, Harry?'

'I can take anything,' I replied.

'Well, we've had a little trouble with your vetting.' He held up his hand at my look of alarm. 'Don't worry, we'll get you vetted. But it will take a couple of weeks. Until then we will have to send you on a course.'

'What course?'

'Platoon Sergeants Course.'

It was one of the most demanding courses in the British Army.

'When do I start?'

'At 1600. Here are your joining instructions. Sorry, but until you're vetted it's best you're off the camp.'

I left holding centre at 0500, grabbed five hours' sleep, drew my equipment at midday and by 1600 was in the Battle School. For the next eight weeks I learnt everything about command and tactics the Army had to teach me. I loved it.

On its completion I was told to report straight to the CO, Lieutenant Colonel Rose. I walked into his room while he was on the phone. He covered the mouthpiece with one hand.

'McCallion? Your vetting came through.' He threw a light-grey beret across the table to me. 'Welcome to the Regiment. Report to A Squadron.'

Even though the beret was two sizes too big I immediately put it on. I felt ten feet tall. Reporting to A Squadron was going to be a little difficult. They were in Northern Ireland. Four hours later I was on a plane to Belfast.

Of all the roles that the SAS have had to perform, their entrance on the Ulster stage is, without doubt, one of the most difficult and definitely the most controversial the unit has performed since its formation. The SAS Regiment had first been deployed in the province in 1969, patrolling the Mourne Mountains, but had quickly been withdrawn. It had been held out of Ulster (despite what Republicans and apologists among the left wing claimed) until the vicious series of sectarian murders in South Armagh prompted its return in 1975. So successful had the Regiment been against the South Armagh Provisionals that the unit had been deployed throughout the Province in a squadron-sized com-mitment of roughly sixty men. In early 1980, A Squadron had its full strength deployed in the Province. Originally squadron troops were dispersed in three localities. This had shrunk to only one location, and a single troop strength. However, 14 Intelligence Company still had three detachments. This arrangement explains why, to this day, inside the specialist world of Ulster's anti-terrorist units, the SAS is still referred to simply as the 'Troop', while 14 Intelligence Company is called the 'Det'.

I joined Air Troop (Free Fall Troop) and quickly settled into the squadron routine. When not on operations, we spent the day on the rifle range or in the gym. Ops were frequent although most, mounted on Special Branch information, were little more than speculative. There was a general feeling in the unit that a certain amount of these were carried out to placate Special Branch before you got a really good job. A really good job came up in Londonderry just two weeks after I arrived. It looked like a dead cert for a contact with the enemy. Twenty men were needed but I was not one of those picked to go. Like any outfit the SAS has a pecking order and as a new boy I was well down the list. My initial sadness in missing out on some action was quickly dispelled. A bigger, better job came up in Belfast.

A unit of the Belfast PIRA, armed with handguns and blasting incendiaries, were planning to tunnel through a wall and attack a bus station in the city. Special Branch had a source, an informer, inside the unit. The remaining members of A Squadron, with reinforcements flown over from G Squadron, were tasked with intercepting the gang and either killing or capturing them. The SAS has no *carte blanche* to kill in Ulster; like any soldier on duty in the Province they are governed by the rules of engagement, the 'yellow card' rules. However, the SAS comprises highly trained, extremely aggressive soldiers, and putting them near armed IRA terrorists is a little like putting hungry wolves next to red meat.

The attack was scheduled for that night. Shortly after darkness fell, I was dropped off from an unmarked car with my Det colleague, who would identify any IRA suspects who passed us. We were dressed from head to toe in black and moved like shadows as we made our way to the roof of a building overlooking the bus station. Below us we had a well-lit, panoramic view of the scene. Our men were already inside the depot, having been inserted during the daylight hours. They waited, hidden in the back of two buses.

Below me a figure walked past the depot's front gate. The DET man next to me stiffened slightly in the darkness and whispered: 'That's the OC of the local PIRA ASU, having a last check.'

I reported the sighting on my personal radio and almost immediately the SAS men inside the buses heard hammering noises from the perimeter wall. The IRA were trying to tunnel in.

For the next hour we waited, and all the while the noise of the terrorists' tunnelling efforts was clearly audible to the concealed soldiers. Then the hammering stopped. Twenty minutes later over our secure radios, we were told the reason why. The wall was reinforced concrete, and they could not break through it. The source reported that the terrorists were in the process of hijacking two cars; the attack would now come through the front gate. I felt the adrenalin course through my body. I would have a ringside seat. I eased the Armalite rifle I was holding into the ready position. They wouldn't know what hit them.

Suddenly, two military Landrovers appeared at the front gate. UDR troops. I swore under my breath and reported their presence to my disbelieving controller. He too cursed and warned the group inside the depot to keep their heads down. I couldn't believe what was happening. The area was out of bounds to normal troops. This was an essential requirement for undercover operations in Ulster. These UDR soldiers should not have been there, but they were. They had left their vehicles and were moving through the bus station in extended line. If they discovered our hidden men, dressed in civvies and carrying Armalites, anything could happen. There was an excited shout from below. Within seconds, two vehicles sped from the depot, tyres screeching. Everything went quiet. We waited for the source to report in. He didn't, not that night, or ever again.

Someone, it was never established who, had come over the UDR radio net and told them that they were in an out-of-bounds area and that a covert operation was underway. The IRA had been monitoring all radio traffic in the area and had picked up the transmission. Our radios were, of course, secure. Any attempt at monitoring them would have been futile.

The entire IRA ASU was confined to a safe house until one of the terrorists' internal security teams was called in. They quickly established the identity of the source. He turned up three days later stripped naked, hands wired behind his back, on the South

Armagh border. Whoever had spoken on the radio that night had cost a brave man his life.

The rest of my first tour in Ulster with the SAS was a lacklustre affair. The missed opportunity in Belfast and the loss of a top source was a bitter blow. I spent hours in the gym, pumping iron and hitting the punch-bag to relieve some of the pent-up rage inside me. Coming from a war of almost constant action to the frustrations of Ulster was a difficult adjustment. Yet on my very first operation with the SAS I had come so very close. I was like a predatory animal that had stalked its prey, only to see it slip away at the last moment. Four weeks later A Squadron's tour came to an end. It was the last full-squadron tour of duty in the Province. Thereafter a single troop detached from the anti-terrorist team would fulfil the role. I returned home for a four-week break, the first I'd had since returning to the country.

Airborne Forces weekend was on in Aldershot and I took the opportunity to go back and renew some old friendships. Standing outside the beer tent I saw a familiar broad-shouldered figure weaving his way towards me.

'Harry,' a broad Irish brogue announced. 'How the hell are you?' It was Leon McKevitt, now a sergeant in charge of the Junior Parachute Company in the depot. He'd put on some weight but still looked magnificent in full Para battledress. He was duty sergeant for the day and his juniors, also in uniform, hovered around him, fetching him the occasional beer and hanging on to his every word. It was obvious they idolized him. I asked him what he had done to pull duty on Airborne Forces day.

'Ah, Harry. I filled the depot RSM in when he was a sergeant, I filled the depot sergeant-major in when he was a corporal and I filled my own colour sergeant in when we were both privates.' He threw his arms wide in exasperation. 'Is it any wonder I'm on duty today?'

It was during this break that I learnt my father had been killed in Lincoln. Someone had the good sense to blow his head off with a shotgun. Then my marriage broke up. I had met someone and fallen in love for the first time. My wife didn't take the news at all well. She complained to my OC, who could not understand my point of view. As a result (hell has no fury) I moved from A to B

Squadron. This didn't particularly bother me. B Squadron was full of larger-than-life characters. There were the Fijians, among them the legendary Tak of Mirbat fame, and Neil G, the Royal Marine sniper, whom I'd met in the New Lodge in 1972. Neil was one of the most natural killers I ever met. He was a crack shot with any weapon and lightning fast with a handgun, and his shooting prowess were admired and respected by all who met him. He was inclined to be gruff, almost morose, while on the training wing in charge of selection. It was not for nothing he got the nickname 'Nasty Neil'.

Bob T, an ex-Green Jacket who was a member of Mountain Troop, was a man I warmed to almost immediately. He was short and stocky, with a shock of close-cropped ginger hair, and came from a military family. His father had been decorated in the retreat from Dunkirk and a brother had risen through the ranks to become a lieutenant colonel. Bob himself had joined the junior leaders as a schoolboy. The first time I met him was in the SAS's Paludrin Club at Stirling Lines, Hereford. Our views on everything seemed the same, and we both lived for only one thing, soldiering.

I had joined 6 (Boat) Troop. Each squadron has four troops – Air Troop, Boat Troop, Mountain Troop and Mobility Troop – each with its own specialized skills. My troop boss was Captain Andy L, who had a masters degree in mathematics and was unlike any officer I had ever met. He talked and behaved more like a ranker than a 'Rupert' (the SAS's derogatory nickname for an officer). The troop staff sergeant was Jakey V, the most senior staff sergeant in the Regiment, who'd fought in many of its previous campaigns. A Scot with a biting line in self-deprecating humour, Jakey had a funny story to cover every situation.

The relationship between Jakey and Andy was very close. Andy really respected Jakey but more than that he liked and trusted him. Whatever Jakey said was gospel to Andy. In turn Jakey had an almost paternal attitude to his Troop Captain.

B Squadron was part of the 'Team', the SAS's anti-terrorist force. Its Mobility Troop was detached to Ulster. Life on the Team was terrific fun. Most mornings were spent in the regimental 'Killing House', practising CQB (close quarter battle) with the 9mm Browning pistol and Heckler and Koch MP5 sub-machine-gun, an excellent close quarter assault weapon, accurate and very reliable. Torches, synchronized with the weapons' sights, were fitted as standard, giving the user the ability to fire effectively in almost total darkness. Afternoons were spent improving personal fitness or shooting on one of the outside ranges. Most weeks we went to the gym for a game of what some called basketball. The object of the game was to move the ball from one side of the gym to the other and propel it into the net suspended midway up each of the two end walls. Beyond that, there was no similarity between our game and the conventional one. We played by jungle rules.

One of the squadron characters was George, or Mad George as we called him. He had been blown up in the Middle East and still had a metal plate in his head. It was the standing joke of one member of the squadron that he knew George had brains because he'd held them in his hands. George gave the impression that he was always on the verge of losing his temper. One day he grabbed the ball and with a yell of triumph began to charge down the gym. He was built like a bull, and I thought it would take a bulldozer to knock him down. From the opposite side of the room another figure hurled himself at breakneck speed at George, an elbow extended like a lance. The elbow struck George just under his ribs. His body deflated like a burst balloon and he collapsed in agony, swearing revenge. His attacker, who had made off, laughing, with the ball, was Mel P, one of the hardest men in the Regiment. He had gained worldwide fame as the first man across the balcony into the Iranian Embassy. I decided I liked B Squadron.

Most nights were free, giving me the chance to catch up with my social life. I avoided my first wife like the plague. She had not taken our separation at all well, and I had hoped that she might leave Hereford, but she dug her heels in and stayed and seemed determined to try and get me RTUd at every opportunity. Apart from this aggravation, for a young man who had just passed Selection life was great. I found the bars convivial and the women in plentiful supply. We had a ball. We had our own groupies, and there was never any shortage, but this did lead to problems, because Hereford is a small town, and the SAS a small unit. Frequently an SAS man would find his divorced or separated wife on the arm of another member of the Regiment. Men who went away on trips returned to find their girlfriends involved elsewhere.

More men have been lost to the Regiment by being RTUd over

women, than from the efforts of the IRA, the Argentinians and the Iraqis combined. One man who had been on highly secret operations made the mistake of telling his wife they were getting divorced. She promptly went to his OC and revealed what she'd been told. He was RTUd the next day. Wives were in no doubt about the power they wielded. When I had left Pat it was my OC, rather than a lawyer or marriage counsellor, she ran to.

I'd been in B Squadron a scant six weeks and hadn't even had time to get a telephone installed in my new flat when I got a knock at the door, just after tea one day, and was told: 'Be in camp at 0530 with enough kit to last you a week. You're going back to Ulster.'

I had a very quick briefing from Andy L. We were going to reinforce Mobility Troop for an extended operation. Twenty minutes later I was on a helicopter and in less than two hours was back in Northern Ireland. We had been sent over for one task only, to ambush a man called Jim Lynagh.

In the early 1980s Lynagh was the most active terrorist in the Provisional IRA. Born on 13 April 1956, a native of County Monaghan in the Irish Republic, he had joined the Provisionals in his early teens. In 1973 a bomb he was carrying prematurely detonated, injuring him badly, but on his release from prison he quickly went back to work. In 1979 he was elected to the Monaghan District Council as a Sinn Fein councillor. He liked to kill up close, happy to use either gun or bomb. Like all brave IRA men, he chose his targets well: off-duty RUC or UDR men sitting with their wives and families; the occasional workman who fed his family by doing stuff for the security forces; people who were generally unarmed and easy prey. Lynagh was the SAS's top priority and information had come in that he was coming north to kill again.

Although he was unaware of it, Lynagh had already survived one SAS ambush. He and five others had walked through it a few months before. Weather, bad communications and incomplete intelligence had conspired to prevent his arrest. Now it was our turn. We were hampered again by poor intelligence. We knew roughly when Lynagh planned to come over the border but we didn't know where, or exactly which target he would hit. IRA scouts had been picked up by surveillance teams near three possible locations so it was decided to insert long-term ambushes in the vicinity of each. My location was a small wood next to a suspected target's house.

For the next four weeks we were sleeping in two-hour shifts, eating cold food, unable to move in the daylight hours and urinating and defecating into plastic bags that were stored in our bergens for removal. It was a really horrible experience, balancing on your heels while you aimed at a plastic sheet. Hygiene was very important in long stays out in the field, and your hands had to be washed thoroughly after every toilet. Quite apart from the health risks, the last handicap you wanted was the runs.

Lying still for hours on end is an art form. If you are not careful your legs become like dead weights and the urge to move them is almost overwhelming. To stop this from happening most of us had little routines. Starting with one leg we would concentrate on moving the toes, then the foot inside the boot, then slowly flexing each muscle of the leg and then repeating the process with the other leg. In this way you helped to prevent both 'dead leg' and cramp. Cramp was a particular hazard as it could literally cost you your life.

We used to rotate the watches so that nobody spent more than an hour actually watching a target. After that even the best of us started to think about other things, like hot food or a warm bath. At night we would use our peripheral vision to watch an object. If you stared at a tree for too long at night it grew arms and legs, then it began to move. When you shot it turned back into a tree. Staring too long at anything at night had caused more than one poor squaddie to initiate an ambush by mistake.

The target I was helping to guard, an RUC Reserve Constable, knew of the threat against him and of our presence near his house. His neighbours, mostly Catholics, did not. One would walk his dog, a large Labrador, near our position and on one occasion the inquisitive hound came right up to me. At a distance of less than three inches man and dog eyed each other suspiciously. I could feel its hot breath as it studied me. Its nose touched my face. Imperceptibly I moved a fraction away from it. It continued to sniff, for after a few days in the field my body odour must have been quite attractive to a dog. I heard a faint call and the dog lifted its head. A silent sigh of relief swept through me. Then the monster cocked its leg and pissed over me. Most of it cascaded off my waterproof smock but some got on to my trousers. I love dogs, but at that moment I could quite easily have strangled the beast with my bare hands.

Lynagh didn't show. Not for the first time, I wished the IRA was more disciplined. If they had been we would have hammered them. Empty-handed, we left. The Team in its present composition was coming to an end and we handed over to our relieving squadron. In January 1982, D Squadron's Mobility Troop ended a run of failed operations in Ulster with a stunning success. For over a year a Protestant terror gang belonging to the UDA had been attacking senior Republican figures. The SAS seldom went up against 'Prod' terrorists. In order to work in an area the SAS would put it out of bounds to normal security force patrols to prevent a blue-on-blue contact. When we tried to do this in Protestant areas the local Prod paramilitaries were almost always tipped off by sympathizers within the locally recruited UDR. In the Regiment we are totally unbiased; a terrorist was a terrorist. To have used us against the Prods on any sort of regular basis would have resulted in UDA and UVF men coming back in coffins. That, in turn, would almost certainly have resulted in some kind of retaliation. The reason for our presence in this case was that the intended target of the UDA attack was Bernadette McAliskey, the former Westminster MP Bernadette Devlin. The RUC's Special Branch knew McAliskey was going to be hit, but not when. A four-man team from D Squadron was dispatched to do a CTR (close-target recce) of McAliskey's home, near the fiercely Republican town of Coalisland. The team, dressed in the uniform of the local British Army patrolling unit, were approaching the McAliskey home when they heard the sound of shots. Rushing forward, they intercepted the four-man UDA assassination squad in the act. Had they been just a few minutes later there is no doubt that one of the Republicans' most outspoken champions, a woman who had once urged Americans to give money to the IRA so that more British soldiers could be sent home in boxes, would have died. Even so, it was a close-run thing. A medic with the patrol stopped the injured McAliskey from bleeding to death.

The UDA terrorists were arrested, charged with attempted murder, and finally convicted in Belfast Crown Court and sentenced to lengthy prison terms. It was a matter of much sardonic comment within Special Forces circles that one of our most determined and outspoken critics owed her life to the efforts of the SAS.

In the early months of 1982 Boat Troop was sent on extensive training, first with the SBS, then diving training with the Royal Engineers and Navy. On one diving exercise, in northern Scotland, we were joined by Big Fred M, the giant Fijian who was shortly to take over as Squadron Sergeant-Major. Fred's prowess as a drinker was legendary but, unfortunately for my Scottish brethren, was unknown north of the border. On a wintry night we went to a local inn for some light refreshment. Arranged along the top of the bar was bottle after bottle of Scotch whisky, at least thirty different malts and blends. Fred surveyed them with admiration.

'Brother,' he announced to the barman, 'that's an awful lot of whisky.'

The barman leant across the solid oak bar while casually polishing a glass.

'Certainly is. We have a little wager in these parts.'

Fred leant towards him, a huge smile on his dark, handsome face.

'And what would that be, brother?'

'Well.' The barmen threw a quick glance at a group of locals seated nearby and tried to suppress a smile. 'If any man can drink a single measure of whisky from each bottle, all along the optics, and still remain standing, he gets his drinks for free.'

Fred's smile broadened. His huge paw slapped the bar hard enough to make the optics rattle.

'Brother, that will do for me,' he said, producing £50 to show his good intention.

Within seconds we were surrounded by the locals. Bets were placed. I managed to get £10 down at two to one. Fred began his assault. Previous stalwarts had tried to drink quickly. Fred was a man who relished a glass of good whisky, so he drank each glass slowly, savouring the aromas and textures and commenting on them. Scottish pubs sell shorts in measures of an eighth of a gill. I calculated that to drink from each of the optics Fred would have to consume at least two and a half bottles. What happened that night remains part of a local legend. Not only did Fred drink the lot, but he started back again before closing time and walked out to a standing ovation.

Towards the end of the diving course I surfaced too quickly from a dive and suffered what felt like a small explosion in my ear. The doctor took one quick look.

'No more diving for you, my lad. It's back to Hereford.' I had a perforated eardrum.

On my return to Stirling Lines I found the Squadron preparing for the annual Flintlock exercise held in Germany. It was universally disliked by Regimental personnel. I went to great lengths to convince the SSM that, because of the injury I had received, I couldn't parachute. Much to my dismay, I was put on the road party.

As I left the old wooden basha, I bumped into a friend of mine from another Troop, Bob C. He asked if I'd been listening to the radio.

'The Argentinians are threatening to invade the Falkland Islands.'

'Where the hell are the Falklands?' I asked.

'Beats me. But, wherever they are, the Argentinians are going to invade them.'

We burst out laughing at the absurdity of it all and headed for the NAAFI.

During NAAFI break Bob and I were joined by several other members of B Squadron. It was good to catch up with the latest gossip. Bob told his Falklands story much to the mirth of all those seated at the table.

'Perhaps they will invade and we'll all get out of Flintlock.'

We were still laughing when one of the Troop Sergeants appeared.

'You're all wanted back in the Interest Room. The Argentinians have landed an invasion force on the Falklands and there's been heavy fighting. It looks like war.'

War. The chance to see some action. I could hardly contain my excitement.

'Do you think this is for real?' I asked Bob.

'Dunno.' He shrugged his shoulders. Then he smiled brightly. 'But I reckon Flintlock will be kicked into touch.'

We arrived at the Interest Room to find most of the Squadron assembled. The room was buzzing. We all felt that a full-scale invasion of a Crown Colony by another nation would justify at least a two-squadron deployment. D Squadron, on immediate call, had already been dispatched to the area. We were the next Squadron in line to go.

Eventually, 'Boss M', our OC, came in with the SSM. He reviewed what we already knew, told us there would be no move that day and that the CO would speak to us the following day. The rest of the day was spent in slightly frenzied preparation for a quick move. That night most of us RVd in the Booth Hotel for a drink, still high with excitement. Then a bombshell was dropped with all the impact of a well-aimed kick in the crutch. G Squadron were being sent in ahead of us.

Around me the atmosphere deflated, to be replaced with bitter recrimination. The CO was ex-G Squadron; we felt we'd been upstaged by the 'Guards Mafia'. Many members believed that the Guards, who form G Squadron, had too much influence in the higher ranks of the SAS and looked after one another's interests first and foremost. I tried to be a little more positive. Perhaps it was only a rumour? But the sight of grinning G Squadron personnel leaving the pub confirmed this was no idle gossip. Talk turned to the possibility of three squadrons being deployed. It was only an outside chance. Most of us returned home that night with the taste of ashes in our mouths.

Next morning I walked through the camp gates to see the massed ranks of G Squadron preparing to leave. The Interest Room was subdued. Boss M came and said that the CO would brief us at 10 a.m.; that G Squadron was going because we were being held back for some special reason. 'Because we're not G Squadron,' someone shouted from the back of the room. There was an angry murmur of agreement. The SSM called for quiet and the room fell silent again. Boss M said he understood how we felt, but asked us to give the CO a chance. We were left to our own devices until that briefing.

The CO bounced in with his usual jocular air, seemingly oblivious to the hostility emanating from the sixty or so men seated before him. This was the man many of the Squadron believed had accepted a medal for the Embassy Siege that should have gone to the previous commander of B Squadron. He informed us that G Squadron had been deployed ahead of us because, having just finished a tour on the anti-terrorist team, we had the specialist training necessary for specific types of operation. We were to be a strategic reserve for a special operation, as yet unspecified. He then asked if we had any ideas about what form this special operation might take.

He got only two replies, perhaps because we still felt we'd been done in. Pete W (who was later to write *Soldier I*) suggested firing Polaris missiles at the Argentinians, without nuclear warheads. One of the troop's Ruperts suggested that we infiltrate mainland Argentina, make contact with the anti-government guerrillas there and use them against the present junta. I remember watching the CO's face and thinking, that's his career in the SAS gone for a Burton. On this less than optimistic note the briefing broke up.

Then we began to train. Boy, did we train. Never before in my military career had I gone into such a continuous spate of prolonged and intense preparation. We spent hours practising four-man drills, troop drills and attacks, and squadron drills and attacks. We shot every weapon in the armoury and when we had done that we got new weapons, American M202s, four-barrelled rocket launchers and 60mm assault mortars. Our normal day started at 0700 and we worked until 2200.

We got daily briefings from the Intelligence Corps, those green-bereted wonders. They went into some detail but almost always ended with the warning that in their opinion the whole thing would be settled politically before any landing by British troops. They were giving the same view only days before the shooting started. These stalwarts failed to realize that the Argentinian junta had staked its very existence on this invasion, and Maggie Thatcher would never back down. I sometimes wonder what the 'intelligence' in Intelligence Corps stood for.

We trained hard, night and day, but in our heart of hearts none of us really believed we would be deployed. Between 10 and 26 April 1982 elements of D Squadron assisted in the retaking of South Georgia. I was on guard duty on the 21st, the night two helicopters crashed on Fortuna Glacier. The initial reports were conflicting: men missing, then hurt, then dead, then missing again. It was with great relief at the end of the night that we heard that, thanks to the heroic efforts of an RAF pilot, all our men had been evacuated safely.

With the retaking of South Georgia our Task Force was within striking distance of the Falklands and none of us expected a long campaign to recapture the islands. This was not going to be B Squadron's war.

On 2 May the Argentinian cruiser *General Belgrano*, escorted by the destroyers *Hipolito Bouchard* and *Piedra Buena*, was attacked by HMS *Conqueror*. The British submarine fired three Mk8 torpedoes at a range of less than three miles, hitting the cruiser twice, in the bow and stern. The stricken vessel sank within an hour, with the loss of more than three hundred men. I woke up to the news on the following Monday. The effect was electric. We were in a war now, and no mistake. I jumped out of bed to put the TV on, elated that our government had finally taken the war to the aggressors.

At the daily intelligence briefing the assessment of the Intelligence Corps boffins and our own superiors was that this show of force would probably force the Argentinians to the negotiating table. It didn't seem to occur to anybody that they might want to pay us back.

Two days later, on 4 May, HMS *Sheffield*, a Type 42 destroyer and one of the new breed of naval ships, was carrying out her escort duties protecting HMS *Hermes*. Three hostile aircraft were seen approaching the ship. In the absence of any other information, they were assumed to be Mirage III Interceptors. They were in fact Super Etendard naval strike aircraft, armed with the latest AM39 Exocet anti-ship missiles. The attacking pilots, aware of the British radar protection screen, were under instructions not to turn on their own attack radar until they were within 40–50 kilometres of their target. As a result the *Sheffield* had little or no warning as the 1455lb missile, armed with a 364lb warhead, hit its starboard side amidships.

The warhead did not explode, but even so the effects were catastrophic. The friction of the Exocet passing through thin steel plate caused a sheet of flame which ignited the main supply tank. In fifteen seconds the destroyer was ablaze. The smoke generated by the fire was responsible for the deaths of twenty men.

The attack sent shock waves through the higher ranks of the Army, Navy and government. At this stage plans had been laid for the retaking of the islands, with a landing at San Carlos less than three weeks away. The plan was to unload Rapier anti-aircraft missiles as soon as possible to give local defence. The Super Etendard had not been brought into the equation; the threat it posed, to the Task Force in general, but most particularly to the carriers, was enormous. If we lost even one carrier the war, for us, would probably be over. The Exocet menace would have to be neutralized. The powers that be turned to the SAS and the strategic reserve: B Squadron.

I heard about the *Sheffield* in a news flash just as Julia, the girl I was now living with, handed me my evening meal. In an outburst of sheer, uncontrollable fury I smashed my fist down on the flimsy wooden table, breaking it beyond repair and scattering my dinner over the floor. Sanity returned almost immediately and I apologized and helped her clean up the mess.

The next morning Boss M told us that it had been decided that B Squadron would train for an assault on the Argentinian mainland, to attack and destroy the Super Etendards at source. Training would begin immediately. We would have about two weeks to prepare for the operation. We were already at a peak of training but this new phase would concentrate on the specific tactics to be employed on the proposed raid. The operation was in essence very simple. It was envisaged that two Hercules C130s would carry the Squadron in, in a move reminiscent of the Entebbe raid in 1976. Once deployed on the ground the Squadron would fan out, destroying the Etendards and any Exocets we could find.

As detailed planning was impossible because we didn't know what we would encounter on the ground, our training concentrated on deploying from our aircraft as fast as possible in the few vital seconds after we landed. My task was to assault the officers' mess and kill every pilot there. If everything went to plan, we would hit them so fast they would be unable to react.

For the next week B Squadron began to assault airfields from northern Scotland to the Midlands and beyond. We practised low flying, combat loading and airfield assaults until we could do it blindfolded. Anyone who's never had the pleasure of low-level flying in a Hercules cannot imagine what it's like. Do it once and you'll never wonder again why sick people's faces are painted green in children's cartoons.

As our training intensified, divisions began to appear in the Squadron. From the start there had been those who'd been opposed to the operation. Most outspoken of these was my own troop staff sergeant, Jakey V. He made no secret of the fact that he believed the operation was ill-conceived and would lead inevitably to the destruction of the entire Squadron. Jakey's views were shared by a large number of the older hands.

Nine members of the Squadron, drawn from different troops, were to be dispatched as an advance force, our eyes and ears on the ground. They were led by Captain Andy L, my troop commander. With him in the hand-picked group were Neil G, the former Royal Marine, and from my own troop Mick F, an ex-Gordon Highlander, a robust and aggressive soldier; also in the group were Taff T, who'd won a DCM on Storm, the SAS's code-name for the Dhofar war of 1972–7, and Pete B, whom I had known since we were in the Paras. As they were preparing to depart, I shook hands with each of them, all that is except Andy. Jakey had been closeted with him in the basha for most of the morning and only as his team was about to depart did he emerge. His face was grim and set. He looked like he was carrying the weight of the world on his shoulders.

They would make their way to Ascension Island, from where they would parachute into the Task Force. Taking off from the *Hermes*, a Sea King helicopter, stripped to its bare essentials, would airlift them to their target area. It would then ditch on the Chilean coast, as if blown off course from the Task Force, to allay suspicion.

Their story was told to me by several members of the group.

On board the *Hermes* the nine men prepared for their insertion close to the main Argentinian airfield that was to be our target. Neil was the weapons man. He'd taken along a variety of armaments so as to be able to kill as quietly as possible. At close quarters he intended to use a Welrod: a single-shot 9mm pistol designed by the Special Operations Executive during the Second World War and still used by the SAS. To test it Neil would creep up behind some unsuspecting sailor and fire the weapon into the night. He was satisfied it worked when the sailor didn't react.

Twenty-four hours before the team was launched Andy came in with an aerial photo of their proposed landing site near a farmhouse. Andy was worried that the locals might hear them land and report to the army. He asked for suggestions. Neil produced his Welrod.

'Don't worry, boss. I'll take care of them.'

Andy stormed out, accusing Neil of being a madman.

The main danger for the team was the take-off from the aircraft carrier as the helicopter, overloaded with fuel, might be unable to gain height quickly enough. The helicopter took off like a plane, then dipped drastically seaward. With barely a few feet to spare it began to gain height and headed towards the Argentinian coast, flying low to avoid the coastal radar. Inside, despite wearing Arctic warfare dress, the team were freezing. The pilot landed within a few kilometres of his target, to allow the SAS patrol to infiltrate on foot. Its door opened. In the distance a flare curved into the air over the sea. Andy decided that this was proof that they had been compromised and decided to abort. The message was passed down the helicopter. Neil was preparing to disembark. Mick F shouted above the din of the 'copter's engine that they were going to Chile.

'Chilly. It's fucking freezing,' Neil shouted back.

The pilot reverted to his alternative plan and put them down over the border in Chile, and flying on the last of his fuel, made the Chilean coast before ditching, as were his orders.

They walked through the night but halted at the sound of approaching hoofs. In the distance a rider approached. Neil drew a bead on him with a sniper's rifle to which a special night-sight had been attached. Eventually the man moved away, unaware of the team. Neil grunted quietly.

'If he'd looked this way he'd have been a one-eyed gaucho.'

The team now tried to contact certain agents in Chile. Most simply put the phone down on them. One did tell them to hand themselves in to the Chilean authorities. Next they tried to make their war RVs – rendezvous points where SAS reception teams would replenish their food supplies – only to find them unmanned. With their rations running low, more by luck than intention they bumped into one of these teams, eating in a restaurant. They spent much of the war kicking their heels in Chile, before being flown back to Hereford without engaging the enemy.

Back at Hereford, all this was unknown to us. We believed the team had been inserted and that all that was now needed was the final go-ahead. The Director told us that the final decision to launch our operation would be taken at Cabinet level.

The opposition to the operation was now openly hostile. One well-known member of the Squadron even went as far as to say:

'We're all going to die to fulfil an old man's fantasies.' It was a direct reference to the Director himself.

Several days later we heard about the ditched helicopter and believed the team had been inserted. I knew it was decision time.

'I think there's a good chance of us going in,' I said to Jakey.

'Aye,' he replied, 'and a good chance we'll all be killed.'

At this stage of the war, like the rest of the country I was glued to every news broadcast. I remember the one that night as if it was yesterday. Cecil Parkinson came out of a full Cabinet meeting to be asked by an interviewer if he had anything to announce.

'Nothing I'd like to share with you,' he said. Less than an hour later there was a knock on my door. It was a member of my troop, Dave W, who lived quite close to me. His face was stern. 'The job's on.' There was no mistaking the tension in his voice. 'Be in camp tomorrow at 0500.'

I got up at 0400, washed, shaved, had a full breakfast and met Dave outside at half past. We drove in silence to the camp. His wife was in the back seat and as I turned to say goodbye at the camp gates I saw the tears well up in her eyes. I got out of the car hurriedly to let them have as much privacy as possible.

We made our way to the interest room where the rest of the Squadron had assembled. Boss M, a tall man with thinning, light-brown hair, drew himself up to his full height and delivered a stirring speech. 'Only one unit stands betweent the Task Force and hundreds of casualties. That unit is B Squadron, 22 SAS. We're going in, with help on the ground if possible, blind if not, but we're going in. Our country is at war and we're needed. I know none of you will let me down.' I felt the short hairs rise on the back of my neck; I took a series of short, sharp breaths. At that moment I would have led a charge against the devil in hell with a bucket of water.

We were told to make our way to the armoury to collect our weapons. I looked around for Jakey, but couldn't find him. I walked outside and bumped into the Director heading towards our Squadron office.

'Is your boss in?'

'Yes.'

'Is he alone?'

I nodded.

'Good,' he replied and brushed past me.

The news began to circulate that Jakey had RTUd himself, believing the job was a suicide mission. He'd submitted his resignation to the OC the previous night when he had been told the job was on. So well respected was Jakey that the news came like a thunderbolt to us all. Groups stopped to discuss the situation. One was addressed by a senior sergeant.

'I think Jakey's right and we should support him by offering to resign also.'

Bob T spoke up angrily. 'What you're suggesting is mutiny. I'll have none of it.'

There was a murmur of agreement. Even while this debate was going on, a fresh shock was delivered. Boss M had been sacked. When Jakey had announced his resignation the OC had in turn voiced his own doubts. The Director had sacked him that very morning. There hadn't been a shot fired in anger against us and already we were shell-shocked. The only good news was that Ian Crooke – Crooky as we all called him – the regimental second in command, was taking over as Squadron commander. He was a no-nonsense, well-respected soldier.

All of this absorbed each man's thoughts as we prepared to leave. Normally at such times, the Squadron is a boisterous crowd shouting jokes and making noisy conversation. On board our bus not a word was spoken as the engines started and as we drove through the camp's gates I stared at the passing streets and wondered, as I'm sure each man did, if we'd ever see Hereford again.

6

THE SAS II

'Deadly Bellies kill!'
Dougie Oram, 14 Intelligence Company

We deployed to the Ascension Islands, landing in the early hours of the morning. We were all tired and most of us were asleep long before our heads hit the pillow. The next morning we set off to our Squadron office, situated in a large tent some hundred metres from our bashas, to receive our first impromptu briefing. The gloom of the previous day had gone and the Squadron was its usual self, full of banter. Crooky ducked out from under the tent. One look at his face told me something was terribly wrong.

'Gentlemen, it is my sad duty to inform you that the Regiment has suffered its largest casualties since the Second World War. A Sea King has crashed while cross-decking troops. There are twenty fatalities. I will now read out the confirmed casualty toll. Trooper Armstrong, Sergeant Arthy, Corporal Begley, Sergeant Bunker, Sergeant Currass . . .' And so the list went on, each name bringing to mind a familiar face we would never see again.

'This news is a blow to us all. Any words I say will only be superficial,' Crooky added. 'There will be no training this morning. Each of you have this time to come to terms with it.' We made our way silently back towards the bashas. Not a word was spoken. It was like a funeral march, and in a way it was.

The next week was one of the most difficult of my life. The operation was on, only to be postponed for twelve, twenty-four or forty-eight hours. One moment we would be sitting in vehicles ready to drive to the airfield, the next the job was cancelled yet again. When I joined the Paras, I was told the story of Arnhem in graphic detail. What particularly fascinated me was that, after a month of postponements the Division had gone in, despite warnings from the Dutch Resistance that two Panzer Divisions were in the area. Now, all these years later, I understood. It wouldn't have mattered to me if the entire Argentinian Airforce was waiting just over the horizon. I just wanted to go. To get the thing over with, one way or another.

Major Crooke knew the effect these delays were having on the Squadron, especially since the Task Force was already suffering losses. If we didn't deploy soon, either the enemy would hit one of our carriers (they very nearly did when they sank the *Atlantic Conveyor*) or the landings would be completed. Either way, the reason for sending us would be gone. The matter came to a head: we would go in twenty-four hours or not at all.

Those twenty-four hours ticked by slowly, each of us absorbed in our own thoughts. At 0600 those who could stomach it ate breakfast. We crowded on to the trucks once again, then drove to the airfield. We loaded the aircraft for the assault, then each of us went to his prearranged position. After all the false starts, I felt calm and at ease now that we were ready to go. I'd never been afraid of death. Sometimes I'd even chased it. I wondered whether this was one of those times. On the faces of my comrades I saw a mixture of emotions: excitement on the faces of the younger ones, grim determination on the others.

A Landrover appeared with several RAF personnel. Crooky was called off the aircraft – I thought to be given last-minute instructions. Then the engines slowly died. The job was cancelled, permanently. The RAF had discovered that the Argentinians had deployed a new radar on a boat just off the coast. The airfield we would be attacking would have too great a warning of our approach. We unloaded and made our way back to the bashas.

A lot has been said inside Special Forces circles about B Squadron and the operation that never was, and much of it has been derogatory. But, when the chips were down, when they told us to go, every man went, even those who thought we were doomed.

Crooky was now desperate to get us forward to assist the other two Squadrons on the Falklands. The war itself was moving swiftly and we were stuck on sunny Ascension Island like a Squadron of

Rear Echelon Mother Fuckers. As we carried on training in the nightmare landscape of Ascension's lava beds, we received news of the other Squadrons – most of it good, but then some very bad.

On the West Falklands a four-man patrol commanded by Captain Hamilton had engaged in a close quarter gunfight with a much larger Argentinian force. The captain was killed, two men managed to fight their way out and one man was missing. I heard the story of the incident from the missing man himself, a member of D Squadron nicknamed the Fonze. He and the captain had been cut off and, with his officer dead, he fought on until his ammunition was expended. Then he was taken prisoner. The Fonze, who had extremely swarthy skin, managed to convince his captors that he was little more than a batman for the officer, 'just brought along to carry his kit and clean his boots'. At the end of the war, they got a shock when a helicopter full of D Squadron picked up the Fonze from their position, and flew away without even accepting their surrender.

Another tragedy happened when a Special Boat Squadron patrol, dressed as Argentinians and well outside their area, walked into a D Squadron position. In the ensuing mix-up one SBS man was shot dead.

The war was nearing its climax and still we hadn't been called forward. Then a new task beckoned: the airport at Port Stanley. The high command wanted it taken as part of the final assault. B Squadron had been trained for it. Hastily we rearranged ourselves for a combat parachute deployment. Once on the Task Force, the actual assault would go in by helicopter. We were to leave in three days – no ifs, no buts. Two C130s plus refuelling aircraft were laid on. This time we would go.

Bob T, the legendary Fijian Tak, myself and several others decided to get drunk and we did so gloriously. At about three in the morning, twelve hours before the off, we were seated outside our basha and running short of beer. As the junior man present, I was dispatched to a nearby RAF basha to drum up some reserves. I returned with a goodly supply and a four-man RAF escort.

Every soldier in the Regiment knows of the battle of Mirbat, where, in July 1972, a handful of SAS men fought off an attack by an overwhelming force of Dhofar rebels. In the battle Tak was shot through the chest several times and the subsequent operations to remove the half ton of lead from his body left him with hideous scars on his back. Not long after our RAF colleagues had joined us one of them leant across and fixed Tak with a purposeful stare.

'Listen, I know who you are, and we know where you're going tomorrow, but what I'd really like to know is how did you get those scars on your back?'

Tak observed his questioner through half-closed eyes. 'Well, you see, when I was younger I used to play rugby, and someone stamped on me in a ruck.'

The rest of us turned, stony-faced, to see what our new friend made of this. He nodded slowly.

'I see. You don't want to talk about it. I can understand that.'

We all burst out laughing.

We were sober by 1400 when we loaded on to the two Hercules. We would be jumping in dry suits because of the temperature of the water we would be landing in. Our equipment would be dropped in containers after us. The flight across was as eventful as the rest. One of our refuelling aircraft could not make the RV and had to turn back, meaning that we lost half of the Squadron, which also had to return. We kept going, and the pilot, with some persuasion from Crooky, made our refuelling point. I could feel the butterflies starting to flutter in my stomach. There was no turning back now.

The lights were dimmed, the rear door slowly opened. We shuffled up to the tailgate, the red light came on, we tensed, then the green. As I stepped out into the cold air I looked below me. I could see several ships and one to my right which had been badly damaged from a missile attack on its bow. I think it was the *Gloucester*, which had been hit by a land-based Exocet the previous night. Fast-moving inflatables were dotted between them, waiting to pluck us up, and I had no sooner hit the water than a hand grasped me and I was pulled aboard. We raced to a nearby frigate from where I heard the sound of the Hercules coming in to drop our fighting equipment.

Over half the parachutes didn't open, so a lot of precious equipment went to the bottom of the sea. It didn't matter to me. I didn't care where my equipment was. I was in the war, that was all that mattered. I turned towards the islands and pointed a dark finger in the direction of the enemy.

'You don't know what's coming,' I whispered.

We went below, got into dry clothing and were given a hot drink. We would be moving in four hours to the *Hermes* to prepare for our assault. We were told to get some sleep. I managed to scrounge a bunk from a friendly sailor. Two hours later I was woken by a loudspeaker message: 'A white flag has been raised over Port Stanley. The war is over!'

I fervently hoped that the message was wrong but within an hour it had been established that the Argentinians had surrendered. To say I was disappointed was an understatement. I had come so close to the action in a full-blown war and the opportunity to fight for my country, only to have the chance snatched from my grasp at the very last minute. I was almost inconsolable and prowled about the ship unable to come to terms with the situation. The frustrations of the last few months boiled up inside me. All those weeks with the prospect of violent action and almost certain death hanging over us had taken their toll. Each of us had steeled himself for a mission of no return and now it had ended in anticlimax. A cascade of pent-up emotions went through me: anger, depression and perhaps, although I didn't recognize it then, relief. I found a quiet corner and for the first time in years had a good cry.

Two hours later we were transferred to one of the naval support ships. I dumped my kit and hitched a ride into Port Stanley with several friends. The defeated army had littered the streets of the small town with abandoned weapons of every sort: rifles, pistols, machine-guns. Crashed Pucara aircraft and Bell helicopters lay about like the discarded playthings of a petulant giant. For the first time I got a close look at the enemy I had travelled so far to fight. They staggered around, hollow-eyed, dirty and hungry, just kids barely old enough to have left school. Whoever had set them against one of the best fighting armies in the world deserved to be put up against a wall. I heard raised voices and turned. Two Argentinian officers were arguing with a young Scots Guards lance-corporal, to whom they refused to give their side-arms. I drifted over to stand a few feet behind the Guardsman. I wore no beret and was dressed in an SAS combat smock, jungle-camouflaged trousers and a blue Royal Navy pullover. My hair was long, the wind blowing it behind me. I had a forty-eight-hour beard and a thick, black, drooping moustache. The Argentinian captain looked over the lance-corporal's shoulder and our eyes met. In his I read arrogance and the bitter anger of defeat. What he saw in mine I don't know but his eyes suddenly widened as he glanced down at the weapon I was carrying: an American M203, equipped with a 40mm grenade launcher, the standard weapon of the SAS. I slipped off the safety-catch. Moving very slowly he handed over his automatic pistol without resistance. Two days later Argentinian other ranks attacked the officers' holding area and burnt it down. They were only dispersed when a platoon of 2 Para, bayonets fixed, moved in to quell the disturbance.

Boat Troop stayed on the Falklands for six weeks after the war in case of an Argentinian counter-attack and were billeted in one of the few B & Bs on the island, the Ross Guest House. We spent the time visiting outlying farms where we were treated like VIPs. A cow would be slaughtered and we would be treated to an impromptu banquet.

We heard terrible stories about how the Argentinian officers had treated their men. On one occasion a lad of no more than seventeen had come up to one of the farms to beg for food. He had been chased into a nearby peat shed and, when he refused to come out, an officer had thrown in a grenade. The farmer showed me where they had buried him. We made a note so that the grave could be located and the unknown soldier's body returned to his motherland.

It was time to leave. At Stanley airport, as we waited for the Hercules aircraft to fly us back to Ascension Island, a Harrier jump jet dropped one of its rockets as it landed. It ricocheted into a group of Guardsmen, seriously injuring two of them. They were still clearing up as we took off.

After a night on Ascension Island we flew back to the UK with 2nd Scots Guards and landed to a tumultuous welcome. Banners were draped across windows, saying: 'Welcome back the heroes of Tumbledown.' A red carpet was laid out and a piper was playing 'Scotland the Brave'. Crooky told us to sit tight until the Guards had left and the excitement died down but a civilian in a pinstripe suit walked quickly up the steps of the aircraft and asked if we were Hereford Garrison.

Crooky confirmed that we were.

'Follow me, please,' said the man in the suit.

The piper was putting his heart and soul into his playing. Senior military officers and civilians lined the red carpet to welcome back their boys. Family and friends were cheering. Down the steps walked Boat Troop B Squadron, long-haired, unshaven, not one of us dressed the same. The piper's eyes bulged. A brigadier at the foot of the steps had already begun to salute. Crooky gave him a quick nod and led us off to the side and into the darkness. I looked over my shoulder. The piper was still looking after us. We were definitely not the Scots Guards.

Four weeks later the Falklands were a fading memory. We were in Cyprus, enjoying ourselves on a Squadron exercise. The divisions in the Squadron over the proposed attack on the Argentinian mainland would take time to heal. Many of the younger, newer members of the Regiment had seen our superiors in a less than flattering light. But the rifts started to heal as we worked and trained together in the sun. Ahead of us lay another anti-terrorist team commitment. Soon Boat Troop would be back in Northern Ireland.

But first there was the Regimental Cross Brief, which happens at the end of every year. Every badged member of the Regiment not engaged on operations is compelled to attend. Here the previous year's operations were discussed in detail, and the prospect of future operations. To B Squadron's horror, nothing whatsoever was said about our intended role in the war or even about the patrol that had been deployed on the mainland. The only reference came from the Director. After his talk he told a story about an SAS officer in the Second World War who was driving along a road when he was informed that his men had been ambushed by the SS. He turned his Landrover round and drove towards the ambush, only to be stopped again by a French peasant woman, who told him the SS was waiting in ambush for him as well. I was, rather naively, waiting to hear how this stalwart did a right flanking assault and single-handedly turned the battle. The Director continued: 'So he drove his Landrover straight down the road . . . and was killed!' I was stunned, and I wasn't the only one. There was silence for several seconds. Then, from behind me, someone shouted in a clear voice: 'Did they make him a brigadier?'

Above the laughter I heard the Director shout: 'But he did his job!' It didn't go down at all well. B Squadron believed it to be an insulting reference to their part in the war. Despite the misgivings of many in the Squadron, when it came down to it we had all been prepared to fight.

We arrived in Ulster in early December, and were hardly off the plane, when the unit we were relieving, Mobility Troop D Squadron, hit a contact. The Fermanagh Brigade of the PIRA had laid a 500lb land-mine on a road close to the border. Mobility Troop had laid an OP ambush on the firing point, on a small hill overlooking the road. The mine was to be detonated by a command wire, attached to a battery pack.

The weather had been atrocious but the SAS ambush team's alertness paid off as a figure was spotted sneaking towards the firing point in the early hours of the morning. The patrol commander waited until the IRA man was about to attach his battery pack before challenging him. The terrorist made a sudden movement, the ambush was initiated and he was hit by two 5.56mm rounds. One entered his upper body and actually ricocheted round the contour of the ribs, to exit on the opposite side, near the hip joint. The wounded man was arrested. At times like these, even the slightest movement by a terrorist can be misconstrued by the ambush party. A sudden twist of the body, or a hand disappearing behind a body, can be read as a hostile act. Apparently his first words to his captors were: 'I demand to be treated as a prisoner of war.' He was duly handcuffed, and later tried and convicted of terrorist offences.

Most of us believed that to hesitate, even for a fraction of a second, in an ambush situation, might prove fatal. All of us had studied old contact reports and in particular the killing of Corporal David Jones, of 14 Intelligence Company, on 16 March 1978. Jones and another Det member had been members of an OP party that had challenged three IRA terrorists. Francis Hughes, a leading activist, had opened fire immediately he was challenged, killing Jones and wounding his companion. Hughes himself was shot and later captured.

The Fermanagh shooting was a great boost to the outgoing Mobility Troop but less so for me as I was about to take over the ambush and had missed the opportunity to get a crack at PIRA.

Two days later we took control of SAS operations in Ulster. Our troop was divided into two teams: Blue and Red. The Blue team was commanded by an ex-Para engineer called John S, the Red by Corporal Tommy Palmer. I had originally been in the Red team but moved myself to the Blue, principally because of the way Tommy drove his car. I expected to die in action, not in a road accident.

An RUC Special Branch officer gave us a detailed brief of the current situation in Ulster, and took us step by step through the weapons, personalities and effectiveness of the various PIRA Active Service Units we might face in the coming months. The ASUs were graded by the number of operations they launched against the security forces. Some were once a month, some once a week, but by far the most active were South Armagh, who on average launched an attack twice weekly. We were warned not to take them lightly; they were heavily armed, highly motivated and well trained. We were advised to treat them like regular soldiers. They were among our prime targets, and if we could get good intelligence we would get a crack at them.

I was particularly interested in what had happened in Armagh city in the years since we had killed James McGerrigan. The Grew family still controlled Armagh, along with the Carrolls. Seamus Grew was dead, killed by the RUC HMSU. Desi was now with the INLA but was serving a short prison term for a weapons offence. Oliver, the youngest brother, was now OC of the PIRA in the city. We were told that the PIRA volunteers in the city did not rate Oliver as highly as his brothers and he was being continually pushed to prove himself.

The briefing given by Chief Inspector Ian Phoenix, an ex-Para and a stalwart supporter of the SAS in Ireland, was filled with riveting information and delivered with more than a touch of humour. Members of Special Forces and Special Branch got to know the PIRA as well as some people get to know their neighbours. We would constantly gossip about them: who was being promoted, who pushed out, who was sleeping with whose wife, but we never talked of them with any respect. To us they were vermin that had to be controlled.

On average SAS troops launched between fifteen and twenty operations in a six-month tour. We expected to have only one contact resulting in an arrest or kill in that time. Just after New

Year 1983, John S and Mick F (the ex-Gordon Highlander who had been on the aborted raid on the Argentinian mainland) and I were sequestered for two days to the 14 Intelligence Company Detachment responsible for Belfast, for familiarization training. We were given a briefing on the operations currently being run in the city and the various operations that had taken place throughout Ulster.

An officer engaged in a surveillance operation in Londonderry on 28 May the previous year had his car run off the road by a vehicle containing four heavily armed IRA members. One terrorist had run to the front of the car, a second, armed with an Armalite rifle, to the rear, while a third, holding a pistol, had walked to the driver's door. Drawing his 9mm Browning automatic, with an extended twenty-round magazine, from a holster in the car's door, the Det man rolled down the window as if he was going to speak to them. Instead, he opened fire. Almost immediately the terrorist behind him opened up with a burst of automatic from his Armalite. His aim was bad. All the shots missed the Det officer but hit his own comrade smack between the eyes. Seizing the initiative, the Det man spun round and fired at him before he could regain control of his weapon, hitting him twice in the chest. Next he turned his attention to the fourth and last IRA man, still sitting at the wheel of their car. Coming under fire from a determined operator, the terrorist sped away. The officer reversed and followed. Behind him lay two dead, Charles Maguire and George McBearty. The third wounded man was captured and later tried and convicted.

The IRA tried to claim that a car full of SAS men had drawn up and opened fire on the helpless IRA men. A .356mm Armalite round had been found in the back of the Det operator's car. Three Ruger rifles, a sub-machine-gun and a 9mm pistol belonging to police officers who were engaged in a ten-minute gun battle when they arrived at the scene to investigate and another IRA ASU had fired on them, were returned for forensic examination as usual. The shooting proved what I had always thought: even if you were outnumbered and outgunned by the Provos, as long as you didn't freeze, they were no match at close range for determination and good training. The SAS sent the Det officer a barrel of beer, and the Army gave him the Military Cross.

Each of us was assigned a Det operator to drive us about for three days to familiarize us with the area. Mine was an ex-2 Para soldier, Brad, who was an old acquaintance. On our first morning out we decided to concentrate on west Belfast. While being driven, I marvelled at the knowledge of my Det companion. He knew practically every street and side road and had an almost encyclopedic knowledge of PIRA activists in the area. There was the local OC, here the commander of the gun team, and so it went on. Suddenly Brad pulled the car over abruptly, his face red with anger.

'Will you stop doing that?' he snapped.

'What?' I asked in surprise.

'Glaring!'

I continued to look at him uncomprehendingly.

'Every time I point out a player, you glare at him. I'm going to have to change this car when I go back.'

Suitably chastised, I tried to control my instincts.

Belfast had changed greatly in the six years since my last lengthy visit in 1977. New housing estates were everywhere. Hard-line Republican areas had sprung up to add to the list of Ballymurphy, Andersonstown, New Lodge and the Ardoyne. It seemed, even in the early eighties, that all the Catholic estates were expanding, while the Protestant ones were contracting.

Towards the end of the day we found ourselves driving round Ballymurphy's maze of small, twisting streets. We slowed to allow an Army patrol to pass in front of us. A soldier, barely out of his teens, stopped to give cover, his rifle aimed directly at my head. I looked into his eyes: it was all there, distrust, wariness, dislike, perhaps even a touch of hate. I smiled; he sneered and looked away.

'If only you knew, son. If only you knew,' I said to myself as we drove past.

A tour in Ulster is actually very pleasant as when not on operations your time is basically your own. I spent most of mine training, getting up at 7 a.m. and running four miles before breakfast, in the gym for a lightweight session before lunch, then a heavyweight session afterwards. After evening 'prayers', I would do an hour of boxing training. By the end of the tour I could bench-press three hundred pounds, run five miles in thirty minutes and nobody would come into a boxing ring with me. I was never as strong or fit again in my life. I'd come a long way from the eight-stone seventeen-year-old who'd failed the Army entrance medical!

We hadn't been in operational charge long before we had a visit from our OC. The SAS were worried their role in Ulster might be subverted by the RUC's Special Support Unit, after what seemed like a string of successful shoots against both the PIRA and the INLA. I was not at all sure the shoots had been 'clean' as no weapons had been discovered. I believed that they would come back to haunt the unit concerned. I was proved correct with the instigation of the Stalker inquiry.

But for the present our OC wanted to know what we needed to get some success. Various options were discussed, including the idea of taking out selected IRA targets. This was dismissed out of hand by the OC. We would only be allowed to engage the PIRA if we caught them actually on a terrorist operation and armed. I summed up our feelings.

'If that's the case, boss, what we need is first-class SB information. You get us the intelligence and we'll do the rest.'

The OC promised to do what he could and, true to his word, operations came up frequently after his visit, and the intelligence was good. But one factor always seemed to prevent our final success: source protection. The way covert operations were run in Ulster, then and now, is quite simple. Source information, whether human or technical in origin, would come into a central controlling body, the Tactical Control Group (TCG), and they would decide which agency should handle it. Unless the threat was immediate, one of the surveillance agencies would be tasked. Once they had built up a picture of the intended target and it seemed likely that an attack was imminent, a reaction force was dispatched. It was at this stage that source protection became very important.

Human sources, agents planted within the ranks of the PIRA, are the single most important asset in the continuing fight against the IRA. Each source has his own handler, either in the RUC or Army Intelligence. The Army handlers, many of whom were only in the Province for two years, were often so determined to make a name for themselves that they overemphasized the importance of their agents. A handler who has a good agent will go to almost any lengths to protect him. Sometimes this can be achieved by convincing the IRA that another member of their ASU is in fact an informer. Given the paranoia inside the Republican Movement it wasn't always difficult.

I know of at least two cases where PIRA volunteers have been 'head-jobbed' (shot in the head) by their own comrades in the mistaken belief that they were informers. Both had given taped confessions to their PIRA interrogators. Once one of the IRA's internal security teams has its hands on you, you'd confess to anything. People may blanch at such actions and some talk of dirty tricks. I personally found it satisfying that we were getting the PIRA to kill their own men. Of course, the PIRA were continually trying to infiltrate Special Branch by getting their own men to pretend to be agents. One operator I met was in no doubt we should kill every 'tout' – the IRA's term for an informer – in Belfast. We'd save the country a fortune and wipe out half the operational strength of the PIRA.

I was woken just before midnight on 2 February. The Det had hit another contact, and at least one terrorist was dead. Almost to a man we got out of bed and crowded up into the OP's room to listen to the story as it unfolded. A Det operator had been surprised and ambushed outside a house by two members of the INLA. He had killed one and wounded the other. The dead man was later identified as Neil McMonagle, a volunteer with the Derry INLA. A week later I was privileged to go to the celebration party and meet the man himself, Paul Dougie Oram. Dougie was already a legend after shooting his way out of an IRA ambush. He related the events on the night. He'd been on foot surveillance outside a house where it was suspected the INLA met. He'd done a walk-past but could see no sign of activity. He was asked to do a second but again he could not confirm any terrorist activity. His controller wanted him to do a third. At this there was a wince from the surveillance operators present. To chance your arm doing a third walk-past in a hostile area was really pushing your luck.

Dougie agreed to do the third walk. Inside the house were some of the most ruthless terrorists then active in the Province. Only two months earlier these same stalwarts had placed a bomb with no warning in the Drop in Well public house and killed eleven soldiers and six civilians. Dougie moved his 9mm Browning from its usual position, stuffed down the back of his trousers, to his front waistband. He always disdained a holster of any kind. As he approached the house a figure leapt from the darkness, pushed him against a wire fence and began to frisk him. Spread-eagled against the fence, Dougie saw a second INLA man approach, carrying an M1 Carbine. Realizing he had to act, Dougie lashed out with his elbow at the man behind him, at the same time using his momentum to draw his own gun and fire two shots at the oncoming gunman. He saw bright-red blood spurt from his mouth and realizing he had neutralized one opponent he spun to confront the second, who was now on his hands and knees. He fired twice, hitting him in the chest, then ran for his car. There was a brief silence from the rapt audience as Dougie finished his story, then one voice piped up: 'Why didn't you finish the other bastard on the ground?'

Dougie fixed him with an unswerving stare then broke into a smile. 'Listen, there were five more of them in the house; I covered the hundred metres to my car faster than Allan Wells.'

Towards the end of the night, Dougie took his leave. A man who would never have fitted the traditional role of a hero: long-haired and overweight, a man you would have passed in the street without a second glance. He had always spurned the trappings of the Special Forces: he didn't pump iron or carry fancy shoulder holsters. But around him were some of the toughest men in Northern Ireland.

At the door he paused. He turned and gave a long sardonic stare and gave us the benefit of his philosophy.

'Marines' – he made a dismissive gesture – 'a load of crap. Paras are pussies, SAS, Sweet And Sexy.' He patted his bulging stomach. 'But Deadly Bellies kill!' Everybody collapsed with laughter and gave him a standing ovation. He was later awarded the Military Medal for gallantry. It was the last time I would see him alive.

Barely three days later we got our first major operation, the chance to hit an entire ASU while they were collecting weapons from a hide. I drove with the Blue Team commander, John S, to the TCG for the initial briefing. It sounded good. Several weapons had come into a clearing hide (the main hide in the area, from which the weapons were dispersed to more accessible hides for the ASUs to use). The source was the IRA quartermaster for the area.

Informers come in three general categories: those who are blackmailed (caught with their hand in the till, or screwing an imprisoned member's wife, either of which could get you head-jobbed); those who do it for the money (some are paid very big money indeed); and finally the very few who turn informer for ideological reasons. This particular source was in the last category, a man who had joined the IRA because he believed in a United Ireland only to see the organization for what it truly was: a pitiless, murderous gang of thugs who were the main stumbling block to any chance of a United Ireland.

We wanted to hit the ASU as they collected the weapons from the clearing hide but the source's handler was totally opposed to this. The weapons would have to be allowed to move to at least two other hides before we could intercept the shooters. Nor would he allow the Army's technical branch to bug the weapons (known as 'jarking') for fear that this too would compromise his source. I was beginning to lose my temper. I pointed out that if we let the weapons out of the hide and into circulation, we stood a very good chance of losing them completely. That was a chance we would have to take, the handler replied.

'And some off-duty UDR man gets it in the back of the head, because you want to protect some damn source,' I said.

At this point everybody was told to calm down, especially me. The SB had their way, we were not allowed to hit the ASU where we wanted too. A week later the weapons were moved and the surveillance team, despite their best efforts, lost them. They went on to be used against the local security forces. To say I was angry didn't even begin to describe it.

Not long afterwards the Det had a major success and threw a party. Chalky, a fellow member of the Boat Troop, and I went along with another man from the troop. Everybody was there, including Ian Phoenix, the SB man who'd given us our introductory talk, with a bottle of champagne in his hand. At the party was the SB handler. I avoided him like he had a contagious disease. Twice he tried to talk to me only to have me cut him dead. At the end of the night he cornered me.

'I want a word with you,' he said, stepping up close. He was slightly taller than me, but I was carrying at least a stone more muscle. People have always said that I look evil and when I have been walking alone at night even some police officers have crossed the street to avoid me. For a man to confront me when I was drunk and angry was unusual. His voice shook with barely controlled anger.

'I know you. I know exactly what you are and where you've been. You may be the hardest man in the troop, I don't give a damn. All you want is a kill, PIRA if possible, but if not, anybody will do – INLA, UVF – you don't care. That man I'm handling has saved more lives than a dozen men like you. His wife is in Sinn Fein and all his family are Republicans. If any of them thought for a moment, just a moment, he was a tout they'd turn him in. The only friend he's got in this world is me.' He stabbed a finger into my chest. 'And before I'll turn him over so that a psycho like you can get another notch on his gun, I'll see a dozen weapons lost.'

Without waiting for a reply, he spun on his heel and stamped out of the room. I was aware of the attention I was drawing and walked to the bar. Chalky joined me.

'Certainly told you, didn't he?'

I threw him a dark look and ordered another drink.

'Tell you what, though,' Chalky added. 'He certainly had you pegged to rights.'

I had to agree: he had.

Social life in Ulster for the troop was great. When there were no imminent operations we had the run of the entire Province. One team would be stood down on alternative weeks and we would visit bars and clubs in safe areas. We became adept at inventing cover stories to explain why we were in Ulster. None of us looked like soldiers, which helped. I was in love at the time, so didn't chase the women with the determined enthusiasm of my colleagues. One occasion found four of us in a bar in Bangor, County Down. I was driver for the night, restricted to shandy. Across the dance floor a vision of beauty appeared, tall, blonde and with a figure Venus de Milo would have scratched her eyes out for if she'd had arms. The shortest member of our group, who'd already been turned down by just about every woman in the bar, decided on the direct approach. Giving her the benefit of a John Wayne walk, he sauntered over.

'Excuse me.'

She surveyed him coolly from beneath half-closed lashes. 'Yes?'

He looked her up and down. 'Do you go to bed on a first date?'

She didn't bat an eyelid. 'Of course I do,' she said with a sweet smile, 'but not with little men like you.'

Completely outclassed, our colleague retreated tactically to the comfort of our ranks and a ribbing that lasted the entire tour.

Halfway through my time in Ulster, frustration and boredom drove me to start taking risks. Armed to the teeth and looking for trouble, I stared to cruise the hard-line Catholic areas of west Belfast. I carried an MP5 with twin thirty-round mags, a 9mm pistol with a twenty-round mag in a shoulder holster, fragmentation and stun grenades and, just for good measure, an Armalite rifle in the boot. I wished fervently for a chance encounter with the IRA or someone to attempt to hijack my car, an illegal road stop – anything. I logged this down as familiarization training. The reality was that I just wanted to hit a contact.

The closest I came to trouble was in the upper Falls Road. I was winding my way through the narrow, winding streets, when my path was blocked by a mechanical digger. As I waited for it to let me pass a nearby factory suddenly disgorged its workforce on to the street. Hundreds of potentially hostile locals streamed past, only inches away. Any chance glance inside the car would have revealed the arsenal I was carrying. I feigned indifference and boredom, even stretching to yawn. The JCB still blocked the road. Surely somebody would look inside the car. My mind raced. If I was spotted, I'd throw the car into reverse. If I was blocked in, I'd get on the radio, get the Browning out and put a few above their heads, and if that didn't work . . . Then the digger swerved to one side and there was a gap. I was past the obstruction in seconds and back out on to the main Springfield Road.

Ministers of the Crown and Secretaries of State for Northern Ireland come and go, but behind them are the people with real power – the Permanent Under-Secretaries. Grey, middle-aged men in pinstriped suits who advise ministers on every subject. One such mandarin came to visit the base. We put on a demonstration of our skills for him and afterwards we were invited to an informal chat. He asked us what he, his department and the minister could do for us. A silence greeted his request. Soldiers have an inbuilt distrust of any politician as it is always our blood that marks their mistakes. Nevertheless we were invited to speak frankly by the OC.

'I'll tell you what you can do,' I said, fixing the civil servant with my most baleful stare. He shifted in his chair. 'You can give us the go-ahead and in six months we'll destroy the IRA and we'll make it look like their fault.'

His reply was the epitome of diplomacy.

'You are of course entitled to your views, and I will ensure that the minister is made aware of them, but I cannot foresee any circumstances in which the current thrust of security force policy in the Province, balanced between the need to keep pressure on the terrorists, but at the same time encourage political debate, will be changed.'

I got some flak from my superiors for my remarks.

Another job came in that looked promising. Intelligence had indicated the Tyrone PIRA were about to launch an operation in the area of Pomeroy, a small but very Republican town. The intelligence had been vague. TCG had dispatched an Army Close Observation Platoon (COP), to lie up in the village. They had reported that six suspicious men carrying heavy bags had entered a house in the town. Within an hour we were in Pomeroy RUC station being briefed. Dressed like conventional soldiers, we infiltrated the town and set up an area ambush around the suspect house.

I was in charge of a three-man assault group, consisting of me, Harry Taylor and Des H, placed directly opposite the house. The hours ticked slowly by towards dawn, which was when we suspected that any attack would be launched. As the first signs of the new day began to spread out across the sky, it became clear that we could not remain undetected in the small town for much longer. We decided to take action. A member of the troop, accompanied by a rather nervous RUC man, went boldly up to the front door and knocked. Around him twenty rifles came to bear. If a car had backfired at that moment, a rain of lead would most surely have engulfed the house.

After several minutes a youth of no more than sixteen appeared. The bags contained musical instruments. Inside the house we found four other very frightened teenagers, members of the band. We apologized and left.

I was the senior paramedic with the troop and was continually called upon to give lectures to other agencies on the treatment of gunshot wounds. I also continued my education at the Army Education Centre in Lisburn. Coming back from a lecture, I made comms to tell base we were on our way. Their reply sent a shiver through me and my two companions. One word: 'Minimize!' A signaller will only give such an instruction if there has been a contact. It means 'Keep off the air. There is an emergency.' It sounded like there had been one as John S was reporting that he could not find the weapon, that the car was a wreck. We headed back to base at top speed. It was not a contact, but a car crash. Tommy Palmer had driven too fast once too often. He was dead and another troop member was seriously injured. His handgun had disappeared and was never found. They had been going on a fishing trip, of all things, when he had lost control of his car at speed on the motorway near Lurgan. It was a tragic waste and affected us all. Tommy had been a wonderful character, and had won the Queen's Gallantry Medal at the Iranian Embassy Siege in 1980, during which he had killed two terrorists.

Finally, as the tour was coming to an end, a job came up which looked like a dead cert. The SB man tasking us, who was the most reliable in the Province, only called the troop when there was the real prospect of a shoot. Two gunmen were to take over a house and a hijacked car would be abandoned outside it. When the RUC came to inspect the vehicle, the shooters would open up with an Armalite and a bolt-action sniper's rifle.

The Det would trigger us by placing an OP in such a position that they could observe the target house and they'd tell us when the gunmen entered. We'd respond and launch our assault.

John S and I put together the plan for the assault. It was simplicity itself. As soon as the shooters entered, we'd attack the target dressed in the uniforms of the local army unit. I would sledgehammer the door open and John would lead two four-man assault teams into the house.

The inside of the house had been recced. There was a narrow staircase leading to the room the shooter would fire from. We had to get up these stairs extremely fast if we were to avoid any casualties.

Our plan did not meet with the approval of the senior RUC

personnel present. They were concerned about source protection. If we assaulted the house before the shooter opened fire the IRA would know that they had an informer in their ranks. The shooters would have to be allowed to open fire first. In all my years as a soldier I had never heard anything quite as stupid. No matter what we said officially, the IRA would know within days that it was not an Army patrol but the SAS who had killed their volunteers. There's no such thing as a secret in Northern Ireland. We pointed out to the senior officer that if we allowed the IRA to fire first, the police unit tasked to respond to the hijacked car was likely, at the range involved, to suffer casualties or even fatalities. His reply shocked us all. He said simply: 'That's a risk we'll have to take.'

We loaded up and prepared for action. I chose an MP5 as my main assault weapon, with my trusted 9mm Browning as a backup. I also took two fragmentation grenades. These had never been used in Ulster and our troop staff sergeant, controlling the job from the operations room, told John to tell me to put them back.

I looked my team commander squarely in the eye.

'John, you won't let me be the first up those stairs. If the opposition drops you, I'm going to grenade them, then I'm going up there to kill every person in the room.'

'You're only going to use them if they kill me?'

'That's right.'

He patted my shoulder. 'That'll do for me. As long as I'm not around to take the flak.'

We moved off in an unmarked civilian van to the vicinity of the ambush. The driver, dressed in civvies, began to read a paper. For the first time we discussed in hushed voices our reaction to the orders of the RUC officer. Each of us gave his opinion. John eventually summed it up.

'As soon as the Det trigger the shooters into the house we go in. To hell with waiting for them to open fire. We go in. Everybody agree?'

We all nodded. We were about to disobey a direct order, but there was no way on God's earth we were going to allow two brave RUC men to be shot, just to protect a source.

The assassination team didn't come. Walking in with their weapons, they spotted a passing police patrol and decided to abort. Two things about that operation remain fixed in my mind:

the courage of the men who were prepared to put their lives and careers on the line for a principle, and the disregard some senior officers in the RUC appeared to have for their men.

The tour came to an end: no kills, no arrests and we had lost a man in an accident. Yet for me it had been a good one. I was promoted at the end of it and I had been involved in every major job that came up, high praise indeed from my contemporaries. I had met two RUC men who were to become lifelong friends and have an important impact on my life, Bill D and Tim M. I had begun, at last, to be able to control the violent mood swings of my past. Beneath the surface the demons still lurked: my forays alone in west Belfast looking for trouble were testimony to that. But at least now I could keep them chained.

I got married for the second time during my leave, to Julia, a Hereford girl. John S was my best man. The reception was a grand affair, with over two hundred guests, in the Paludrin Club. The sergeants had a formal dress dinner later that night at 2100. Fred M, the giant Fijian, was still drinking with me at the bar. My staff sergeant, Pete, gently told him that the RSM required him in the sergeants' mess. Fred's reply showed the warmth, character and strength of the man.

'Tell the RSM I'm indisposed. I'm drinking with my brother.'

He threw a huge arm across my shoulder.

In late November 1983 I was sent on a Squadron training exercise in the Sudan. It was a land of grinding poverty and civil war. Only the armed forces seemed well fed. For the first time, I saw human beings dying of hunger. Once, while out on a recce, driving around looking for possible mortar sites for a proposed exercise, I stopped at the side of the road to make a brew and have something to eat. I was aware that I was being watched, and turned slowly. An old man was studying me, his body ravaged with hunger. Rags, dirty and covered in flies, did little to shelter his thin frame from the merciless sun. His eyes met mine then fixed on the sandwich I was about to eat. He clasped his hands together in a motion of prayer, then held them towards me, pleading for food. I handed it over, then made him some hot, sweet tea. We sat in the shade of my Landrover and I watched him eat. He ate like all those who are truly starving, with excruciating slowness, relishing every bite. I found what little other food I had and handed it over, then climbed back into the Landrover and as I drove off gave him a half wave, which he returned. In the wing mirror I watched him, still standing looking after me. Neither of us had spoken a word.

While in the Sudan we did joint training with the local forces. They were of a very poor standard. Once, while we were trying to teach them how to operate an 81mm mortar, they fired the weapon so badly that three rounds went wild. We had a spotting team out: the first round landed only a hundred metres from them, the second was closer still. We held our breath as we waited for the last. When it landed we called the observation post. They didn't answer. We stared at the radio with heart-stopping intensity. Then it broke into life.

'It's OK. It missed us . . . just.'

We also got the opportunity to get some good diving training in the local harbour. The water was warm and crystal-clear. It was also filled with things that wanted to take a king-size bite out of you. Chalky was my partner and on one occasion we were diving on the wreck of a Second World War freighter, still loaded with ammunition. As we swam round its bow we encountered a large piece of the superstructure that had broken away from the main vessel. It formed a kind of artificial tunnel. Chalky led the way in, and he had gone barely a yard when a huge, black Moray eel darted out of a hole in the wreck's side as he passed, its mouth open, revealing rows of small, razor-sharp teeth. It took a snap at Chalky's leg, missed and turned swiftly to look at me. I was frantically reversing, making incoherent gurgling noises. The creature, well over six feet long, darted back into its hole. These beasts are extremely territorial and will attack anything that swims past their holes. Chalky was extremely lucky not to lose part of his leg.

My closest call came after I had just completed some underwater demolition work. Dead fish, killed in the explosion, filled the water and I was so engrossed in checking that all my charges had fired that I forgot to keep a close watch. Around me, a shadow drifted lazily by. I froze. Less than a yard from me was a five-foot shark. I got into my support boat with the speed of a Trident missile.

I was the diving supervisor and as such was responsible for training the local Sudanese team. When they arrived I noted that their weight belts were pieces of string with lead tied to them.

We refitted them with our equipment and they turned out to be excellent divers.

Our main training, contact drills and live ambushes, was done in the desert. SAS training is always as close to actual combat as the Regiment can make it. Mel P, of Iranian Embassy Siege fame, was running the exercises and he helped prepare an 'A type' ambush. In this, an SAS speciality, great reliance is put on the use of improvised explosives and ordnance. I had been chosen to blow four 81mm mortar bombs that had been converted into improvised claymore mines. This was to be done under combat conditions at very close range. As I pressed the detonating device all the air was sucked out of my body, my ears seemed to explode and for a microsecond I felt totally disorientated.

Then the pain hit me – sharp, hard and hot. My right leg seemed to be on fire. Looking down I could see blood and yellow mucus seeping through my combat trousers. My shin bone had been split up the middle like a cracked cricket bat by a half-inch piece of shrapnel. The large tendon running down the front of the shin had been shattered. I was told later I had lost four inches from it. The pain was indescribable. In movies when the hero gets shot he rolls over, lights a cigarette and calmly continues shooting at the oncoming bad guys. I had been shot before, but never through the bone. I screamed for the doctor at the top of my voice. What happened to me afterwards is lost in a morphine-induced haze. I have been told I was evacuated across country and then operated on in a makeshift field hospital. By the time I came to, I was in a hospital in the UK. I had three long and painful operations to repair the damage to my shin.

While I was recuperating I heard that A Squadron had killed two members of the PIRA near Coalisland. Although still on large amounts of morphine, I persuaded a friendly nurse to get me a couple of cans of beer for a toast. This had been the Regiment's first kill in Ulster since November 1978. In the five intervening years a combination of bad luck, bad intelligence and, it has to be admitted, some poor soldiering had enabled the IRA to escape us. Now, at last, we had a success.

The operations on my leg complete, I was discharged from hospital. I was told it would take me six months before I could walk properly. Six weeks later I was doing three-mile runs.

By mid-January 1984 I was in Qatar with the rank of captain, helping to train the country's Special Forces in SAS techniques. It was good work, though a little frustrating. The Army was mainly mercenary, drawn from all over the Middle East. In its ranks were Egyptians, Sudanese and even some Lebanese straight from their own terrible civil war.

Like all professional soldiers, I follow wars wherever they are fought, always keen to learn a lesson that might save a life. I had watched with fascination as the Israeli Army, vastly outnumbered, had won victory after victory against the combined might of the Arabs. After less than a week training the Qataris I realized the Israelis had won because the opposition was of an extremely poor standard.

My first unarmed-combat lesson illustrates just some of the problems we faced. Trying to motivate my class, I was building myself up to a climax, showing the vulnerable points of the body and the killing blows used on them.

'You have to have aggression,' I almost screamed.

Turning, I found half of them were holding hands with one another. I almost wept. A change of tactics was in order. I decided that a picture is worth a thousand words so I asked for their strongest man to come forward. A hulking brute with the shoulders of a giant lumbered towards me. He had been a wrestler in civilian life. I told him to get me in a bear hug. He obliged – his strength was quite exceptional. I hit him with a concussion blow on either side of his head and he collapsed. The class were like excited children, dancing up and down with glee, asking to see it again. My victim was less enthusiastic, being only semi-conscious. From that time on I at least had their attention.

It was while we were training that news flashed to us that Dougie Oram had been killed in Ulster. Dougie and another Det operator had been in an OP which had been compromised. Three IRA men had sneaked up behind them and the first they knew was a voice saying: 'You're Brits. Stand up.' Dougie and his companion had stood and turned to face them. For the briefest of seconds there was silence, then with the speed of reaction that had made him a legend, Dougie went for it. He managed to get his gun out and fire before the opposition could react, wounding his two adversaries. His companion also started to draw his gun. The IRA pair, Hogan and Martin, opened up, killing Dougie and seriously wounding his companion. The Intelligence Company backup reacted in seconds. Both Hogan and Martin, still armed, were engaged and killed. The third IRA man got away.

We continued to train the Qataris and slowly managed to hammer them into shape. It was extremely difficult to get them to concentrate for more than a few minutes. Urgency didn't seem to exist in their world and no matter how much we tried to get them to understand that in a contact speed of action was vital, they always did everything in slow motion. Despite this, by the time I had to leave, they were a half-decent fighting unit and later distinguished themselves in the Gulf War. At the airport they came to say goodbye. It was hard to appear gruff and unemotional, as I had grown to like them, despite everything. The last one to shake my hand was the huge Sudanese wrestler.

'Sir,' Ibram announced proudly to the assembled listeners, 'after you hit me, I had a headache for three days.'

Normally at the end of training the host nation gives a present of a watch to the members of the team. Mine was sent on to me. I'd had to leave early, as Gran had been taken seriously ill. I visited her in Glasgow. She was in a very bad way. I stayed with her two days until she was out of immediate danger. It nearly broke my heart to see her so ill. I'd tried to see her as often as I could over the past few years but inevitably with the work I was doing and the constant trips overseas, the visits had become less and less. Now she was only a shadow of the warm, loving human being that had been the rock of my childhood. Her mind wandered constantly and in the moments she was lucid all she talked about was how proud she was of me and how much she loved me. I wanted more than anything for her to understand how much she meant to me. Then she would drift away again. I can only hope she understood.

Returning from leave in late 1984, I had only three weeks in Hereford before I was abroad again, this time back to Malaya, jungle training. The trip gave me a chance to meet some of the new members of B Squadron. They seemed a good bunch, particularly a little Scot called Jocky. He was an ex-paratrooper and I took to him the minute I met him. He had a great sense of humour and consumed life like it was all going to end tomorrow. He was a pure warrior, wanting only what a fighter needs: a war, a drink and a woman, although not necessarily in that order. Des summed him up well: 'If you broke that man in half, he'd have paratrooper through the middle.'

Jocky's approach to life could be summed up by an incident in a Singapore bar. We had been having trouble with some Americans and it looked for an instant as if a battle would break out. Through the crowd lumbered one of the biggest men I have ever seen in my life: a bald giant, well over six foot, and at least eighteen stone of muscle, with arms like corded tree trunks. It was the bar's bouncer. Jocky took one look at him, and launched himself up to attempt a head-butt. His head bounced harmlessly off the big man's chest. He looked down at Jocky with faint amusement, as the rest of us rushed forward. I reckon it would have taken all of us to stop him tearing our little comrade apart.

'You don't want to be doing that, son,' the giant said in a soft, lilting Irish accent. 'You'll only get yourself hurt.'

He turned out to be a really great guy who had been in the merchant navy and jumped ship, started off as a bouncer in the bar, married a local girl and now was half-owner. He ushered us away from the Americans and drank a few beers with us. Nobody was in any mood for starting trouble as long as he was around.

It was on this trip that I saw the first real change in SAS contact drills. The shoot-and-scoot tactics of the past were being replaced by more aggressive drills, using more firepower.

Towards the end of the two-month trip, all the Squadron's medics, under the command of the regimental doctor, undertook a 'hearts and minds' operation in the north of the country, close to the Thai border. These operations are as essential to operations as any to actually kill the enemy and had been important factors in all SAS campaigns, with the exception of Ulster. Only by gaining the confidence, trust and respect of locals could any army hope to win in a guerrilla war. It was mainly for this reason that SAS medics were upgraded in the late seventies to paramedic standard, to enable patrols to deal with the variety of diseases and injuries encountered in remote corners of the world.

The area we were working in was still considered hostile as it had only recently come back under total government control. We had a platoon of Malaysian army troops to guard us and carried a full complement of ammunition. Although no doctor had been in the area for well over six years, most of the tribesmen were in good health. There were some worm infestations which we traced to a bad water source and treated. The people we were dealing with, especially the children, were kind and curious. It was a totally fulfilling job.

I have one passion: I love a cigar at the end of the day. I ran out of mine two days before we were due to fly out. I happened to mention it to one of the older tribesmen, and within ten minutes I had a hand-rolled native cigar. I lit it just as the sun began to set. Two puffs later I was on cloud nine, high as a kite. The doc was called. It was pure marijuana, my first and last experience of it.

October 1984 found me once again on the anti-terrorist team, this time as the second in command of the method of entry and assault team, under my good friend Pete B. Pete had been in the Parachute Regiment with me. Handsome, softly spoken and intelligent, he was everyone's idea of what an SAS NCO should be. He'd been on the ill-fated advance party during the Falklands war. In many ways he was an excellent foil to me and Des H, the other ex-Para who was part of our team.

Des was a big, tough soldier with a devil-may-care attitude. He was covered with tattoos, even on his backside. A mop of unruly curly brown hair, a self-deprecating sense of humour and a ready smile made him a hard man to dislike. He was even more hard-line than me about what the SAS should be doing in Ulster. On one drive to an exercise he put foward his latest idea for destroying the IRA.

'What we should do is just grab an IRA man every month and make him disappear. They'd never know it was us and panic would spread through the ranks.'

Pete shook his head. 'The Government would never allow it. They don't even like it when we shoot them with guns in their hands.'

'Wouldn't work anyway,' I put in.

'Why not?' Des asked.

'The opposition would soon switch on it was us. We'd hand them a propaganda bonanza. You'd have even moderate Catholics joining up with the IRA.'

'If we did it right they would never know,' Des retorted.

'Of course they would, they're not stupid. We might get away with it once or twice but after that they'd have banner headlines in every national newspaper. Besides you couldn't keep something like that a secret. There are no real secrets. Sooner or later somebody would leak it to the press and we'd all end up in the dock.'

'Well, what's your solution?' Des demanded.

'I haven't got one. The IRA are losing. Day by day we're grinding them down. It's not a great priority because, although the government will never admit it, we have an acceptable level of violence. As long as the PIRA don't get too out of hand we'll just contain them until they get so damn tired they'll give up.'

'Huh,' Des sniffed. He'd expected more backing for his theories from me. 'Look who's preaching self-restraint. You're one of the most violent men I know.'

'There's a big difference between you and me, Des. When you go across to Ulster you think that by killing IRA men you'll solve the problem. I just kill them because I like it.'

The assembled audience burst into laughter.

We were called upon to do countless demonstrations for visiting VIPs. They always began the same way. They'd be taken to the small combat room in the Killing House, where the boss would explain that it was in this room that all SAS men began to learn about close quarter combat. The boss would normally sit on a table surrounded by three targets. Outside, dressed in black assault overalls and carrying MP5s, a three-man snatch squad would wait. The boss would build up to the climax of his presentation.

'We believe the CQB can best be summed up by the initials SAS. We believe SAS should stand for . . . Speed, Aggression and Surprise.'

On that, three men would burst in on the back of a stun grenade. Two would engage the targets around the boss whilst the third pulled him out. Normally we could do it in 2.5 seconds.

B Squadron's 7 troop (Free Fall Troop) now had the Northern Ireland commitment. Theirs was to be an eventful tour. It started with an operation just outside Portadown on 12 October. An IRA hit team had planned to assassinate a UDR major. Acting on SB information Free Fall Troop conducted one of the most dangerous operations the SAS are asked to perform: a substitution job. A member of the troop took the place of the intended target, acting as a stalking-horse to draw the terrorists out. The man who volunteered for this job was Al Slater, an ex-Parachute Regiment sergeant. A man of intelligence and huge good humour, Al had joined the SAS only the year before and was already earmarked as a man who would go far. I had taken an immediate liking to him.

The operation was a disaster, for many reasons: the SAS interception squad, waiting in nearby lanes, were triggered too late, resulting in a car chase through narrow, twisting roads. The troopers inside the cars could not lean out of the windows to fire at the IRA gang in their van, and tried to fire through their own car windows. Only one hit was recorded on the van. The IRA, from a more stable platform, poured a withering fire on their pursuers. Tragically, as they abandoned their car, a passer-by, Frederick Jackson, was killed in crossfire.

On the team we had a visitor, a member of the USA's élite Delta Force, Marshall B. He was a born-again Christian and the very best pistol shot I ever saw. His introduction to pistol shooting is still fresh in my mind.

'We in Delta Force believe there is nothing in the anti-terrorist field that we can teach the SAS. In pistol shooting, however, we know we can teach you a lot. Please observe.'

He turned towards the target, produced a fifty-pence piece and placed it on the back of his hand. He turned his hand to let it fall. Before it hit the ground, he had drawn his government-issue .45 Colt, and put two rounds in a two-inch circle of a target ten metres away. I let out a low whistle of admiration. He turned back to his attentive audience. 'I am only an average shot in Delta Force. By the end of this training, all of you will be up to my standard of pistol shooting.'

At the time I didn't believe him, but I was wrong. I can now draw and empty a twenty-round mag from my Browning into a two-inch circle in under three seconds, at twenty metres.

While with the team, Marshall converted a member of the Squadron to Christianity. He is now an Army chaplain.

On the morning of Sunday 3 December I was preparing for a trip to the north of England on a team exercise when the phone rang.

'Harry, it's Des. Have you heard the news?'

'No.'

There was an intake of breath from my friend at the other end. This was going to be bad.

'Al Slater's dead.'

Just outside Kesh in County Fermanagh, Al and two other members had stopped to put up an immediate roadblock. They were reacting to information that a fugitive ASU was about to launch an operation that would result in multiple security force casualties. The weather was absolutely dismal. As they waited, a lone man approached them through the heavy fog. One of Al's companions, Pete S, challenged him to halt and in reply the man made a hushing sound. Pete challenged again, this time saying, 'Halt, security forces.' The man took off across the fields, pursued by Pete and the car commander, Cyril K. Al decided to put up a parachute flare, but as he did so he came under fire from close range. Hit in the shoulder, he spun and engaged the enemy, firing his rifle one-handed, only to be hit again in the chest and head. A warrior to the last, he went down shooting defiantly.

Pete and Cyril captured the runaway and brought him back to the car. They were totally unprepared to find Al dead on their return. The fog had blanketed the noise of the gun battle. Their prisoner panicked and tried to escape. He was shot dead, both Pete and Cyril believing he had grabbed a weapon. He was later identified as Antony McBride, an ex-Irish Army sergeant and a leading member of the Provisional IRA.

By the worst of all possible luck Al had stopped his car directly opposite an IRA ambush where they had planned to lure a police patrol on to a land-mine and kill all the survivors. McBride had been setting the charge.

Al's return fire wounded one of his killers and as the gang tried to escape across a nearby river another, Kieran Fleming, went into a deep hole and drowned.

News of Al's death hit me very hard. The Regiment had only ever lost one man in Ulster: Captain Richard Westmacott, killed in action in Belfast in May 1980.

That afternoon I travelled up to Cottingham in Hull to meet a man called Reg Clucas. Reg was a self-made millionaire and an inventor of the highest order – perhaps the nearest thing the Regiment ever had to its own Q from the James Bond films.

Anytime we had a problem we went to Reg and he fixed it. Among his inventions was the 'grit-grot machine' for removing bricks almost silently from walls, and the Hatton round, a special shotgun round that we used to remove doors without risk to anybody standing behind them. That night we had a wake for Al. Reg put a pint at the end of the bar for the warrior who wasn't there. Reg's hospitality was legendary, and we needed it just then. I will always remember my stay with him with fond affection.

Four days after Al's murder, our spirits were lifted a little by news of a success. Two members of the Derry PIRA, Daniel Doherty and William Fleming, brother of Kieran, who had drowned after taking part in Al's murder, were shot to death. Initially we thought it was an SAS job, but it turned out that the Det had shot them. The Det operators had been on a routine surveillance when they had picked the two up on their way to murder an off-duty UDR man at the Gransha Hospital. Both terrorists were on a motor-cycle and, when it became clear that they were not only armed but intent on murder, were engaged. Although it by no means evened the score for Al, it did make us feel a little better.

It was approaching Christmas and Regimental Cross Brief Time. Every year at the latter event we had a guest speaker. This year's would leave a profound and lasting impression on me. He was a lieutenant colonel in the United States Air Force. He stood and surveyed his silent audience.

'There isn't a man in this room who can't be made to talk,' he said, then paused to take us all in with a measured gaze. 'I know who I'm talking to, and I know there are some very tough men here, but if you're captured by an enemy who knows how to use torture you will be made to talk.'

He told his story. In the early 1970s he had been in a flight over North Vietnam. His plane was shot down and he was captured by North Vietnamese. His right arm had been broken by a bullet and this became the initial focus of his interrogator's attentions. A slight smile played on his lips as he remembered.

'That was OK. It was so numb I couldn't feel anything. They could twist and turn the damn thing all day.'

His interrogators became more artistic. Broad leather straps were produced and his hands tied behind his back. The straps were passed over his arms and thrown over a beam and he was suspended three or four feet above the ground. Over a period of time the weight of his body caused his arms to dislocate. His tormentors would come in and reset his shoulders and do the same thing again. This went on for twenty-four hours. When they still did not succeed in making him talk they came up with something new. The straps were passed over his head and through his now bound legs until he was rolled up into a tight ball, and then he was thrown into a corner. It was at this stage he nearly died. Unable to move he had started to vomit and almost suffocated.

'At this time I didn't give a damn. In fact, I wanted to die.'

The guards came in, undid his bonds, cleared his airways and drew him back into a ball again. After a couple of hours of that, he informed us, you talk, even if it's only to curse your captors.

'The secret is to talk without giving information and retain your honour.'

The rest of his talk concerned the four years he spent in the prisoner of war camp called the 'Hanoi Hilton': the beatings, tortures, executions and his survival, and ultimate repatriation to his homeland.

When he had finished the CO stood, but before he could say anything the massed ranks of the SAS rose to give a truly brave man a standing ovation.

B Squadron were beginning to wind down in Ulster, and G Squadron, who would replace us on the anti-terrorist team, were just beginning their build-up training when an operation suddenly turned up from a most unexpected quarter.

The Gambia was the object of a military coup. Neighbouring Senegal was sending in an armed force to return the president to power and was requesting a small team from the SAS, no more than three men, to advise them. Major Crooke and two corporals from the team were dispatched within hours. G Squadron had argued that their men should go. The CO's reply became something of a catch-phrase within the Regiment: 'No buts, it's got to be B.'

The three men quickly made themselves at home with the Senegalese troops and within days were entering The Gambia with them. Their presence was soon needed. The former president's wife and family had been taken hostage by the rebels. What happened next was sheer SAS genius. A frontal assault on the rebel base might well have resulted in the death of the entire family so a note was smuggled into the base, telling the president's wife to request a hospital visit. As Crooky expected, the family were only guarded by two men on the visit. The first they knew of the presence of the SAS was when they found themselves looking down the barrels of the corporals' 9mm Brownings, above which were two sets of ice-cold eyes. Crooky's quiet voice requested the president's wife and family to come with him. In less than a minute they were whisked to safety. Both rebels were held prisoner by the SAS, who feared, correctly, that if they were left to the mercy of the Senegalese they would be shot.

With the release of the first family, the Senegalese launched a major assault and rebel resistance quickly crumbled. The SAS men were in the thick of it and one of the prisoners from the hospital actually carried and reloaded a rifle for one of the corporals, so terrified was the man that he might be shot if left alone. The three not only helped in the attack but their presence and calm authority prevented many atrocities after the rebel surrender. In less than a week they had rescued a family, put down a rebellion and helped restore a government. Crooky was awarded a DSO. Both corporals got MMs.

We handed over the anti-terrorist team's functions to G Squadron. The role is transferred officially once the incoming Squadron has completed its build-up training, and with it all weapons and equipment. As the handover was taking place, the Det were in action again in Ulster, this time in Strabane. On 23 February another routine surveillance operation, trying to locate a hidden terrorist hide, ended with three members of the Det walking almost headlong into three IRA men, who were returning to the hide the Det were searching for after a failed ambush on an RUC patrol. In the resulting gun battle three Provos, Michael and David Devine and Charles Breslin, were killed. Automatic weapons, including for the first time improvised rocket launchers, were recovered at the scene.

Bad as things had been, it was about to get worse. Three members of G Squadron, newly arrived in the Province, got lost in County Tyrone near the Republican town of Carrickmore. Taking a wrong turn, they ended up in a scrapyard run by a Republican family. Their car was quickly surrounded and in the ensuing scuffle they ran away, leaving behind their car, maps and a weapon. These were young and inexperienced operators under the command of a lance-corporal but even so, their actions brought the Regiment's performance in the Province into sharp focus.

The success of the Det and the failure of the troop on operations caused a crisis of confidence in special forces circles in Ulster. Senior SAS officers were dispatched to find out what was going wrong and to assure others, especially SB, that it would be put right. Long-laid plans were brought forward. No longer would a troop be detached from the Squadron committed to anti-terrorist operations. At long last the Regiment recognized that Ulster was a special area of operations. From now on, Ulster would be a year-long, voluntary posting. Those who volunteered would undergo extensive training and selection. Within a year of the Carrickmore débâcle, the very best men the Regiment had to offer were in Ulster, just waiting for a crack at the PIRA. But it was too late for me.

Being part of a small élite band of men, quite exceptional men, was an experience that had changed me. It had forced me to exercise self-discipline, for the first time in my life. There is no real formal discipline inside the SAS. Rank meant very little. Below the very senior non-commissioned officer ranks, everybody called you by your first name and you in turn called them by theirs. Ruperts were, of course, a different animal and although they were never saluted they were always called 'boss'. Bob T best summed up our feeling towards them. 'Ruperts come and go and get their medals, but we're here for ever.'

Except in combat, senior ranks seldom give direct orders, yet what they want done always gets done on time. Fighting between badged members was absolutely frowned on and in most instances the culprits were lucky if they were only fined; very often they would suffer the dreaded fate of being RTUd.

In this relaxed atmosphere, self-discipline has to be developed to its highest level and for the first time I realized that I couldn't solve every problem with my fists.

I loved the Regiment but if I stayed I would leave the Army in my early forties, with a wealth of experience but still only a soldier, perhaps trapped in the circuit of bodyguard and security jobs. I didn't want that. I applied to the Royal Ulster Constabulary and, after a detailed interview with three senior officers and passing the RUC's entrance examination, was accepted. More than anything else the RUC offered me the chance to continue my own private little war with the IRA. Like everything in my life the idea to leave had come on me very quickly. I'd never planned anything and once I had got the idea into my head that was it. It seemed to many people that I was giving up a lot, but I couldn't really explain it to anybody, perhaps not even to myself. All I really knew was that I needed a new challenge. I was to report to the RUC's Enniskillen Training Centre on 5 August 1985.

Two days before I was due to leave the Regiment, I got the saddest of all news: my Gran had died. I travelled to Glasgow for the funeral. In the church I wore my full SAS uniform for the last time and as they lowered her coffin into the grave I took off my sand-grey beret and placed it on the coffin. With tears in my eyes I stood to attention as the person who had meant more to me than anyone was lowered to her rest.

I was discharged the next day. It was late April. I had well over three months before I had to report to Enniskillen. I filled the time by working as a bodyguard for the Sultan of Brunei. I was a qualified bodyguard instructor, but Kevin Costner and I didn't seem to have much in common. The work is mind-numbingly boring: long hours standing outside doors in hotels and outside restaurants. Hours spent trying to concentrate and keep on your toes and not just watching the clock. It takes a great deal of effort to remain alert under such conditions. There are compensations: staying in the Dorchester Hotel and eating at restaurants like Anton Mosimann's, but Hollywood it isn't.

SAS men are much prized for this type of work. The Regiment trains many of the bodyguard teams responsible for the security of heads of state worldwide. The people who employ SAS bodyguards want to know they are safe, but they don't want the intrusive protection of large, heavy men who overreact to the slightest provocation. When you hire an ex-SAS man you get the best, someone who can stay quietly in the shadows and will only respond to a real threat.

The Sultan of Brunei is a striking figure of a man, handsome and urbane and always quietly spoken. He was a fine employer. It meant a lot to me and my fellow ex-SAS men when he paused, as he frequently did, to thank us for the work we were doing. Once, when he had a big win on the tables, he stopped to hand out some of his winnings to the men on the door.

The only non-SAS man on the bodyguard team was Tony E, who now runs a pub in Hereford. He was an ex-Para and an extremely able man who kept us continually amused. He told us how he'd once argued with another paratrooper about which way a revolver cylinder turned. Tony had said the right, his companion to the left. Following a practical demonstration by his companion, Tony was proved correct, and got a .38 bullet in his stomach for his troubles.

At the end of the job I was offered a full-time position as part of the Al-Fayed protection team. It was a very tempting offer but I declined politely.

As I sat on the plane taking me to Belfast airport, a quote from H. G. Wells kept running through my mind: 'If your present does not please you, you can change it, perhaps not for the better, but at least for something more interesting.'

7

THE RUC

*'There are three religions in Northern Ireland:
Protestant, Catholic and police officer.'*
Commandant, RUC Training Centre, Enniskillen, County
Fermanagh, 1985

Walking through the gates of the Royal Ulster Constabulary
Training Centre was like taking a step back in time. The base
had been used to turn out recruits for the RUC since the force
was formed and before that it had been an operational camp for
its predecessor, the Royal Irish Constabulary. The main buildings
were of grey brick, three storeys high, with sloping grey slate
roofs, and the front of the principal building was dominated by
a massive parade ground. The camp was on an island surrounded
with water on three sides, and the surrounding countryside was
breathtakingly beautiful. It was Saturday 4 August 1985. The next
day the course members would assemble and we would take the
oath and be sworn in as RUC constables.

As I had a free evening I decided to find out what the town of
Enniskillen had to offer in the way of entertainment. The town was
small, with hilly, winding roads. I found a small restaurant and had
an excellent meal, then decided to wander round the local bars. The
people were friendly, the beer excellent. I moved from bar to bar
making casual acquaintances and small talk. I told anybody who
asked me that I was a tourist down for the fishing. At 11 p.m. I
found myself in a small bar, well off the beaten track. After last
orders the doors were locked and the publican continued to serve.
I was enjoying myself. Then they started to sing Republican songs.
I was in a Nationalist pub, probably filled with IRA members.

I couldn't help but laugh; there I was, an ex-SAS man, sitting drinking with my sworn enemies, people who would have killed me without a second thought, had they only known who I was, and we were all having a good time. Ulster is a crazy place. I finished my drink, refused the offer of another, and made my way back to barracks.

We gathered early on Sunday morning. Three things struck me within minutes of meeting my fellow recruits: their youth (most were under twenty-one), their commitment (all were hard-liners as far as the Republican Movement was concerned); and the fact that most of them seemed to come from police families. After morning tea, we went to the main hall to be addressed by the commandant.

All of us should think carefully about the oath we were about to take, we were told, after which our lives would never be the same again. There are three religions in Northern Ireland: Protestant, Catholic and police officer. Once we put on the uniform we would become so-called legitimate targets for many terrorist groups. On or off duty, our lives would constantly be at risk. Friends we had known for years might avoid us and conversation would change as we entered company. In our dealings with all sections of the community we must be fair and uphold the highest standards, both on and off duty. This was the life we had ahead of us. We were given a last minute to think it over, then sworn in as probationary constables.

We were formed into squads, for drill, physical training and classroom work, then issued with uniforms. We would not get guns until after basic training. I felt naked in Ulster without one. Our drill instructor was Jimmy D, an ex-Irish Guardsman, with a barrel chest, a drill voice that would have made any RSM proud, and a heart of gold under a bluff exterior. Every recruit knew him as he was a permanent fixture in the depot. My classroom tutor was Sean H, a gentleman in every sense of the word.

Among my fellow recruits was a former Reserve Constable who was sporting the Queen's Gallantry Medal. I asked him how he had got it and the answer took me straight back to my old stamping ground in Armagh. Oliver Grew, still OC PIRA in the city, had not yet gained the respect of his fellow volunteers, so he decided to launch a major operation to show that he was as good as his brothers. A land-mine was laid, and detonated as a UDR patrol vehicle passed over it, injuring four soldiers. What the waiting IRA men did not see was an armoured police car coming up the same road. Thinking the mine had been for them, they started to reverse and in doing so saw two armed men run across the road. They called on them to halt and when they didn't one of the RUC officers opened fire, killing one IRA man instantly. The other terrorist threw himself into a ditch and called out he was surrendering. It was Oliver Grew. He was arrested and charged with attempted murder.

Our day quickly fell into a neat routine. In the mornings we had to prepare ourselves for a detail inspection, what in the Army is called a muster parade. Every RUC recruit is familiar with the morning practice of 'patting down'. Our bottle-green uniforms attracted dust like a flower attracted bees. I was patting down a friend of mine, Sammy G, when there was a tremendous explosion from the direction of the town centre. I bounded towards the window. The whole world seemed to disintegrate in thunderous red and yellow flashes. I could see the roof of the squat, grey-brick building opposite collapse amid a series of rapid explosions. The noise was deafening, a cacophony that vibrated the floor, walls and even the very air we were breathing. 'Mortar attack, everybody down,' I yelled, turning to shove Sammy towards safety.

There was a cracking thump as our windows blew in, showering us with glass. I looked at Sammy, and burst into a fit of almost uncontrollable laughter. He was trying to scramble under a bed, his hands and feet burrowing furiously like some demented hamster in the bottom of its cage. He looked like he was trying to dig his way through the concrete floor with his bare hands. Despite his energetic efforts, he was getting nowhere fast. The explosions continued as the mortars landed around us. As in all violent situations, the seconds become elongated, time itself seemed to expand. I was aware of the most minute detail: Sammy's frantic scrambling; stunned incomprehension on another recruit's face; a single bead of sweat frozen on his upper lip; my own heart, beating like a drum against my chest. The camp's siren sounded – a long, droning wail – belatedly warning us of a terrorist attack.

I did a visual check of my fellow police officers. They were in shock, their eyes wide with fear, their faces reminding me of trapped springbok I had seen in Africa. I could see no sign of any actual physical injury. For perhaps a second we all lay in silence, each of us thanking whatever god we believed in that we were still alive. Then, as the oldest and most experienced, I decided to take control. 'Right, everybody up.' My tone would have done credit to any sergeant-major I had ever served under. I grabbed one man, then another and got them to their feet. 'Follow me.'

Outside we found ourselves confronted by a scene from Dante's Inferno. Recruits were staggering about, some covered in blood, all in shock. The air was heavy with the sharp stench of ammonium nitrate that the PIRA used to fill their bombs. Smoke twisted into coils and drifted slowly upwards. Unexploded mortar bombs, ugly oblong tubes, lay scattered about the yard. The main barrack block had taken the brunt of the attack. Smoke streamed from its roof. The centuries-old walls of the building seemed actually to have been distorted by the explosion, bulging outwards.

Behind me another recruit, an ex-UDR man, arrived with a set of sheets to use as improvised bandages. I sent my room-mates towards the assembly point and looked at my companion. He had the control that years of military discipline instil in people. I could trust him. I nodded. 'Let's go.'

We ran the short distance to the main building. Entering it, we found our vision restricted by smoke and dust, and in the gloom I bumped into the first casualty, a young recruit from the squad immediately in front of us in training. He had a large piece of wood stuck through his forearm, and was holding the injured limb with his other hand. I grabbed him, dark-red blood from his arm spilling on to my pale-green RUC shirt as I steadied him. He was barely twenty, and his legs shook with the pain and the trauma of the moment. He tried to talk, but no words would come, the pupils of his eyes had dilated with fear, tears welled down his face and he shook his head as if trying to wake from some terrible nightmare. We got him out of the door and while my fellow rescuer gave him some first aid, I re-entered the building. Visibility was so poor, I wished fervently for a torch. From not far away I heard the sound of coughing and moved towards it as a second figure loomed out of the semi-darkness, staggering down the stairs. He was in a state of confusion, his eyes glazed over in a mixture of fear and shock. As I got hold of him, he felt to me like he was close to collapsing.

The injured recruit clung to me like a drowning man to a lifebelt. I could feel his body being convulsed by involuntary waves of nervous shudders, so I made soothing noises as I steadied him. Suddenly an overwhelming wave of anger swept over me, a rage at the animals who had done this. I threw my charge's arm across my shoulder and put my arm around his waist and walked him slowly through the darkness to the safety of the daylit doorway.

Outside he slumped against the barracks wall, his head thrown back as he gasped in great draughts of air. 'Are there any more inside?' I asked him. He shook his head and tried to speak, but was convulsed by a spate of coughing. Finally he took in a great gulp of air and said: 'I don't know.' I patted him on the shoulder, and grabbed a recruit who was running past and asked him to take my charge to the medical aid point. I looked up at the building above me; clearly there was some kind of fire in the roof where the mortars had impacted. I nodded to my ex-UDR man and we went back inside and began to search for any other injured comrades. The damage was incredible, even on the ground floor, where water was cascading over the tiles making our footing in the darkened room treacherous. Outside the siren was still droning on. I wished somebody would turn it off.

On the next floor the damage was worse. Walls had collapsed into corridors, and doors, beams and personal equipment was strewn everywhere. At every moment I expected to find a body crushed beneath the debris. As I stepped over some rubble I tripped on something metallic. Cursing, I bent and looked closely through the gloom at a six-foot-long black metal object, flat at one end and tapered at the other. An unexploded Mk10 PIRA mortar.

My companion and I swapped glances, then both of us, for some unknown reason, burst into laughter. The moment of madness was brief, for the smoke was thickening, stinging our eyes and clogging our throats, tasting acrid. The fire in the roof seemed to be getting worse, and we didn't know how long we had before it would spread and force us to give up our search.

The middle floor was bad but the top floor was a disaster area. Huge wooden beams had collapsed into rooms and corridors. At times we both had to crawl under rubble in order to check rooms. Heat from the fire above was also starting to become a problem. In many cases doors were blocked with rubble, forcing us to kick them in. We called out continually for any survivors but when we got no reply, we feared the worst. I kicked the last door open only to hear another metallic clunk. Another unexploded bomb. Finally we had satisfied ourselves that there was nobody left injured and got ourselves out of the increasingly thickening smoke. Once outside we blocked the door. A sergeant from the guard squad ran past and I grabbed him and told him the main block was clear and that there were unexploded mortar bombs inside. We then rejoined our friends at the assembly point on the outskirts of the grounds.

Viewed from a distance the damage seemed immense. A cloud of dense, black smoke hung over the training centre, yet I was amazed to discover that, although we had twenty-three injuries, one of whom was serious, nobody was dead. We were very lucky indeed. The squad who would have normally been in the upstairs rooms of the main accommodation block patting themselves down, had just been returning from early-morning swimming. In fact they had seen the terrorist escape after the mortars had been launched into their own sleeping quarters. A part-time member of the guard squad even got his gunsight on the bomber as he fled to a waiting getaway car but didn't fire because he could see no weapon. The mortars had been fired from a flat-bed lorry rigged so that it took only one man to drive it to the scene and set a simple but deadly device which, when activated, fired the mortars automatically. (The terrorist was later shot dead by two of my friends in the SAS, much to my delight.) One of the recruits later described to me the sight of the mortars travelling towards the camp and his friends as being like: 'A rain of long, black objects. The sky seemed to be full of them and for a second they all seemed to be suspended in mid-air, then they dipped slowly towards the ground and my friends. I thought you would all die. I closed my eyes and prayed to God.'

Most of these young RUC recruits were under twenty-one. Many required counselling after the attack: one of the unseen products of the terrorist war in Ulster. That night we kept the bar in the camp open late and had a party. I was proud of the young recruits there that night, for although they had been through a violent baptism of fire, not one of them spoke of resigning. The mood was one of defiance, and an urge to finish training and get on with the job. It was a merry band of recruits who went to bed that night. Next morning's parade was a different matter. Hardly any of us had a complete uniform and with our hangovers into the bargain, we were a very sorry sight. The commandant put his head out of his half-ruined office and told us to get off the parade square.

Several days afterwards I was asked by one of the training sergeants about my actions during the attack. I related my activities, praising my fellow adventurer, the ex-UDR man. I gave no other thought to what I believed to be no more than idle curiosity. A week later I was to get a shock. I was called away from class by the sergeant and put in front of the chief inspector.

What had been my actions on the day of the mortar attack, I was asked in a very authoritative voice.

Again I related my actions.

Had I read standing orders, relating to actions to be carried out in the event of a terrorist attack? I was beginning to feel slightly uneasy.

'Yes,' I lied in a not wholly convincing way.

'What does it say about what to do after a terrorist attack?'

I thought back to the thick book I had read the day after I had entered the depot.

'Go to the assembly area?' I offered optimistically.

The chief inspector fixed me with an unswerving stare. 'And what did you do?' I remained silent, having learned from past experience that if you're getting a telling-off the best approach is not to give the other person any ammunition.

'I'll tell you what you did. You chose to disregard standing orders and enter a building that was on fire, taking with you another recruit. Do you realize you could both have been killed?' He shook his head slowly and threw a glance at the sergeant behind me. 'What am I to do with the man, Sergeant?'

The sergeant, a man I respected immensely, answered in a quiet, measured voice: 'Well, sir, you know my views on the matter.'

For several seconds the chief inspector stared at me, then spread his hands as if to say the matter was out of his jurisdiction. 'I'm afraid I have to agree with you, Sergeant. Constable McCallion, we are putting you up for a gallantry decoration. Your actions, although expected, are in the highest tradition of the RUC.' He held out his hand and said: 'Well done.' I was stunned.

Subsequently I found out that several of my fellow recruits had made statements recommending me for some kind of recognition. In due course both my ex-UDR friend and myself were highly commended for bravery, the only RUC recruits ever in the history of the force to be decorated while in training.

The rest of our training, with which I was very impressed, was uneventful. The standard of physical fitness was high, and the legal training detailed and absorbing. In the final written exam I passed fourth out of the seventy or so remaining recruits. I now had to complete a four-week firearms course and then I was posted to Tennant Street RUC station. Tennant Street is probably one of the busiest police stations in Europe. Situated in north Belfast, an area that has seen one out of every four murders in the entire Province, it is bang in the middle of a hotbed of every type of terrorist crime. Some of the worst Loyalist murder gangs in Northern Ireland were operating in the area embracing the Shankill Road and the satellite Protestant estates of Ballysillian and Tyndale. The Shankill Road is the cockpit of Loyalism, and had always been a difficult area for the police to patrol. As early as the turn of the century a well-known local joke went:

'Who's that you're hitting, John?'

'A Peeler.'

'Hold him so that I can hit him too.'

'Get away and find your own Peeler to hit.'

The first RUC man to die in the present troubles, Constable Arbuckle, was shot to death by Loyalist extremists during a gun battle on the Shankill Road in 1969. As if the area didn't have enough problems, across the dividing line of the Crumlin Road sat the fiercely Republican Ardoyne, where, I was soon informed, two very active PIRA ASUs were waiting to have a crack at us. The two communities were separated by a 'peace wall' (or environmental wall, as the city council preferred to call it) but this did not prevent easy access by murder gangs on both sides.

Housing in the area ranged from ultra-modern developments to run-down back-to-back terraced houses built before the war. Each area was dominated by murals depicting the virtues of particular paramilitary organizations. Some of them were quite beautifully done, others crude and cruel. But all of them served as a warning to the other side: from the Catholic Ardoyne's

'Our day will come' to the Protestant Woodvale's 'All taigh's are targets.'

Perhaps the cruellest of them all was a faded depiction of a shooting incident that happened in the 1970s. An RUC man had observed some youths acting suspiciously on waste ground near the Lower Ormeau Road, an active IRA area. He had challenged one of them and he had turned quickly. The youth had been holding something and in the darkness the officer thought it was a gun. He opened fire and killed him. It turned out that it was a paintbrush. The youth had been painting 'Up the PROVOS' on the wall. A local wag had immortalized the incident by writing 'Up the PRO . . .', then dragging a line to the base of the wall and drawing a body there.

Driving through Tennant Street station's guarded front gate, I glanced at the squat two-storey building that was to be my home for the next two years. The sentry box that had once been on top of the flat roof had gone, but the bullet holes from the UVF gunman who had fired at it back in 1972 were still visible. My section sergeant was Seamus L, a Catholic and a fine and dedicated police officer. The rest of my section consisted of the usual cross-section of people you find in any group. Some were strong, some weak, some wanted to work hard and advance, and some just wanted to sleep at the first opportunity. Coming from organizations which entirely comprised highly motivated, aggressive people, it took me some time to come to terms with the fact that not everybody was as committed as myself.

The Anglo–Irish Agreement, signed by Margaret Thatcher in the early part of 1986, was intended as a step forward in the Ulster conflict. The Protestant community saw it as a complete betrayal. For the first time, they thought, a foreign government (in the shape of Dublin) would have a say in their affairs. Although I was new on the streets of the Shankill, I could feel the tension build as the date of the signing approached. Police officers were 'advised' by certain 'Loyalist' politicians to go sick on that day or face the consequences. The Protestant areas were about to explode, and we were smack in the firing line.

Most of us believed the Anglo–Irish Agreement was wrong. Even Margaret Thatcher concedes in her memoirs that she might have 'gone too far'. The Protestant community regarded it as a betrayal, as did most RUC officers. The sense of disloyalty was all the more acute, all the harder to bear, because Thatcher, a committed Unionist, was signing it. This was the prime minister who had faced down the miners, won a war six thousand miles away and had the strength to stand firm against the IRA during the hunger strikes. It was as if a close and admired friend had suddenly thrust a knife into your vitals. Many of the constables in Tennant Street resigned from the Police Federation in protest. A police force can only police an area with consent. Areas like west Belfast or Crossmaglen are not policed: they are patrolled. Traditionally we had always enjoyed the consent of the Protestant community but with the stroke of a pen we were robbed of it.

As an outsider, I didn't feel the pressure quite as much as the local lads. They lived in Protestant communities and drank in Protestant bars, and each of them, in the build-up to the signing, faced mounting demands that they join the protest by going sick or resigning. Thankfully, on the day we had no more than the average number of officers report sick, because that day the Shankill exploded. Riots broke out everywhere. We had no sooner managed to get one under control, than another broke out. At first it was just running, stone-throwing mobs which scattered as soon as we drove our armoured police wagons at them but as darkness fell on the first night, gunmen began to appear. The first shoots were cowboy affairs, lone gunmen with a pistol or shotgun blasting at us from side-streets. I very quickly became adept at telling which missiles were bullets winging off the side of the armoured car and which stones. A man with a double-barrelled shotgun jumped out and fired both barrels at the vehicle behind. We were right in the middle of a riot, petrol bombs coming at us from every angle. I watched the gunman disappear back into the crowd. One of my companions said I looked like a rabid dog eyeing steak it couldn't get at.

Near midnight, the front vehicle of a two-car patrol was lured into a deliberate ambush in Ballysillian. A land-mine was detonated as it drove past (fortunately only partially detonating), then gunmen opened up with high-powered rifles. This was no cowboy shooting. We were given instructions not to dismount unless we had no other option. It was during this terrible period of unrest that I was first called a 'black bastard'. As I'm as white as a ghost, I wondered why the rioters chose that particular form of abuse to hurl at me. One of my compatriots enlightened me. When the RUC had just been formed, their uniforms had been of a much darker green and they had worn long, black overcoats.

The violence died down in the early hours of the morning. Most of us slept in the station as the area was still too tense to risk driving out in a civilian car. The Shankill looked like a war zone but the extremists hadn't given up yet, seeing us, the RUC, as Dublin's bully-boys. We would have to pay.

The first police officer's house caught fire at about 1 a.m. Systematically they set about burning out of his home every officer who lived on the Shankill Road or the nearby estates. Firemen coming into the area to put out the fires were stoned and petrol-bombed. I went to one incident, and found a fifty-year-old reservist sitting in the middle of the street while his house blazed. A silent, hateful crowd of fifty or so people watched it burn from a distance of only a few feet away. As I got out of the armoured car I looked carefully at their faces. I shall never forget the look of smug satisfaction. I went over to the Reserve Constable, a big man who was crying like a baby. They'd held him at bay until his house was well and truly alight. Even so, he had dashed inside and saved a few meagre belongings, although he had burned his hands badly. As I helped him to his feet he pointed towards the silent crowd and said: 'They did this to me, my neighbours.'

I picked up the pitifully few things he had saved. A single stone landed next to me. I looked round slowly. The crowd still had that look on their faces. I wished so much for a platoon of Paras in riot gear.

On the walls a new piece of graffiti appeared, reading: 'Come home to a real fire. Join the RUC.'

A little after 9 a.m. we received a call from a new location: the Ardoyne. Someone was wrecking cars in one of the side-streets. Normally a police patrol with Army backup would have been sent in to investigate, but with a full-blown riot still going on in the Shankill, we had no one to spare. Luckily the call went unanswered. The PIRA had laid a well-planned ambush and the wrecked cars were just a come-on. Had anybody reacted they would almost certainly have been killed. That night, if you wore the bottle-green uniform of the RUC you had no friends in Tennant Street's operational areas.

The riots lasted three days but the legacy of bitterness and hatred inside the Protestant community against the RUC was to last much longer. Despite everything, our casualties had been relatively light and with the streets now reasonably calm I could go about learning the business of being a police officer in Ulster. For the first time in my life I had to deal with the effects of violence, instead of simply inflicting it. The area was dominated by violence of every imaginable kind. The paramilitaries had the community, on both sides of the Crumlin Road, by the throat. Protection rackets flourished. Those who contravened the 'laws' of the paramilitaries were kneecapped. 'Normal' crime was also endemic. On average we had two robberies and five burglaries a day. I often wondered how anybody could live in such areas, yet I met them daily, people who just wanted to go to work and bring up their families as best they could.

Tennant Street RUC patrolled the area vigorously. The station had four sections, divided between morning, late and night shifts, and one resting. On a normal day each section would put out armoured and 'soft-skin' vehicle patrols and a foot patrol. In addition we had specialized patrol groups for the Ardoyne and Ligonel. In times of particularly high sectarian tension or when serious rioting broke out, extra men were brought in. Our immediate reserve were the DMSUs, District Mobile Support Units. On mobile patrol each constable took turns being an observer, and was *de facto* in charge of the vehicle. It was his duty to complete any files that resulted after the shift and to carry out any investigations. The paperwork was a slowly growing mountain that constantly threatened to engulf us. Yet I loved being an observer. My colleagues thought I was slightly strange.

In the aftermath of the riots our morale suffered. We were being spat at continually in the street and many of us had lost confidence in our own superiors. At one policeman's funeral the chief constable was hissed at by the mourners. Morale was also affected by the Stalker inquiry, which was drawing to a close with the prosecution of several officers for murder. All were acquitted. Lord Justice Gibson, who would himself be murdered by the IRA, had even congratulated the RUC men for bringing the men they had killed 'before the highest court of justice'. We viewed Stalker as a meddling outsider, an Englishman who didn't understand the first thing about the problems we faced. A conscientious and dedicated police officer he may have been, but the only people who benefited from his inquiry, as far as we were concerned, were the Provos. I believe Stalker got it all wrong. Instead of trying to convict the constables and sergeants who had pulled the trigger, he should have concentrated on the lack of command and control that was evident in the operations. If you are a member of a specialist unit and your superiors tell you a car contains armed gunmen who will kill you and you believe that a split-second delay will cost you your life, then it's their fault if the operation is a disaster and unarmed terrorists get killed.

Even as the streets of Belfast were in turmoil, with RUC men being murdered by the IRA and burnt out of their homes by the UDA, the inquiry was still trying to force the chief constable to hand over a tape recording about a shooting in a Tyrone hayshed. To us that seemed madness. I talked to one of the HMSU (Headquarters Mobile Support Unit) men involved in the shooting who had actually listened to the tape. He maintained that it contained nothing that could have incriminated any of the RUC men involved, and in fact reinforced their version of events. The only controversial thing in the tape, according to him, was after the shooting when one of the RUC men had suggested finishing off one of the wounded men, which he believed could be put down to 'over-enthusiasm'.

About a month after the agreement, the UVF in Ballysillian decided to show its disapproval. It began to kill Catholics. Over the next six months we had a sectarian killing or attempted killing on average once a week. The first murder I attended was in Ligonel, where the caretaker of the social club, a man by the name of Scullion, was the victim. Mr Scullion had not been a big man in life. In death he looked nothing more than a bundle of rags, the wispy grey hairs on his head doing little to cover the gaping holes left by the two .45 bullets that killed him. As I looked at what was left of the sixty-five-year-old I said to my sergeant: 'That's an awful big gun they used to kill such a little man.'

I was in the police vehicle that was sent to deliver the news of Scullion's death to his wife. As we neared the family home I still could not find words to tell the old lady that her husband of many years was dead. My driver had a suggestion.

'Why don't you start by saying: "Are you the widow Scullion?"'

Graveside humour at its worst, but that day, as on many other days, it helped us to cope with the horror of the situation.

Some of the attempted murders were so inept they would have done justice to a Mack Sennett silent comedy. The UDA twice tried to murder a Sinn Fein man who lived on the Oldpark Road. The first time, two gunmen walked in with automatic pistols, fired twenty shots from a range of less than four feet and managed to hit him once, in his heel. The second time was worse. Wanting to leave nothing to chance, they brought a shotgun. As the two were getting out of the car one accidentally discharged both barrels, hitting his companion in the buttocks. The Sinn Fein man took the hint and moved.

The man behind the campaign was the leader of the UVF in Ballysillian, James Bingham. I met him under unusual circumstances. As the Crumlin Road winds its way into the countryside it curves back upon itself in a tight loop known appropriately as the Horseshoe Bend. Several near-fatal accidents had occurred because horses had been allowed to wander on to the road from a nearby field. Motorists had swerved into ditches and collided with oncoming cars to avoid them. I was instructed to investigate, find the owner and prosecute him. It seemed, at first glance, to be a straightforward police assignment.

My inquiries met with a wall of silence and, although I did not recognize it at first, fear. I could not understand why the locals in the nearby Ballysillian and Forthriver Estates clammed up every time I tried to find out who owned the horses. After a couple of weeks of fruitless enquiries, I realized only the UVF could inspire such a reluctance to talk.

James Bingham owned a pet shop in the area. I approached him about the horses. Initially he denied any knowledge of their ownership. He was a tall, broad-shouldered man, with long, curly, light-brown hair. Several times in our conversation he went to great pains to stress that he had connections with local politicians and that he was, to use his term, a 'hard-line Loyalist'. I informed him that as I couldn't discover who owned the horses, they would be confiscated, held for six months and then sold at auction if no one came forward to claim them. He stood up and came over to where I was standing and towered over me.

'I wouldn't do that if I was you,' he said in a low voice.

I smiled. 'Why not, Mr Bingham?

'Because I wouldn't like it.'

We eyed each other for several seconds. 'Is that some kind of threat?'

'I don't threaten people. You know what I am. I wouldn't like it if those horses were confiscated.'

I removed my body armour to reveal my medal ribbons.

'Do you see these, Mr Bingham? I got them fighting wars. I got them for killing people. Men who would have eaten you for breakfast. If you think a jumped-up UVF thug like you scares me, you're wrong.'

His face flushed with anger. I replaced my hat and walked to the door.

'If those horses aren't removed within twenty-four hours, I'll have them confiscated.'

The horses were gone the next morning.

Bingham began to ask questions about me. Whether he was just curious or was planning some action against me, I never knew. Two weeks after our chat, three IRA gunmen attacked his house and Bingham was shot dead trying to run upstairs to a secure room. After his assassination two innocent Catholics were shot dead, one in front of his wife as they left midnight mass. The gunmen told her as he left: 'One of ours died last night, two of yours will die tonight.'

In the days following the murders the area was tense. The aftermath of the Anglo–Irish Agreement riots, the sectarian killings and Bingham's murder made our job as police almost impossible to carry out. The superintendent of Tennant Street invited the local 'civic leaders' to meet him for a coffee, to discuss the situation. I was on the front desk as they trooped in. Among them were UVF and UDA gangsters and racketeers, some of the worst scum in the area. People who were getting rich, and taking winter holidays abroad, paid for by the suffering of the people of the Shankill.

Barely two nights later, I was asked to drive the superintendent. I'd only known him for a relatively short time. My stony silence in the car promoted him to ask me if anything was wrong. I never ask anybody if I can be frank, and I answered: 'It's that meeting you had the other day, sir. You know the kind of men they are. How can you sit down and drink tea with them?'

The superintendent thought for several seconds before answering; when he did his voice was measured, but tinged with irony. 'Harry, we only police the Shankill with the good grace of the UVF. Everyday I have to send two middle-aged beat officers down the Shankill Road, and every day the UVF could walk up behind them and shoot them in the back of the head. Before I'll walk behind those men's coffins I'll sit down and have tea with the devil himself, even if it makes me sick to my stomach to do it.'

I think that then, for the very first time, I began to see the realities of life in Ulster. The longer I served in Tennant Street, the more apparent it became to me that some of the views I had cherished since my first tour were completely wrong. Black and white had becomes shades of grey. Terrorists, whether Catholic IRA or Protestant UVF, were part of their communities. To us they were 'players', 'targets', people who had to be removed from society. But in their areas they were young Sean who lived next door, or big Frank who drank next to you every night. The communities might not agree with them, but an attack on them was an attack on the herd.

By now I was into the routine of shift work and overtime. A fourteen-hour day was not uncommon. In fact, we were never really off duty. We carried our .357mm Ruger Magnum revolvers at all times. I never let mine out of arm's length.

The PIRA had launched an offensive against off-duty police officers. In 1986 twelve RUC men were killed, many when they were most vulnerable, in their own homes. The regular killing of police officers was causing us all concern. The IRA offensive had also spread to the Ardoyne area, which had been quiet for a couple of years. When a local member of the IRA unit had become an informer – one of the first 'supergrasses' – his evidence had enabled the RUC to round up most of the active IRA men in the area.

The RUC had attempted to emulate the successful use of supergrasses by the Italian Police Force in their fight against the

Mafia. The idea was a simple one: catch a terrorist who faces a long prison sentence, and persuade him to give sworn evidence against his comrades in return for immunity and a new life in a foreign country. It had worked well for them but the system collapsed in Ulster because evidence given by the terrorists was eventually discredited on appeal. Most of the terrorists who turned supergrass were shown to be habitual liars, it was little wonder the courts could not rely on their evidence.

Nevertheless the Black trials as they were called (after Christopher Black from the Ardoyne) resulted in most of the IRA ASUs being rounded up and incarcerated while waiting for an appeal hearing or going OTR (On The Run). With the collapse of the supergrass system many of them had returned. In addition Martin Meehan, a killer who was legendary amongst Republicans in north Belfast and had always dominated the Ardoyne, had finished serving a fourteen-year jail term for kidnapping an alleged informer and was back in the area. His return spelt trouble.

In the Protestant calendar 12 July was the most important occasion: the anniversary of the Protestant King William III of Orange's victory over the Catholic King James at the Battle of the Boyne in 1690. Marching bands from all Protestant areas walked in procession into the city centre. In Tennant Street on that day in 1986, nearly five hundred police officers had assembled to police the parades.

It was rumoured that the IRA in the Ardoyne had kidnapped a soldier. First it was thought to be a member of an Army patrol, then an SAS man. The rumours became wilder by the second. We were called on to parade and the Chief Inspector of Operations addressed us: 'The IRA have snatched an off-duty soldier from the Ardoyne shop fronts and he is being held somewhere in the Ardoyne. We believe he is still alive but if action is not taken quickly, he may be killed. Consequently the Army has sealed off the Ardoyne. You will enter in force and search every house. If anybody refuses to open their door to you, you have the authority to force an entry. This has to be done fast. Remember, somewhere in that area there is a very frightened man who is depending on you.'

In seconds we were briefed and minutes later some five hundred uniformed RUC men invaded one of the strongholds of Republicanism. Most people simply opened the door to our knock; when they didn't we kicked the doors down and searched the houses quickly. Less than ten minutes after we had entered the area a patrol, two doors up from me, hit the jackpot. Entering what seemed like a deserted house they found a TA soldier tied to a chair in an upstairs room. I arrived in the house a few minutes later. A look of combined terror and relief crossed the man's face. He was crying and smiling all at once, his voice barely intelligible. He bore the signs of a terrible beating and it looked to me as if his jaw had been broken. As he was being led from the house, there was another shout. Three men had been found hiding in the attic of a nearby house and one of them was Martin Meehan. They had escaped by the back door of the house where they had been torturing the soldier, as the front door was being forced. We had little time to savour our joy at the release of the soldier and the capture of Meehan. An explosive device was found with a command wire attached. The area had to be quickly cleared.

Back at Tennant Street the full story of the day's events was relayed to us. The soldier, a member of the Territorial Army, had been snatched by locals as he walked past the Ardoyne shop fronts and quickly handed over to the tender mercies of the IRA. One leading IRA man in the area, known as Butcher, wanted to kill him quickly and laid a command-detonated mine next to his body. The mine was laid but Meehan wanted to interrogate the TA man first. He was still doing so when we burst in. Quick action and decisive leadership had resulted in a man's life being saved and one of the most dangerous men in Ulster being captured. Meehan was later given another fourteen-year jail sentence.

Despite our success in the Ardoyne our relations with the Protestant paramilitaries in the area, in particular the UDA, Ulster's largest paramilitary organization, remained tense. About a week after Meehan's capture I was in charge of a mobile patrol called to investigate a burglary in a well-known UDA drinking club. The break-in had obviously been carried out by kids. The footprints were from trainers, and judging by their size I reckoned that the culprits couldn't have been more than fifteen. Only cigarettes and some bottles of spirits had been stolen. As I was taking a statement I got a nudge in the back from my colleague. Turning, I found myself confronted by three men all wearing black leather jackets. Two were about my age, early thirties, of medium height and build.

But it was the third who dominated the group. He stood just over six foot but was built like a mountain. Our eyes met and I read arrogance, dismissal and a little madness there, and when I met his gaze without looking away, something else: challenge.

The barman hurried over to the three men and there was a quick, subdued conversation as they turned to leave. The mountain glanced over at me, his face twisted into a sneer. 'You won't have to worry about this one.'

I was about to go after him but my partner restrained me.

'Let it go, Harry.'

'Who the hell are they?'

'UDA. The big man is Billy Dixon. He's their top enforcer.'

'What did he mean, we don't have to worry about this?'

'It means they have a good idea who did it. They'll find them and kneecap them.'

'I should have arrested him.'

'We'd need more men. Last time we had to arrest Dixon it took half a section of DMSU to get him handcuffed. Even then when we got him in the cells he kicked the cell door off, and that was embedded in two feet of concrete. Besides, you haven't a case. What he said could have been taken any way. Finish taking your statements and let's get out of here.'

Two hours later we got a call to the lower Shankill. In an alley we found two kids of barely sixteen writhing in agony. Billy Dixon had been as good as his word.

Dixon and I had not liked each other on sight. Partly it was because I was an RUC man and he was a thug. I knew deep down inside me that I would have trouble with Dixon if he ever got the opportunity. As I watched the two young lads being helped into an ambulance I swore to myself that he was not going to get the better of me, no matter what it cost. I had two more run-ins with him before the year was out. Every time I met him he raised my hackles.

On 25 April I decided to take my first leave back in Hereford since joining the force. Julia had moved to Belfast with me and we were anxious to see friends in Hereford. After taking the overnight Larne to Stranraer ferry I drove down to England through the night. As I was entering Hereford in the early hours of the morning I switched on the radio and heard that one man had been shot dead and another seriously wounded in a shooting incident in Fermanagh. I knew instinctively that it was the SAS. An hour later the dead man's name was released. I felt a savage burst of glee: it was Seamus McElwain, the man we were told was responsible for the mortar attack on the RUC depot while I was in training. McElwain had been captured by the SAS only to escape from the Maze prison in a mass break-out. Since then he had been killing with abandon on the Fermanagh border. That night I went to the SAS social club and was told the whole story.

An Army foot patrol had found a command wire running across a field. Instead of stopping the patrol they had carried on and reported it when they were a safe distance away. A two-man SAS team, two good friends of mine, were dispatched to make a close-target reconnaissance of the area. They found the wire and traced it down to a 500lb mine then back to the firing point. They called in the main ambush party but before it arrived two armed men approached. Both were engaged and in the resulting gun battle McElwain was killed. Both SAS men were later decorated with the Military Medal. I bought a bottle of champagne to celebrate.

Back in Tennant Street things were a little quieter, although there were still sporadic attacks on innocent Catholics by both UVF and UDA hit teams. In the Ardoyne the capture of Meehan had taken the wind out of the PIRA's sails, but they were still dangerous. After the murder of a Catholic taxi driver, who had once been an auxiliary IRA man, by the UDA, a three-man hit team had killed a top UDA officer in the Ligonel Road. There had been no operations against us but a hardened IRA killer was about to be released who would revitalize the IRA in the area and increase the threat against us dramatically.

The beginning of 1987 found me on attachment to the Ardoyne patrol, the specialist police unit which dealt solely with this Republican area. Most ordinary police patrols never ventured into the Ardoyne's maze of narrow streets. The Ardoyne patrol operated daily. We checked all the licensed public houses in the area, assisted the Army in searches and carried out our own. Very quickly we began to get to know the players in the area. The hatred the Republicans had for us was almost beyond imagination. Once when I was patrolling past a well-known IRA man's house he went inside and dragged out his four-year-old daughter. Pointing at us, he said: 'They're bad men. They're the ones you must stay away from. They're the ones you have to warn Daddy about.'

I wondered then if there could ever be any kind of peace in Ulster.

By late March the Ardoyne was becoming increasingly dangerous. Intelligence had informed us that two ASUs had been reactivated and had already aborted several ambushes. The prime mover behind this upsurge in the terrorist threat was Laurence Marley, a professional terrorist who had spent most of his adult life either on the run or in the Maze. He'd tried to evade custody so often that his nickname in Republican circles was the 'Great Escaper'. I saw him only once, briefly, from the back of an RUC patrol vehicle. He was kneeling on the pavement outside his home mending a bike and my attention was drawn to him by the driver. Through the observation slit I looked directly into his eyes. I don't believe I have ever seen such a look of unadulterated hatred in my life. I remember saying to myself: 'This is a bad one, Harry.'

On 31 March two youths went into a bakery on the Ardoyne shop fronts, produced a handgun and left with the day's takings. An RUC patrol vehicle, commanded by a depot colleague of mine, Nevin B, was tasked to the scene and arrived only minutes after the 'robbery'. The baker ran out to meet the approaching RUC vehicle and in doing so probably saved Nevin's life. As they walked back towards the shop a Reserve Constable, Peter Nesbit, who was acting as gunner, got out and moved to a vacant doorway to give cover to the commander.

Peter was what was known in the RUC as 'a good-living man'. He didn't smoke or drink and was a scoutmaster with the local troop. I remember him as being outgoing and friendly. His kindness was well remembered by all Tennant Street station. A bachelor who lived with his mother, he had joined the Reserve Force simply because he wanted desperately to help his community.

As Nevin walked into the relative safety of the bakery, a 20lb bomb was detonated behind the unsuspecting Peter, killing him instantly. The explosion blew his body halfway across the street.

A command wire had been run out of the back of the shop, along an adjoining alleyway, to a house in the street behind. A terrorist with a radio had been positioned in the houses opposite and he had signalled when the target was in the killing area.

My patrol had almost walked into the same ambush two nights previously, when a postbox directly opposite the ambush had been vandalized, and letters scattered across the pavement. We hadn't left the safety of our patrol vehicle.

I arrived at the scene about five minutes after the explosion. The driver of the RUC vehicle was shocked almost into incoherence. Nevin, although badly wounded and shaken, was still in control. We set up a defensive perimeter, a ring of protecting officers now augmented by the Army against the possibility of a secondary ambush. We set about collecting forensic evidence, and Peter's decapitated body. A large, vociferous Republican crowd soon gathered. Within minutes, a suitably gory painting had been etched on a gable wall with the legend 'Nesbit's lost his head' beneath it. As ever, it was not the swaggering teenagers among the jeering crowd who caused the most offence, but the middle-aged matrons of hate.

Even as the forensic evidence was being gathered our intelligence was reporting that Marley had detonated the bomb. His house in Havana Gardens was raided and the IRA Godfather taken into custody. But we had no evidence to link him directly to the explosion. He was released within hours. We relied on sources within the Ardoyne, local people, some of whom were actually in the PIRA. Of course, none of them would be prepared to come forward and give evidence in open court but the information they provided was nearly always spot-on.

Marley's release was not the end of the story. He had only recently been released from the Maze and hadn't yet turned his home into the kind of fortress most prominent IRA men lived in – complete with steel plating on the door, iron bars and bulletproof glass at the windows. On the afternoon of 2 April a car containing three men was driven slowly into Havana Gardens and stopped outside Marley's home. Marley was expecting a visit from a senior IRA killer nicknamed Bootsy. Two men knocked on his door. The IRA chief asked who was there and started to walk down the short hallway toward the door. Perhaps some instinct for self-preservation took over because he stopped and again asked who was at the door. The two men, members of the Mid-Shankill

UVF, produced a sawn-off shotgun and a 9mm Browning High Power pistol. The terrorist with the shotgun blasted a hole in the door. The blast knocked Marley off his feet. The second UVF man shoved his handgun through the shattered door. In all, ten shots were fired at the prone figure. Only one hit him, but it was enough. He died a few hours later in hospital.

I heard the news at home and although off duty drove immediately to the station. The atmosphere was electric. I had never seen so many smiles on police officers' faces. In the Ardoyne things were different. The death of Marley sent shock waves round the small, fiercely Republican population. Marley was a well-known figure in the community. A neighbour, a man who drank in the same pubs as they did, who went to the same chapel, whose children played with their children. An attack on him was an attack on the herd – and the herd closed ranks. In the hours after his death, crowds of angry, sullen young men and women gathered at street corners, suspicious of any passing vehicle and openly hostile to any security force patrol.

The Ardoyne PIRA was determined to give Marley a full military send-off, complete with guard of honour, plus tricolour, black beret and gloves on the coffin. The RUC's policy at this time was to brook no display of paramilitary paraphernalia at funerals. The scene was set for confrontation. On the morning of Marley's funeral it looked to me as if the entire population of the Ardoyne had turned out. Republicans had bussed in from all parts of Belfast and even further away. The RUC too was out in force, with Divisional Mobile Support Units out in strength. At mid-morning Marley's coffin was carried from his home, complete with full IRA regalia. The RUC in massed ranks at the bottom of the short garden refused to let it proceed further. There was a tense stand-off. Then, slowly, the honour guard carrying the coffin turned and went back into 9 Havana Gardens.

As the door closed, the first brick was thrown. In seconds we were in a full-scale riot. I was in the thick of it. A seething mass of frenzied bodies and projectiles hurled themselves at our shield wall in seemingly endless waves. Bricks crashed down on us and we started to sustain casualties. I heard the sound of baton guns, which fire rubber bullets, opening up in reply. My whole world was encompassed in a ring of jeering faces as I struggled to keep my feet. Some of our assailants had ripped up steel spikes from nearby fencing and emerged from the crowd like medieval lancers. If we hadn't been in heavy body armour, some of us would have died. I was armed with the short baton, almost useless in such conditions, and if I could have drawn the .357 Ruger at my side, I would have done. Then, almost as suddenly as it had begun, the crowd broke up, leaving the cordon around Marley's home panting, shocked and bruised.

The riot degenerated into a series of small running battles between groups of ten to twenty youths and patrolling RUC vehicles. As night fell the first petrol bomb was thrown and we were pulled out. The stand-off continued until the early hours of the morning, when the gangs drifted slowly away to get some sleep and ready themselves for round two.

The RUC had learnt its lesson from the previous day: it was out in force at Marley's home. Half the DMSUs in the Province were there, armed to the teeth and ready for anything. At midday the door opened. Marley's coffin, carried by eight bearers, all prominent members of the Ardoyne PIRA, started to emerge. It still carried the black beret, tricolour and gloves. Some DMSU personnel pushed forward and tried to grab the tricolour. The two IRA men at the front started to reverse, while those at the back still tried to push forwards. If the situation had not been so tense it would have been comical. Finally, the men at the rear realized what was happening, put themselves into reverse, and Marley's coffin again disappeared into his house. We all waited.

The crowd seemed to draw in a collective intake of breath, then threw themselves at us with an anguished howl. We had greater numbers and were better prepared this time. A policewoman, a member of a DMSU, got a little ahead of her male colleagues. An enormous local youth landed a haymaker squarely in her face, felling her instantly. Her outraged colleagues advanced like an avenging praetorian guard, knocked the youth to the ground and dragged him by his heels to a waiting RUC vehicle, where they no doubt delivered words of caution about his behaviour.

In the midst of the onslaught one of the IRA pall-bearers, a noted IRA activist, appeared outside Marley's home with a megaphone and called for calm. He claimed that the RUC wanted a confrontation and asked the crowd not to give us an excuse to brutalize Irish people. Volunteer Marley, he confirmed, would not be buried until he was allowed to be buried with dignity.

The rest of the day was tense though uneventful, but as night fell the rioting started again, this time more earnestly. The local boys had been joined by travelling thugs from west Belfast. We were pulled out again; Intelligence believed that the Ardoyne PIRA was planning some kind of revenge for the Marley shooting, either against us or Shankill UVF. The night became a series of running battles which went on until around 4 a.m.

The whole of Republican Belfast was now in a state of high tension. Nothing excites the Irish psyche like the death of a martyr. Perhaps not since the hunger strikers had Belfast been on the verge of such total anarchy. There had been no shots fired against us in the Ardoyne, but in nearby west Belfast and the New Lodge, the security forces were being shot at regularly. The RUC was calling in further reserves and Republicans were converging from all over Ulster.

The next day found the biggest crowd yet outside Marley's house. Thousands had gathered. We'd increased our numbers and the morning was spent in an ugly stand-off as Senior RUC officers negotiated with the PIRA. Eventually a face-saving compromise was reached. Marley's coffin would be draped with a tricolour, but no black beret or gloves. In addition two ranks of RUC personnel would walk alongside the coffin to prevent an IRA guard of honour forming. The funeral could proceed.

The coffin was finally borne from the house and taken on the long walk from the Ardoyne to the Holy Cross Church on the Crumlin Road. Throughout the route, vicious, ugly fights broke out between the marchers and the accompanying RUC officers, but the coffin eventually reached the Crumlin Road and went beyond our jurisdiction. I was standing on the Crumlin Road as it passed on its way to the chapel. I could see only Peter Nesbit's shattered body.

Peter's funeral followed two days later. The IRA disrupted it by issuing a series of false bomb alerts. As the coffin finally arrived at Roselawn Cemetery, on the outskirts of Belfast, members of the security cordon became suspicious of a car parked at the gates. It exploded as they approached. Six officers were injured, mercifully not seriously. The IRA issued a statement through its Republican

Press Bureau that as long as the RUC failed to allow Irishmen to be buried with dignity they could not expect to bury their own dead with dignity.

The threatened revenge for the killing of Marley took place some three days later. Frenchie Merchant, a long-time member of the Shankill UVF, was standing in his usual position, outside the UVF's political party offices, when a car containing four men drove slowly up the road. Two Armalite rifles appeared from the windows and before their target could react, they opened fire, riddling him with .223mm bullets. He was dead before his body hit the ground. The car proceeded slowly up the Shankill, its occupants howling with laughter and firing their weapons in the air.

We expected the UVF to hit back for Merchant's murder and worked every hour God sent putting up roadblocks and mobile patrols to prevent a spiral of tit-for-tat killings. Slowly due to our constant pressure and swamping of the area, the tension died down, and both sides of the Crumlin Road subsided into their usual state of sullen watchfulness.

Some three weeks later, on a pleasantly warm, early summer afternoon, I was in a mobile patrol in Ballysillian.

'It's quiet, isn't it?' I murmured to the driver.

He grimaced. 'Don't ever say that. It's bad luck.'

As if to emphasize his words his radio burst into life, directing us to a victim, possibly of a shooting, in a stream near the Tyndale housing estate. As the driver swung his vehicle around and switched on the two-tone siren, he threw me a withering glance.

'Now see what you've done.'

What remained of the victim was lying half in, half out of a small stream. No sectarian murder is pleasant but this was one of the worst. The dead man had not been shot: his head had been crushed with a breeze block. A trail of blood led us back up the small hill to the Tyndale Community Centre, a grandiose name for the squat, single-storey building. Tyndale was probably the worst estate we had in the area. It was a dirty rabbit warren of run-down houses and filth-covered streets. The UVF dominated the Shankill and most of the other satellite estates, but the UDA, still legal at the time, and its sinister killer gangs who called themselves the Ulster Freedom Fighters (UFF), controlled Tyndale. The man in charge of them was known as the 'Window Cleaner'. Tyndale was his own personal fiefdom, and he ruled it with an iron hand.

The Window Cleaner was a man of middle years and medium height, powerfully built. He wore dark-tinted glasses over a squat nose that had been broken more than once. The IRA had tried to kill him with three rounds from a Thomson sub-machine-gun. His survival had only enhanced his reputation. He'd got his nickname early on in the Troubles. Accompanied by an accomplice carrying a ladder, he had gone to the homes of isolated Catholics, placed the ladder against the bedroom window, climbed up and gently knocked. When the unsuspecting victim had gone to investigate, he had been shot at close range. Special Branch believed he had killed twenty-one men using this well-tested technique.

I got my first view of him as I crested the hill. He was sitting on a wall, watching our every movement. The dead man was, inevitably, a Catholic, a middle-aged pigeon-fancier. He had driven a friend home and been invited up to the Community Centre for a drink. Once his religion was discovered, his fate was sealed. What possessed a Catholic to go into Tyndale at all, let alone the Community Centre, I'll never know. His death had been particularly brutal. He'd been beaten until he was unconscious, then dragged down to the stream and bludgeoned to death. The depravity and senselessness of it all touched something raw deep down inside me. I was having to deal with such random acts of violence on an almost daily basis, and it hurt.

My old friend Bob T was over on a year's attachment as second in command of the SAS detachment in Ulster. On Friday 8 May we had arranged to go out for a drink but by 6 p.m. I still hadn't heard from him. At 6.30 I knew why. He was at a little police station in County Armagh called Loughgall.

The operation in which the SAS smashed two complete ASU's of the East Tyrone Brigade of the PIRA was the most stunning success achieved against the IRA since the start of the campaign. They were led by a sergeant-major from B Squadron, with Bob T as second in command. It had been mounted on pure intelligence (information supplied by our own forces on the ground) not 'source' information. One of the terrorists killed was in fact a long-time Special Branch source, Michael Anthony Gormley, whose nickname within the Special Forces was the 'Banker' because he was reputed to have been paid more than £80,000 for information over the preceding years. He'd been selling out his comrades and double-dealing Special Branch by taking part in operations to kill members of the security forces to protect himself from detection by his fellow IRA men. He'd not warned his handler about Loughgall, which had led many to believe the operation was not going to be mounted. Among the IRA dead was James Lynagh, the IRA assassin the SAS had hunted for so long. The operation was a tremendous fillip to morale within the security forces in general, and the RUC in particular. At last, we believed the war was being taken to the enemy. It also had the effect of soothing Loyalist nerves, still strained about the Anglo–Irish Agreement. I only hoped it would last.

On the ground I had my own success. On the Shankill no vehicle could deliver spirits or beer without the risk of being hijacked. The alcohol would disappear into the cellars of many illegal drinking clubs run by the paramilitaries. I was baby-sitting one such delivery when a general call went out about a vehicle in the area. The controller had no sooner finished his all-points warning when it came right round the corner. I jumped from my police car in front of it.

The two men inside it looked frightened, with good reason. Between the front seats were two files, crammed with photographs of IRA and Sinn Fein members. The men were on their way to target a Republican working on a city centre building site. My action probably saved his life. The UDA men later faced a multitude of terrorist charges, including fire-bombing stores in Dublin. They were convicted and sentenced to long periods of imprisonment. The chief inspector in charge of the operations congratulated me on the arrest, and that meant a great deal to me.

Stolen cars were a menace. Hardly a night shift went by without us being involved in a car chase with joyriders, a term the RUC refused to use officially. The problem had become so endemic that the force had set up a Province-wide stolen car squad. A senior officer of the squad appeared on a television interview during which he was asked which make of car was the easiest to steal. Without hesitation he named it. There was an immediate outcry from the makers, who publicly challenged the RUC to explain their statement or publish a retraction. The car squad offered to prove it was so.

A demonstration was set up in Musgrave Street RUC station. The company in question supplied its latest top-of-the-range model, with thief-resistant locks. That morning, just around the corner in Belfast Magistrate Court, a young joyrider, well known to the squad, was due in front of the magistrates, facing charges of 120 cases of 'taking and driving away'. He was from west Belfast, and had been stealing cars since he was twelve. The squad asked him to do them a favour, in return for which they would put in a good word with the magistrate.

'What do you want me to do?'

'Break into a car.'

At Musgrave Street the company's Ulster management, security expert and head of European sales waited. In walked the two members of the squad. Between them, dressed in faded demin jeans and a torn leather jacket, swaggered their 'expert', all five foot two inches of him. When he saw the car his eyes lit up with anticipation. He was asked if he needed any special tools. He shook his head, 'Naw, just a screwdriver.'

The car's locks were supposed to delay a thief for five minutes. The Belfast boy was inside and had it started in less than twenty seconds. The company's security expert was appalled.

'Those locks are triple-lever locks,' he pointed out.

'Yes,' the car thief acknowledged, studying the tip of his screwdriver. 'I thought it was a bit stiff.'

By now even I was beginning to feel the strain. The long hours of police work and the gut-twisting tension took a terrible toll. Many officers drank to excess, and one member of my station used to turn up drunk regularly. He was a decorated hero and had been a fine policeman. It was terrible watching him slowly unravel. Heavy drinking and firearms is always a very unstable cocktail. Suicides from gunshot wounds were a tragically common affair. Two members of my own depot squad, the RUC recruits I had gone through training with, died by their own hand, and so did a member of Tennant Street. If they'd had to throw a rope over a beam, or go into a garage and start a car, they might have had time to think again, but their gun was always close and so easy to use. Just one squeeze of the trigger and all the pain was gone. The RUC set up an operation health unit to try to deal with the situation, but it was still a serious problem when I left the force.

Late on a Saturday night I was part of a road stop outside a notorious Loyalist bar on the Shankill Road. While standing just inside an alley with an old reserve police constable for company, I saw a door at the end of the alley open and a figure start to lumber down the dark tunnel towards me. It was Billy Dixon. I felt a stab of fear as I saw the monster recognize me. I had two options: to retreat to the comparative safety offered by my fellow officers, or stand my ground. I stood my ground and pulled my Ruger revolver for the first time in my police career. Whether Dixon was going to start something or not, I don't know. I didn't give him a chance. When he was within arm's reach I pushed the nasty little magnum revolver under his chin and pulled the hammer back on to single action. His eyes widened. He knew enough about guns to know that the slightest pressure would set it off.

'Walk round me, Dixon,' I said softly.

Like two people engaged in a macabre dance, we edged round each other in the semi-darkness. Dixon threw me a look of hatred and continued on up the road. I let out a long-held breath and reholstered my weapon.

'Would you have shot him?' my companion asked.

I shrugged. 'What do you think?'

'I think you would have shot him.'

'So did he.'

A week later I was on a course to be assessed for the RUC's E4A Department. E Department is responsible for intelligence gathering, and among its sub-departments is E4A, specializing in human covert surveillance. I've always been an avid news listener, trying to catch the BBC's 7 O'clock News broadcast whenever I can. The third item that morning was of particular interest. A man had been shot to death in north Belfast while working on his car. He'd been named as Billy Dixon. I doubt whether my companions could understand my sudden whoop of joy, particularly since I'd failed the course, because of my erratic driving.

8

THE RUC II

'We're all so proud of you.'
Prime Minister Margaret Thatcher to author,
Carrickmore, County Tyrone, 1989

Nineteen eighty-eight opened with two events which altered my life considerably. I had been studying for the RUC sergeant's exam for over a year. Passing it, and thereby qualifying for promotion, made me believe that academically I could achieve anything. The second was that Julie walked out on me. It was completely unexpected. She left two days before my exam, saying she needed some time on her own. In retrospect, I can hardly blame her. I had been so wrapped up in my work I had completely neglected my home life. Love is like a shiny ornament, but to keep it bright you have to care for it and I had forgotten to.

There is no easy path to reconciliation. If you chase a woman, you chase her away, and lose your self-respect in the process. If you ignore her, she thinks you don't care. I handled it worse than most. I'd never really been in love until I met Julie, who was just twenty-one. Our love had exploded like an atomic explosion from the first moment we met. In the years we were together she'd been my lover, wife and best friend. Taking her from the security of her friends and family to Northern Ireland had been a tragic mistake.

Thinking back, it would have been best for both of us if I'd simply recognized that what we had was over and let her go. It would take me nearly two years to come to terms with the loneliness and rejection I felt. The only solace I had was my work and I threw myself into it, working every hour I could whether I was getting paid or not.

The month after I had passed the sergeant's exam, I sat next to Seamus L in the station canteen. He was reading up on the gaming laws.

'What's up, skipper, going to sit the inspector's exam?'

'No, every station in Belfast has been told to crack down on illegal gaming. The paramilitaries are making a fortune out of the machines they have. I've been told to brush up on the law and mount an investigation.'

'I studied the gaming laws for the sergeant's exam. What do you want to know?'

For the next ten minutes I lectured my sergeant on the complexities of the Northern Ireland Gaming Act. Seamus stared at me.

'You should be doing this. You know the law by heart.'

'I'll do it if they let me.'

'I'll have to clear it with the superintendent. Be back in five minutes.'

Seamus was as good as his word. He was back in three. 'You're elected. Mount your investigation.'

For the next six months, I had complete autonomy and could draw on the full resources of my section. The paramilitaries had machines everywhere: video stores, newsagents, snooker halls. They were using fun machines, designed strictly for amusement. When a customer gained enough points, he was paid out in cash from behind the desk. I sent plain-clothes officers into the various establishments armed with bags full of ten and fifty-pence coins and from them I learned exactly where the incriminating books were held. At the end of my investigation, I launched a series of raids, in conjunction with C13, the anti-racketeering squad. I netted five machines, each with a turnover of at least £20,000 per year – £100,000 in total out of the UDA's pocket. That took me right off their Christmas-card list.

March 1988 was a momentous and bloody month in Ulster's troubled history. It started in Gibraltar. Three IRA volunteers, on a murder mission, Mairead Farrell, Danny McCann and Sean Savage, were shot to death by B Squadron's anti-terrorist team. Control was only handed over to the SAS, a member of the team told me, when Farrell paused on her way back across the Spanish border and put her hand inside her handbag. It was believed by everybody that she was priming a bomb left in a parked car.

Regardless of what any investigative reporter says, both MI5, who were trailing the trio, and the SAS believed that the car left by the terrorists contained a bomb.

In Tennant Street we had a party. McCann, in particular, was a man we would not mourn. He was an expert pistol shot and specialist close quarter assassin who'd killed many an off-duty police officer.

But things had only just begun. At the funeral of the terrorist a rogue UDA hit man, Michael Stone, attacked the mourners, killing three of them. The effect on Republican areas was traumatic. Funerals play a big part in the Irish psyche, perhaps even more so in Republican circles. On the night after the shooting in Milltown cemetery, we were up to our necks in rioters and petrol bombs and our orders were to simply contain and not arrest. Fortunately the initial riots died down and not too many of us had been injured. We had been getting stoned and petrol-bombed all night and in the early hours of the morning, my driver spotted one of the stone-throwers making his way home. He called him to the door of our vehicle.

'You're one of the bastards that have been stoning us all night.'

'No, I'm not.' The youth's denial was unconvincing.

'Yes, you are.' Without any warning the driver head-butted him. 'Get yourself home,' he shouted as the youth staggered away.

We drove on in silence. It was broken by the driver.

'I wish I hadn't done that.'

Ah! Remorse, I thought.

I was wrong. He pulled the vehicle over to the side of the road.

'I've got stars in front of my eyes. Can't see a damn thing.'

As the next IRA funeral approached, something close to hysteria swept threw the Catholic areas of Belfast. The RUC were adopting a low profile in allowing the IRA to police their own funerals. It was a policy that was to go tragically wrong.

As the IRA cortège made its way through west Belfast, a car suddenly drove between the mourners. Soon it was surrounded by a frenzied mob. A shot was fired, the mob jumped back for a second then set about the car with renewed fury. In the end, two men were taken out and shot dead. They were Corporals Derek Wood and Robert Howes.

I was at home watching the event on television and my first thought was that it was our men in the car. I rang the SAS Belfast HQ and spoke to a friend of mine who confirmed that the men in the car were not SAS or Det. Everybody believed it was another Protestant paramilitary attack that had gone wrong.

My phone didn't stop ringing all afternoon as friends called me from all over Ulster and the UK to make sure they weren't SAS. The disgust everybody felt about the way the two men had been killed was evident. Many who spoke to me that day had tears in their voice. Much has been written about these deaths. Some investigative writers claiming unnamed sources have tried to suggest that they were members of an ultra-secret special force unit known as FRU. Such claims are balderdash. The two men were signallers, plain and simple.

Their reactions show they had no special forces training, and the limited armaments they were carrying – two pistols, with twelve-round mags – is also testimony that they were not SAS or any other secret unit. When they were surprised and drove into the crowd, they were more scared of damaging their car than getting out of the situation. When they opened fire it was only with a single shot and even then it was too late to do any good. An SAS team would have tried to ram their way through and would have opened fire a lot sooner. The IRA men in the crowd might still have got to them but they would have had to climb over an awful lot of bodies to do so. Why were they there? Nobody really knows, but the best guess is that they were simply on a swan. Perhaps they were engaged in a hand-over. One had only just arrived from the UK. Maybe the old hand was showing his replacement round west Belfast; a bit of bravado that cost them both their lives.

On the ground the reaction was one of revulsion. One old lady stopped me in the Ardoyne. 'Son, I thought we couldn't sink any lower until I saw what they did to those two wee boys yesterday.' There were tears in her eyes. 'It's terrible, simply terrible.'

It was the first time I had ever heard anybody in a Republican area express sympathy over the death of a soldier.

The RUC decided to prosecute everybody who had taken part. In what has become a textbook example of how to investigate an outbreak of mob violence, a video was made from various recordings of the incident. It was sent to every station in Northern Ireland and gradually every person on the video was recognized, arrested and prosecuted.

One of the leading IRA figures in the Ardoyne, 'Cleaky' Clarke, the man who had thrown his arms around Corporal Woods as he had tried desperately to escape, was among those arrested. When he opened his door to find us waiting outside he said simply: 'I've been expecting you.'

In April I was attached to Tennant Street CID for six months. I was no sooner in plain clothes than a major murder investigation was launched in Tyndale. It had all started with a drinking session in one of the local bars – most of the Tyndale UDA were there. The Window Cleaner was drunk. He had a volatile temper at the best of times and combining it with drink was like mixing nitrogen and glycerine. For reasons nobody could identify he attacked the father of his own second in command and when the UDA man tried to intervene to prevent the old man being beaten to death, the Window Cleaner turned on him. The attack was so savage the man was unconscious in seconds. But it didn't end there. The Window Cleaner dragged the still body of his lieutenant outside, went to a nearby building site and returned with a breeze block. He dropped it on the man's head, killing him instantly.

When we arrived shortly afterwards I could barely tell that the body had once belonged to a human being. Within seconds we were told who had committed the crime. The normally close-mouthed community was stunned at the senseless brutality and the murder of one of their own. We dispatched a uniformed patrol to the Window Cleaner's house. They found him burning his clothes and arrested him. It looked like one of the worst killers in north Belfast had finally overstepped the mark; we had four witnesses willing to give us a statement, including the bar owner. The Window Cleaner was charged and remanded in custody.

When the suspect is a member of a paramilitary organization, we would normally expect some intimidation of the witnesses but Special Branch believed that the UDA would not back the Window Cleaner on this one. It came as something of a surprise when the first witness turned up at the station to withdraw his statement. The Window Cleaner's friends in Tyndale had not deserted him, no matter what the rest of the organization wanted.

One by one the witnesses retracted their statements, until only the bar owner was left. He was given round-the-clock protection, and I was part of the team that looked after his wife and young family. A handwritten note was delivered one morning. It listed where his wife worked, where she shopped and where his kids went to school. It ended: 'need we say more. Retract your statement.'

The barman retracted and a week later the Window Cleaner, a man who had murdered one man and left another brain-damaged in a crowded bar, walked free. I felt my stomach turn over with revulsion when I saw him once again on the streets of Tyndale. However, he did not stay in the area long. Rumours were about that friends of the dead man were bent on revenge. The Window Cleaner left the Province for England, where, I believe, he still lives.

Shortly after his departure we had yet another murder in the Tyndale Community Centre. This time the victim was a Protestant woman. Nobody could say exactly why she had been killed. She'd been drinking heavily and there were suggestions that she was believed to be a police informer. Whatever the reason, she was dragged outside and bludgeoned to death with a breeze block. This time we were able to identify her killers and arrest them. CID investigations of this kind follow a set pattern; even though the force was facing an unprecedented terrorist onslaught, crimes were solved by painstaking, routine legwork and good police work.

House by house, door by door the neighbourhood was combed. It was soul-destroying as many refused to answer questions and others were openly hostile. But, even in Tyndale, there were those who, although not prepared to give a statement, would tell us who'd been in the club that afternoon. The fact that the dead woman was a Protestant also helped to loosen a few tongues. Our own knowledge and intelligence, gleaned from frequent siting reports around the club over many years, also helped to identify possible suspects. Gradually a list was drawn up of who had been there that day.

Every person who was identified was questioned. Many were arrested and taken to Castlereagh holding centre, where all major murder investigations took place. Hours of questioning resulted in isolating a group who were drinking with the dead woman. After that it was only a matter of time before each one started to blame the other for the murder. This had been a spontaneous, drunken act of violence, rather than a planned sectarian killing. None of the participants had prepared an alibi and forensics could link many of them to the murder scene. The saddest part of the whole affair was that nobody could say with any certainty why they had decided to kill the woman.

The killing was the last straw for the Community Centre. There had been four murders connected to it in less than a year. We got a court order and demolished the place.

The IRA in the Ardoyne were once again causing trouble. There had been several shooting incidents against the security forces. The most active IRA man in the area was the Butcher, the man who'd wanted to kill the captured TA man eighteen months earlier. An anti-robbery/burglary patrol was driving up the Crumlin Road towards Tennant Street when they noticed a group of men acting suspiciously in Rosemount Street. Turning into the street, they saw the men were armed. They called for backup, which wasn't easy as they only had a hand-held radio and couldn't lift it to their mouths because the gunmen were only feet away. No planned operation could have worked better. Two RUC vehicles swept in from opposite directions, trapping the gunmen between them. I was on duty as unattached personnel – those who were only attached to the CID and not full-time members of the squad – pulled a lot of night-work. Behind a wall I found an over-and-under sawn-off shotgun and a home-made sub-machine-gun. By amazing good fortune we had trapped a UVF hit team. Later they confessed that their intended target was to be the Butcher.

Even though he was an IRA killer, the Butcher had to be warned that he was under threat. We were to mount an operation to go into the Ardoyne and inform him the next day. I happened to look out of the window. The man himself was getting out of an armoured police vehicle below me. He'd been picked up in west Belfast, suspected of targeting RUC stations for terrorist attacks. It was the greatest irony of them all.

On 1 July the Butcher launched an operation in north Belfast on North Queen Street RUC station. A small SAS team were waiting, but owing to several bad planning mistakes the ambush was unsuccessful. An innocent passer-by was killed in the crossfire. The Butcher escaped, but with a deep bullet crease in his side courtesy of the Regiment, to remind him how close he'd come. He's now on the run in the Irish Republic, but still very active and one of the SAS's major targets.

Although my work was going well, I was still feeling the loss of my second wife. Then something happened in Tennant Street that allowed me to see life in a different way. It started simply enough. A mother and her sixteen-year-old daughter came into the station to complain that the daughter had been assaulted on her way home from school. She had been quite badly beaten and had a cracked lip and black eye.

She told her story in a faltering voice, pausing occasionally to gather her thoughts. My instincts told me there was more to this than simple bullying. I tried to press her but every time she threw a frightened glance at her mother and clammed up. I asked her mother to get us all some tea. Alone I tried again.

'What really happened?'

Tears started to well in her eyes. I tried again, speaking softly.

'Is it something you don't want your mother to know?'

She nodded, still crying. I couldn't handle this. It was a job for a trained policewoman. I stood to leave, telling her that a female officer would conduct the rest of the interview. She looked up at me, a face like an angel's, tears streaming. It all came out in a rush: the assault, the rape, the hurt. I knelt beside her and told her it wasn't her fault. All the pain I had suffered in my life seemed like nothing compared with what this poor child was going through. Her mother returned and I met her at the door.

'Talk to your daughter. She has something to tell and please, be gentle.'

I left them alone while I fetched a policewoman. Such cases were handled by a special RUC squad.

I don't think I ever quite looked at things the same way again. Seeing that ravaged innocence, feeling that pain, made me face some of my own demons, face them with a strength I didn't know I had.

During my stay with CID, I had formed a good friendship with a long-time CID man, Nigel K. A huge man, he must have weighed close to twenty stone. His very presence in an interview room was intimidating. A mobile uniformed patrol, responding to a call about intruders in a house in Ballysillian, found two men hiding under the stairs. One of them was a long-time UVF thug about whom we had enquiries from other stations in connection with a string of robberies. We had absolutely nothing on the other man. Nigel and I conducted his interview.

The man's story was simple, if tragic. He had been drinking in a local pub, when the UVF man, whom he knew casually, suggested that he could 'earn a little extra money' with him on a job. The next thing he knew he was helping him break into a house. Nigel didn't believe a word of it and suggested that he was in fact a professional burglar. The man denied this. Nigel put him through a verbal wringer for at least two hours, offering him the chance to unburden himself by telling about the rest of his burglaries and getting them TIC (taken into consideration) at his trial. The man stuck stubbornly to his story. We took a break outside the interview room.

'I think he's telling the truth,' Nigel said. 'You get a statement and finish up the investigation. It's pretty straightforward.'

Both elected for trial at Belfast Magistrates Court, and three weeks later, just before the end of my CID attachment, I attended the court as investigating officer. I went down to the cells to speak to our man before he appeared in the dock. As I turned to leave he caught my arm.

'Will you speak up for me in court?'

His face was anxious, strained. He looked like he was pleading for his life.

'Why should I?'

'Look. I've never done anything like this before, and I won't do anything like it again. I'm trying to get out of the area by swapping my flat with my sister, who lives in the south of the city. If I go to prison, I won't be able to get the house swap. I'll be stuck there.'

I considered what he had said, studying his face.

'Do you know who I am?'

'I know you're a tight man. Everybody says you're a man not to be crossed.'

'If I speak up for you, you'd better get out of the area. Also, if I find that you've got arrested again, for anything, I'll make it my mission in life to make sure you get the maximum sentence possible. Do you understand?'

He nodded.

'OK, I'll speak up for you.'

'You won't let me down.'

'You have my word, that should be good enough.'

In the court the man's lawyer was running the defence that his client was drunk on the night. It was no defence at all. The magistrate was unimpressed and said so.

'The public have a right to have their property defended. I see no defence here at all and I think that . . .'

I tugged the defence solicitor's arm.

'Could I speak with the magistrate?'

I was sworn in. I turned to address the magistrate.

'It is true that the defendant was drunk on the night in question but there are other matters I think should be drawn to the Court's attention. From my investigations, I am sure that the man was acting under the influence of people who want to drag him into their world of crime and thuggery. The defendant knows this. He is trying to get away from their influence by swapping his flat and moving to another area. Your Worship, I know I'm not supposed to give an opinion as a police officer but with your permission I'd like to.'

The magistrate nodded slowly.

'If the defendant stays in this area, he will eventually come under the influence of these men and come before this Court on far more serious charges than those he faces at present. That is not in my interest as a police officer, nor, I venture to add, this Court's.'

There was absolute silence in the Court. The magistrate turned to the defence lawyer. 'Now why didn't you say that?'

The courtroom burst into laughter.

The defendant was remanded for probation reports. I made my way out of the Court. The defence solicitor caught up with me in the hall.

'That was a fine thing you did in there. Many a police officer would have thrown him to the wolves, considering the company he was arrested with.'

'Everybody needs a chance.'

Nearing the main door, I felt a tug on my arm. I turned. A

young girl, barely eighteen, stood at my elbow. For a second my heart stopped. I thought it was the same girl who had come into the station to report her rape. I looked at her enquiringly.

'I'm his sister. I've just been on the phone to my mummy. She asked me to thank you for what you did.'

I nodded and walked outside. It was a bright, sunny morning. I lit a cigar and inhaled deeply. I've had good days and wonderful days, days when I felt my heart swell with pride, but that day I remember better than most.

A week later I was back in uniform. We had a call to a hit-and-run accident on the Crumlin Road, just opposite the prison. When we arrived, we found an abandoned car and several wrecked vehicles. It looked like some drunk driver had lost control, smashed into the parked cars and run off to avoid arrest. I was 'gunner', armed with an M1 Carbine to protect the driver and observer, a newly arrived probationer. While the driver parked we set about sealing off the road so that he could carry out his investigation.

I heard a shout from a sentry-box in the front of the prison. 'The man who was driving the car just ran down that side-street.' A hand pointed towards the lower Shankill. 'He's just under five feet eight inches tall, blond hair, wearing a white T-shirt.'

I shouted my thanks, handed my rifle over to the driver for safe keeping and ran down the street to look for him. Stepping off the Crumlin Road into the dimly lit side-streets that surround it is a dangerous thing for any lone man, even a police officer, and perhaps I should have known better. I rounded the corner at the bottom and found my suspect; he fitted the description to the letter. There was only one problem: he was standing in the middle of a group of about twenty youths, asking for their help. They turned towards me as one.

I didn't even have a radio to call for backup. I had two choices: retreat or advance. I walked swiftly into the midst of the group and put my hand on the man in the white T-shirt.

'You're under arrest for reckless driving.'

I turned him fast and began to frogmarch him back towards the main road, thankful for the weight training I'd done over the years. The swiftness of my actions had taken the group by surprise. They trailed along behind me like a pack of wolves, hungry but wary.

If I could just get him back on to the Crumlin Road, I would get support from my other two officers and the sentries in the prison. Everything was going great, I had about seventy metres to go. Then my suspect began to complain. 'You've got no evidence to arrest me.'

'Yes I have!' Sixty-five metres to go.

'You can't arrest him without evidence!' a tall youth of about twenty shouted. His companions murmured their assent. They were in the centre of the narrow street, walking abreast of me on the pavement. They were getting bolder, inching towards me.

'Stay out of this. It's police business.' Fifty metres to go. I glanced towards the well-lit road ahead. My charge took this moment to throw his arms around a lamppost.

I tried to pull him off but he hung on grimly. The group had me surrounded on three sides. Their leader was almost within arm's reach.

'He's on his own,' he said softly.

There was a low growl from his companions. For only the second time in my police career I pulled my revolver.

'I'll shoot the first one who takes a step forward,' I said, keeping both the gun and my eyes fixed on the man who was doing all the talking.

'You won't shoot,' he said, but this time his voice lacked conviction.

'Yes I will.' I swung my gun in a wide arc, forcing them to jump back. The suspect decided the time was right for him to lend a hand, or foot. He began to kick me in the shins. I yelled at the top of my voice for my companions. There was a nasty giggle from the group leader.

'They won't hear that. You're on your own. Let your man go and we'll let you go . . .'

There was a shout from the Crumlin Road. Round the corner came six heavily armed young police officers. It was a DMSU that had stopped to see if they could help. They charged down the street like the Seventh Cavalry. My tormentors scattered, melting into the darkened side-streets. As the leader of the pack rounded the corner he turned and shouted back towards me: 'You were lucky, you black bastard.'

I thanked my rescuers and marched the man back to the crash scene, where I handed him over to the probationer.

'Throw the book at this one. I want him done for everything, drunken driving, assault on a police officer, obstruction, and being born ugly.'

November saw another rise in tension in Protestant areas. Nobody knew the immediate reason but it could all be traced back to the Anglo–Irish Agreement. In Ballysillian the demonstration quickly degenerated into a full-scale riot. The Ardoyne patrol's vehicle, one of the largest and heaviest armoured vehicles we had, was trapped in a side-street. In seconds it was swamped. Rioters clambered all over it. One observer later said it was like the Zulus attacking Rorke's Drift.

As the unit tried to reverse, a rioter slipped from the roof and they drove straight over him. The crowd went berserk. Patrols were removed from the area. The paramilitaries were getting the guns out. I was in the lower Shankill as observer in charge of an armoured mobile patrol. My inspector was out on the ground with us. Our area was quiet, the streets eerie in the silence. The controller came on the air.

'I'm sorry, DT80, a rioter has been run over. Somebody has to find out how badly hurt he is.'

He directed us to the casualty department of the Mater Hospital. The inspector and I found the place in turmoil. Injured from the riot in Ballysillian were pouring in. I managed to get the attention of a passing doctor.

'A rioter has been run over by a police vehicle. Can you tell me how he is?'

'Basically, he's dead.'

I threw a quick glance at the inspector. This meant trouble.

'. . . we're trying resuscitation but, quite frankly, it's hopeless. He'll be pronounced dead within the next few minutes.'

'Have you got a name?'

He shook his head. 'No, but those people over there brought him in.'

Sitting apart from everybody else were three people, a man in his early thirties wearing a leather jacket, and two women of about the same age, both of whom were crying. I took a deep breath and walked over.

'My name's Constable McCallion. Are you related to the man who was injured in the accident in Ballysillian?'

The man looked up at me, his face twisted with grief and anger.

'You black bastards, you've murdered my brother!'

I met his accusing stare without turning away. Slowly I coaxed the dead man's particulars from him. It was one of the hardest things I ever had to do. When I had the information I paused. 'I know this isn't going to mean too much to you and in no way is it any comfort, but for what it's worth I am truly sorry for your loss.'

I got no reply. As we were walking back out, I saw the doctor deliver the news that the injured man was dead. There was a howl of grief. About an hour later I had to deal with a mugging. An old lady of over seventy had had her face smashed almost beyond recognition for the £5 she had in her purse. It was a bad night all round. I didn't sleep very well. My dreams were filled with images of screaming faces, looking accusingly at me. In my dream I tried to help but found myself swamped and sinking.

The next afternoon as I drove into Tennant Street the streets around the station seemed empty. At our briefing we were told, as if we needed to be, that the area was tense. All patrols were doubled in strength. At supper break, two local SB men joined me at my table. After some small talk one of them looked at me and asked: 'You going to be patrolling the lower Shankill tonight?'

I nodded.

'Keep on your toes. The UDA have threatened retaliation for the death of that lad in Ballysillian last night.'

'They're always threatening retaliation.'

Both men gave me a sombre look. 'This time they mean it. We're telling everybody: stay alert.'

As we patrolled the street, I saw that the SB were right. Everybody was indoors. The very walls seemed to be waiting for something to happen.

They set us up well. A small barricade had been placed across a street. As we manoeuvred to get round it, I heard a whoosh.

'What the hell is tha . . .' I began to say.

They opened up on us from close range with at least two weapons. There were three of us in the back of the vehicle. The constable nearest the door threw himself on the floor. Just for a second, I was back in the SAS. I lunged for the door to get to my attackers, tripping over the supine figure of my fellow police officer and banging my head on the door. Cursing, I tried to get it opened. It was locked. People were screaming at me not to open the door; I was oblivious, all I wanted to do was get at the gunmen outside. The driver put his foot down and we were out of it and back on the main Shankill Road. I sat down dejectedly.

Back at Tennant Street we surveyed the damage to the vehicle. In all twenty-three shots had hit us and only the armoured plating had prevented death or injury. We made statements about the attack and all of us forgot about the whooshing noise we had heard shortly before the gunmen opened up. The next day CID arrested a local UDA volunteer, Samuel Hinton, in connection with the ambush. He had fired a flare at our vehicle and I knew then what that noise had been.

At the UDA man's trial, I was the only police officer willing to say that I had actually heard the sound of the flare being fired at us. This was of great importance as Hinton's only part in the ambush was the firing of the flare: the shooting had been carried out by two other UDA men as yet not apprehended. Without my testimony, there was little to prove it had been fired. I was cross-examined for nearly half an hour by the defence barrister, about why I had not written down the information in the immediate aftermath of the ambush. I stuck to the truth. The judge was convinced. Hinton got twelve years.

Two days later a top UDA man was brought into the station, for what I didn't know. I was SDO (Station Duty Officer) and was taking the opportunity to complete some files. The UDA man came to the front desk to be released. I looked at him with thinly disguised disgust.

'You people make me sick, do you know that? You're out rioting. Two days ago you shot up my police vehicle . . .' A thin smile played across his lips.

'. . . and while you're doing that, this little old lady was beaten half to death for a few pounds in her purse.' I showed him the photograph and the smile left his face.

'This is your community and you let this happen to a defenceless old woman. Like I say, you make me sick.'

Unforgivable behaviour on my part. I think the job was starting to get to me. About a week later, a local thug was found, shot in both elbows and legs. Around his neck was a handwritten sign saying: 'Mugger of old ladies.'

I decided I needed a break from the city. I was dog-tired; the shift work and the extra hours were having their effect on me. I wasn't sleeping well when I was off duty and was suffering chronic indigestion all the time from rushed meals and nervous tension. I asked for a transfer to one of the border stations and was offered Carrickmore in County Tyrone. I accepted.

The previous August, the SAS had ambushed a three-man IRA ASU just outside the town. A man had pretended to be an off-duty UDR man whose vehicle had broken down. When the IRA men turned up to kill what they thought was a helpless victim, they found they were the prey and not the hunters. At the end of a sustained burst of fire Gerald and Martin Harte and Brian Mullin, all leading members of the Tyrone PIRA, were dead. The shooting had taken the wind out of the local IRA and they had been stood down until an internal inquiry was carried out into how the SAS had set them up. I was interested to see what the Carrickmore PIRA would do about this setback.

The town of Carrickmore is situated on a high hill, known locally as the Rock. The RUC station had been built in response to Protestant political anger after the IRA had taken over the town in a publicity stunt in the late seventies. Over twenty uniformed and armed IRA men had set up roadblocks and it even has its own Republican garden of remembrance. There were only two Protestant families in the town and no shopkeepers would serve the RUC or any member of the security forces. Being there made you feel you belonged to an army of occupation, not a police force.

Even so, the routine was much more relaxed, almost restful. We spent three days on duty. We had to be helicoptered in as the roads were too dangerous to travel on. There was very little crime, so paperwork was minimal. It was a little like a holiday, except that outside the safety of the camp, hostile natives continually watched us with thinly disguised contempt. That apart, the days drifted into each other and I quickly became accustomed to the area and its inhabitants. I was able to put faces to a lot of names, in particular a very active IRA man called Baldy Quinn. He had shaved his head to claim compensation. He vowed the loss was due to his treatment by the RUC after being detained by them. The town of Cappagh was within our patrol area, and it was as nasty a nest of violent Republicans as you could hope to avoid.

Our section sergeant was Derek V, who had a relaxed, easy way of running things that made him a pleasure to work with. Among my colleagues was Con L, whose knowledge of the area was almost encyclopedic. He could tell you the names and history of every person in the area, even what colour the curtains were in their houses. The section comedian was Kenny A. Once, when I was having a heated argument with another section member, he turned to my adversary and said: 'Why don't you hit him? There's enough of us to hold him back and you'll look like a big man.'

In early 1989 we had the local government elections. The exercise of democracy takes an unusual turn in Ulster. My section had to guard the polling station in Sixmiletown. Inside the main voting room, all major candidates had a representative, including such deadly enemies as the Democratic Unionist Party and Sinn Fein. One of the Unionist candidates, a local farmer, had a brother, a sergeant in the RUC, who was murdered on his way to visit him. We knew who had killed the police officer and so did he. Three men walked in and stood around the Sinn Fein man. I saw the Unionist candidate's eyes harden. Two of the three were believed to have been responsible for his brother's death. Their conversation finished, the two men looked over at the farmer and smiled. The farmer looked at me, pain and anger etched in every line of his face. I looked away, helpless.

Our Divisional Headquarters was Omagh RUC station. On 6 February a Reserve Constable stationed there had a lucky escape when a terrorist who was trying to plant a bomb under his car was blown up when it prematurely detonated. The explosion ripped away half the man's face but he still had the energy to yell at the ambulance man: 'Keep those black bastards away from me.'

An RUC patrol arrived and the Reserve Constable's shock was compounded when they told him the identity of his attacker. His name was James Connolly, a youth who not only worked at the same firm but whom he'd often given a lift to work. The reservist had even shared his food with him.

Easter was one of the most important dates in the Republican calendar, and Carrickmore was the centre of the Republican commemoration. Inside the garden of remembrance, some three to four hundred were gathered. Facing them were three rows of hard-faced RUC men. Over five hundred police were drafted in annually to deal with the crowds, mainly because the authorities feared a paramilitary show of strength if they didn't parade in force. The area's leading IRA men were there, Baldy Quinn and his ASU from Cappagh, plus our own local bad boys.

A big, nasty-looking individual turned to glare at me as he walked past. I smiled back, and for a second I saw a look of almost total madness cross his face, then he carried on. Stokes gave me a nudge.

'Do you know who that is?'

'No.'

'Desi Grew.'

I looked after the tall, brooding monster.

'Are you sure? I thought he was still inside.'

'He got paroled a month ago.'

'Evil-looking bastard, isn't he?'

'Aye, and he's left the INLA to rejoin the PIRA. No police officer in Tyrone or Armagh will be safe until he's back inside.'

The oration by a leading Republican figure was long and rambling, filled with the usual promises of victory and threats of actions to come. The crowd waited for the piper to play the last post. He hadn't arrived. They stirred uneasily. Every organization has some weak links and the Carrickmore PIRA had theirs: a young man who was so stupid they would never trust him to do anything of importance. But he had a trumpet and could play the last post. He approached the OC of the Carrickmore PIRA. In desperation, he was dispatched to get his instrument. The crowd grew silent as the trumpeter began to play. No two notes were the same as he struggled on. A police officer began to giggle. The sound was infectious, and started to spread through our ranks. The senior officer tried to stem it.

'Quiet, show some resp . . .' The trumpeter blew a particularly off-key note and the officer collapsed into laughter, running for the safety of the nearby police car. Our ranks dissolved. In front of us, the hardened killers of the IRA were staring at the bugler, willing him with all their might to stop, for God's sake. As the parade broke up, the intrepid musician passed me. I couldn't resist a comment.

'Well done, son. I've never enjoyed a Republican parade so much. Your playing is a credit to your organization.'

His reply is unprintable.

Our area was also patrolled by both the Army and UDR. An RUC officer had to accompany all UDR patrols and sometimes the Army ones. I had been out with a couple of Army patrols. They were good value, keen as mustard. I could never remember being so young.

I was told to take out my first UDR patrol, whom I met in Lishnasharagh army base and was briefed on their patrol route. They wanted to visit a farm occupied by a well-known IRA activist. That was OK with me. We were landed by helicopter near the vicinity and began to patrol towards it.

The weather was awful: driving rain and high wind. The patrol was in three bricks of four and I was in the centre. As I entered the farmyard I was faced with a scene of terrible intensity. Under a swinging light the IRA suspect stood surrounded by three UDR men with the wind whipping their hair. What they were saying I can only guess. The IRA man saw me enter the farmyard and his eyes closed momentarily as if in a silent prayer of thanks.

The next minute, the yard was filled with sheep. They had been penned up when I arrived. A UDR man next to me said: 'While he's rounding them up he won't be making any bombs.'

Another UDR man stood by a huge funnel-shaped hopper of grain. His hand went to a lever to dump the grain on the floor.

'Stop!'

He froze at my shout. I turned to the senior NCO.

'Tell your men to make a quick search and then get into that wood at the edge of the farm.' I pointed to a nearby copse.

Ten minutes later I had the patrol gathered around me. I was cold and angry. 'I'm in charge of this patrol. You are my responsibility. It's obvious that I haven't made my position clear to you. From now on, if I see another act of mischief I'll personally have the culprit prosecuted for criminal damage, and I'll make it my aim in life to see that every NCO here is busted so far back he'll be saluting bus conductors. Do I make myself clear?'

There was a low mumble.

'I'll take that as a yes. Now let's get on with our job.'

As the patrol commander led us away from the wood it struck me that ten years ago I might have been the one letting out the sheep. I had certainly changed.

The days in the country drifted, each much the same as the last, long hours spent tramping through fields and manning roadblocks. There were small ripples that disturbed the daily routine. I had an ammunition find, a bag of AK47 rounds, in a field. The section relieving us lost a weapon just outside Sixmiletown. It was handed in by a Protestant civilian. Before I knew it a year had passed. I applied to Ulster University to do an HNC in police studies, and was accepted.

Towards the end of 1989 two rumours swept the base. First, the Carrickmore PIRA, long inactive after the SAS had killed three of their men, was once more a threat. The terrorists' own internal security teams had cleared all their major operators of involvement in the setting-up of the ASU, although they still did not know how the SAS had got the information to ambush their men. We could expect some kind of action from them before long. Second, we were going to get a visit from a very important person. Nobody knew who.

On the day of the visit, the Army was out in strength. I was in charge of a patrol but we were told to stay back at the station. All police and military personnel were lined up to meet our still unidentified guest. The helicopter landed as the Secretary of State stepped out. I felt slightly disappointed. Then from behind him stepped the slight figure of Margaret Hilda Thatcher. Despite my misgivings about her signing the Anglo–Irish Agreement, she remained a heroine to me. A woman with more balls than any two men in her Cabinet, with the guts to face down dictators and tyrants, both at home and abroad. As she stood in front of me I was amazed how small she was. I held out my hand.

'This is a great pleasure for me, Prime Minister.'

Her face broke into a warm smile. 'We're all so proud of you.'

I felt ten feet tall. Her visit lasted less than an hour, then she was in the helicopter and away. As it took off one of my colleagues said: 'That went well.'

'For what we are about to receive,' I replied.

'What do you mean?'

I nodded up to the hill overlooking the station. Several of the locals were staring down at us.

'This is one of the heartlands of Republicanism. That lady let ten of their men die on hunger strike. She's number one on their hate list. Do you think they'll let her visit here and not do anything?'

It didn't take long for me to be proved right. We had a cleaner who lived locally, one of the two Protestant families in the area. As the shopkeepers would not serve police officers he would saunter down to us on Sunday mornings, take any orders for papers and so on and then drive back up into the town and get them for us. On the Sunday after Maggie's visit there were at least eight armed IRA men waiting for him at the shop. They put a 200lb bomb in his car, then told him he had five minutes to deliver it. They had his wife and she would be shot if he deviated one inch.

Our cleaner drove the short distance back to the camp at breakneck speed. At the gate he was incoherent: all he kept saying was: 'The wee men are after me, the wee men are after me.'

The gate sentries let him drive into the barracks and park his car directly under the sentry post. We got him into the operations room, but minutes flashed by before we got it out of him that there was a bomb ticking away in his car. Stokes, with complete disregard for his own safety, ran to the sentry and pulled him to the safety of a blast wall. Seconds later the bomb exploded, badly damaging the sentry post, but thankfully injuring nobody. The IRA had told us what they thought of the Prime Minister's visit.

Only two weeks later, I was returning from Ulster University, technically still on duty, driving through the outskirts of Belfast. I decided that things were going OK. I had no doubts I would soon be promoted, and pretty soon I could start studying for the inspector's exam. My career was the most important thing now and as long as I had that, everything else would fall into place. I was approaching a crossroad. The lights were green. I drove across, at about thirty miles an hour. Out of the corner of my eye I caught sight of a car careering towards me. A white car, with a startled grey face in front of the steering wheel. I stamped hard on the brake! My car's tyres screeched like demented cats. But there was no way to avoid the collision. I ducked my head.

A thought flashed through my mind: What a bloody stupid way to go.

My head hit the windscreen, thousands of tiny needles of pain laced into my skull. In the half-remembered second I thought I'd be thrown through the windscreen. I could feel my body going forward, the glass of the windscreen clawing at my face, then my chest hit the steering wheel. There was pain, sharp and fierce. What little air I had left in my lungs was forced out. Strangely I could hear nothing. Not the traffic outside, or even my own scream. Then I was travelling backwards and soft, comfortable blackness engulfed me. I woke up with a white light in my eyes.

'Try not to move,' a soothing voice said beyond the light. 'We think your neck is broken.'

I tried to talk but my tongue felt like it had been rolled up in Velcro and covered in dust.

'Can you move your arms and legs for me?'

I tried. Panic swept through me. I couldn't feel them, let alone move them. A gurgling sound, unrecognizable as my voice, escaped my lips. Someone rinsed out my mouth.

'I can't feel them,' I croaked.

'Don't worry – it's probably just shock. Feeling and movement will come back gradually. Can you tell me your name?'

I told him my name and address and that I was a police officer.

'I guessed that from the revolver in the shoulder holster. Don't worry about your gun. The local police have it.'

That was a relief.

'You've been unconscious, so we can't give you anything for the pain for twenty-four hours, but as soon as we can, we will.'

I wasn't in pain. An hour later it started. It wasn't too bad at first but as the night wore on it became steadily worse. My entire body was in agony, and it was all the worse because I couldn't move. Sleep was impossible. It came to an end with a large injection of pethidine, and blissful unconsciousness. I barely remember the next week as I drifted in and out of drug-induced sleep, counting the minutes and watching the clock between injections and the blessed relief they brought.

From my doctor and the police officers investigating the crash I was able to put together what had happened. It seemed that a little old lady of nearly seventy had stalled her car at the traffic lights. Restarting her car, she forgot that she was still in gear and took her foot off the clutch, so that her car jerked forward over the crossroad, directly into the path of my car. I had not been wearing a seat belt (RUC officers are excused from doing so both on and off duty in case they are ambushed by terrorists and have to get out of their cars in a hurry) and had been thrown forward, my head going through the windscreen, then backwards over the front seat to hit the back window. I had ended up between the front and rear seats. My car was a wreck. So was my body. There was no bone damage, thank God, but the muscles in my back had been torn to shreds.

Three days after the accident the officer in charge of the investigation came to see me. He wanted to avoid prosecuting the old lady if at all possible, for at her age she would be unlikely to get her licence back if she lost it. He wanted to caution her and asked me what my thoughts were. Having her lose her licence would not get me my health back, so I agreed that she should be cautioned only.

Two weeks later I managed to convince the doctor to let me go home. I was still on my own, but I could count on the support of some of my neighbours and friends. I felt like a cripple: I could hardly walk and many times my back would lock, forcing me to lie down wherever I was. Many nights I spent lying on my living room floor, unable to get up the stairs to my bed. The pain was always with me. The painkillers prescribed by my doctor seemed to have little effect, and sleep was only possible with heavy dosages of sleeping tablets. I had gone from running five miles three times a week and spending just about every day in the gym, to being a bed-ridden invalid. I had lost my work, the impetus of my career. The thing that had held me together and given me the motivation to keep going was gone. Despair loomed. I sat in darkened rooms, sometimes drinking heavily, in spite of the fact that I was taking painkillers, pondering life's injustices. My only company was a Dobermann I'd had since he was a pup. I had never been given to self-pity. Whatever cards had been dealt me, I had played them. Any time I had fallen, I had been able to pick myself up. But this was different. For the first time in my life I was facing something I couldn't physically challenge, pain I could not conquer. At times it seemed about to overwhelm me, threatening my very sanity. One night the pain was so intense that neither drink nor painkillers could ease it. My Ruger revolver was next to my hand. I thought how easy it would be to end it all: the pain, the loneliness, everything. My dog padded across and put his huge head on my lap. I picked up the gun and threw it to the other side of the room.

From that moment I started to get better. Salvation, or the start of it, came from a very unusual source. I started to tell myself stories, and after a time I began to write a particular one down. Eventually, the story book took over my life. In time I was starting to write at 9 a.m. and would still be at it at midnight. I began to sleep without the aid of sleeping tablets. For the first time the pain in my back became somehow tolerable.

My friends too were a help. Bill and Ian would call and take me out, as would the only civilian friend I'd made since my arrival in Ulster.

Nineteen-ninety dawned. My condition, although much improved, was still pretty bad. Two incidents in close succession, forced me to rethink my position. A police officer who, like me, had been injured in a car crash and was on crutches, was murdered at his home and I was compromised on a hospital visit. Someone who had access to my personal file and who was connected to a top IRA man recognized me as a police officer. I had never feared an IRA attack until then. I had always believed I was worth any four of them. But, in my present condition, a one-armed midget with a cap gun could have taken me out. I decided to return to Hereford until I recovered.

I was still writing and was able to walk again without a stick. The pain in my back was still there, but I had grown so used to it I could almost ignore it. I didn't really know what the future had in store for me. I doubted that I could go back to the RUC, but my belief in myself had returned.

One of the things I had most enjoyed about being a police officer had been the cut and thrust of court appearances. I decided I would work towards a law degree and ultimately apply for the Bar and become a barrister specializing in criminal law. With this in mind, I took the first small step by enrolling on Wolverhampton University's part-time LL.B course.

Being back in Hereford also allowed me to catch up with the Special Forces. There was a scandal: over a period of two to three years, a number of women all over the United States had been raped in their own homes. The MO had always been the same and all the attacks had shown a high degree of planning and preparation. The intruder was athletic, always wore a hood and seemed to be an expert in methods of entry. One police officer, through painstaking investigation, managed to link all the assaults and, more importantly, put together a detailed description of a car seen near several of the attacks. The car was eventually traced to Marshall B, who had taught the Regiment pistol shooting in 1984, the born-again Christian who had converted one of our own men during his tour of duty. A surveillance operation was set up and the Delta Force NCO, a decorated hero, was caught trying to break into a house where a woman was staying. His erstwhile friends in Delta Force observed that he had a perfect alibi. Because of his religious beliefs we always said he would not be going out drinking and partying but preferred to remain at base reading his Bible.

Apprehended, the man faced over thirty counts of aggravated rape. He was, because of his previous service to the state, held in a relaxed prison regime, until escape equipment was found on him during a snap search. He is now inside a maximum security jail serving several life sentences. One girl who had known him when he was in Hereford voiced all our fears. 'Do you think he was raping girls while he was over here?'

In September I began studying for my law degree. I took to learning like a duck to water, enjoying every minute of it. I felt that I was starting totally afresh, but the past still kept intruding. One evening on my way home I went into a bar for a quiet drink and walked right into a celebration. Several normally stony-faced SAS men were almost dancing with joy. I asked what the occasion was.

'Haven't you heard? We got Desi Grew last night.'

Grew and another IRA man, Martin McCaughey, had been on their way to kill an off-duty RUC man in revenge for the Loughgall shootings. They had been shot by the SAS. McCaughey had survived a shoot-out with a member of 14 Intelligence Company, although a bullet had pierced one of his ears. The Det operator was unscathed despite both local and IRA claims that the two SAS men had been killed in the contact. Grew had once boasted that he would drench Armagh in police blood after his brother was shot dead by the RUC. The reign of the family that had terrorised Armagh and Tyrone for nearly twenty years was over, with two brothers dead and the third serving life. A lot of RUC men could sleep safer in their beds.

I threw myself into my studies, trying hard to understand the complexities of Contract Law, Tort and Trusts. I barely noticed Christmas and New Year. By April 1991 I was revising for my first exams and one night sitting up late, I put on the midnight news. A man had been shot dead in South Down in what was described as a 'clash with the RUC'. I didn't know it at the time but the shooting was to effect me very personally.

I sat my first law exams in June that year, and passed in all subjects. I was still rejoicing when I had a visit in August from a member of the local Special Branch. I was under threat. The IRA had my name and present address and I was advised to move. It had all begun in April with the shooting of the IRA man Colum Marks in South Down. Marks was a professional terrorist, who was believed to have killed four UDR men in Armagh city the previous year. His speciality was the horizontal mortar, a weapon cable of inflicting terrible damage even on an armoured vehicle.

On the night of 10 April a friend of mine from the RUC's E4A Department had been keeping surveillance on a house from which it was believed an attack would be mounted. Just before midnight he saw a figure, sneaking along a hedge carrying what seemed at first to be a heavy bag. A passing car caught the man in its headlights, and he froze, then dropped to the floor. In those few seconds the RUC man realized what the man was carrying: a horizontally fired mortar.

He radioed in and was told to hold his position. A reaction force was sent. Marks bolted towards the E4A man, who called to him to stop. When he didn't he fired a warning shot and when the terrorist still didn't halt he fired a burst of five rounds, hitting him with three. Marks fell, hit in the head, hand and abdomen. He died from internal haemorrhaging, despite the efforts of the RUC men to render first aid.

The E4A man watched him die. Killing has never really affected me. It's what I'd been trained to do from the moment I entered service. For police officers it is a different matter: they have not been through the long hours of training and indoctrination. For a police officer, even in the specialist squads, a death is a much more personal thing, especially when it's close up and you have to confront the consequences of your actions.

Four weeks after the killing of Marks, the E4A man in question lost his personal diary, having left it in a car in the city centre. An act of carelessness, probably caused by the after-effects of the shooting. Nevertheless the book with my name in it ended up in the hands of the PIRA. I decided to move away from Hereford. It was a difficult decision as the town was the nearest thing I had to a home. I applied to Leeds Metropolitan University for a place on their full-time law degree course and moved north in time for the new year.

My health was slowly improving. I could walk again without limping and had stopped taking painkillers. On 23 May 1992 I was formally discharged from the RUC on medical grounds with an exemplary conduct record. I wrote to the chief constable to express my sorrow at having to leave the force prematurely. I ended the letter with these words: 'In a time when it is fashionable to criticise the police, your officers display a courage and integrity that is an example to everyone. It has been my honour and privilege to serve with you.'

The RUC had been extremely good for me. During my service I'd had experience of dealing with people, and knowing their suffering, without which I doubt that I would have been able to surmount the flaws in my own character. The quiet courage of the rank and file I served with was also inspirational. They were not specialists, hand-picked and selected, yet each man in his own way, by doing the roughest police job in the country without fear or favour, displayed an individual bravery that at times was awesome to behold. Unassuming men, who do a thankless task, in a troubled land.

After my exams, in June 1992, I had a call from an old friend, now in the security business. There was a job on in London. Was I available? I was hardly fit, but that did not matter: my expertise could be put to good use in the operations room. I agreed to go down. It was an excellent four weeks, almost like a B Squadron reunion. I caught up with all the gossip and learnt of the recent deaths of two members of the Squadron. Ivan, an ex-member of Mountain Troop B Squadron, was with both men shortly before they died. He and Paul Hill had been on a training team in South-East Asia at the time.

Paul Hill was the ex-paratrooper who had joined us shortly before the aborted raid on Argentina. He was on R&R and died in a hotel room, from a heart attack induced by a drug overdose. To this day nobody knows for sure what happened. Many believe he was murdered as several tourists had been killed by drugs administered by women and then robbed of all their belongings. Certainly Paul's close friends believe that is what happened to him. Another explanation is that he was taking steroids to enhance his weightlifting. From what I've been told, as he was last seen in the company of two dubious women who vanished after his death, there is at least some credence to the murder story. In all probability we will never know. What is certain is that because of the secrecy of the mission he was on, there was never a full investigation.

Big Joe Farragher's death was surrounded with even more mystery. Joe had been one of the members of B Squadron who had started 14 Intelligence Company – a man of immense physical strength and courage. Once, after a mine explosion in Oman, he had helped evacuate the wounded and then gone back on patrol. Three days later he had asked the doctor to look at his arm. It was broken in two places. In Ulster he had been working in west Belfast, alone and on foot. The car that was supposed to pick him up was delayed, with the result that Joe had to stand for half an hour at 'Highjack Corner' in the Falls Road. The local IRA had become suspicious, but he had looked so ferocious no one had dared go up and challenge him.

Joe was the staff sergeant in charge of Mountain Troop and died on a climbing exercise in Botswana, but the story really begins many years earlier, when the first white explorers were pushing into the heart of the country. The area is dominated by three rounded mountains, worshipped as gods by the local Bushmen. All animal life in the vicinity of these mountains is held sacred. Anyone who killed one would be doomed to die himself by the spirit of the mountains. The first white expedition into the country had asked permission to climb the mountains. They had been granted it, with the proviso that they observe the local taboo on hunting. This they had promised.

Unbeknown to the expedition leader, a separate column of his men had been hunting in the area, right up to the foot of the mountains. They started their climb the following day. There was an horrendous accident in which two climbers were killed. The expedition members buried them in a cave on the mountain, and with them a bottle containing a prayer seeking the forgiveness of the gods of the mountain.

In 1986 B Squadron were on exercise in the same area. Ivan, one of the very best mountain climbers in the Regiment, told me he'd climbed the smallest of the hills the day before Joe died. According to him, it was an eerie experience. He felt as if some malign force was trying to shove him off. It was bright sunlight when he started his climb, but at the summit, almost without warning, the skies darkened and there was a tremendous downpour.

The night before the members of the Mountain Troop were to begin their climb, Ivan warned everybody about the local taboo. Despite this, Joe and another troop member went hunting for rabbits, killing two. When they returned to camp the local guides shunned them. As far as they were concerned, they were dead.

The next morning the climb began. Joe was never a great climber. He tackled every mountain the same way he lived life, by using his vast reserves of strength and courage to overcome all obstacles. Unfortunately he took one of the hardest routes up the mountain and even his great strength could not compensate for the skill needed for such a hazardous climb. He fell and his body landed in an almost inaccessible part of the mountain. With little regard for his own life, Ivan recovered Joe's battered body and abseiled with it strapped to him down a sheer drop of almost two hundred feet.

That afternoon the Squadron drew up in full uniform in front of the mountain that had killed Big Joe. A prayer seeking forgiveness was put in a bottle and placed in a cave in the mountainside. The men spent a minute in silent prayer for their comrade and dispersed.

I had listened to Ivan's story in silence, and now, despite the warmth of the room, I felt a sudden chill. My mind was on a silent hillside, in a land far away, and gods who should be left to sleep.

Studying had now become the focus of my life. Like all mature students, I felt a little self-conscious about being the oldest person in class but that quickly passed.

The law itself was fascinating; each area had its own problems and its own remedies. From a tenant's right of occupancy to a suspect's right to silence, each subject I learnt broadened not only my knowledge but my understanding of the complex legal relationships each of us enters into every day without realizing it.

The classes were not without the odd bit of humour. On one occasion we were discussing the law on libel. In order for a case of libel to proceed, the guilty party must 'publish the libel' – that is, it must be seen by a person other than the person libelled. The question before the class concerned a famous case in which a husband opened his wife's mail and read allegedly libellous remarks. Our tutor went round the class asking whether our spouses opened our mail. When she came to me I replied: 'My first wife did. That's how she found out about my second wife.'

An essential phase of all legal training is the student's attachment to legal organizations. Through the summer break in 1993 I was fortunate to be offered a place on the Government Legal Services 'Look and Learn' scheme and was attached to Customs and Excise. On our first morning we were briefed by the enforcement branch of the organization. The figures they gave us were appalling. If you bought a kilo of cocaine in Colombia, it would cost you less than £2000. This could be sold wholesale in London for £40,000. If you had a distribution network you could sell it at £83.00 a gram, at the then current street price, and make a profit of £81,000. Most cocaine is 90 per cent proof, so it is adulterated with some innocuous substance like glucose to produce twice the volume. A grand total of £164,000 profit from your original investment. With such profits it's little wonder that we are losing the war on drugs.

Shortly after our lecture we were taken to London's Docklands City Airport to see Customs staff in action. During the tour we were told that Customs had received intelligence that a French-speaking Nigerian was about to attempt to bring a consignment of cocaine into the UK illegally. Almost as soon as the words were spoken a man of African appearance was plucked from the line of incoming travellers. Naturally we thought the whole thing had been staged for our benefit. But we were wrong, for a rapid analysis of the man's urine revealed traces of the drug. He protested that he was merely a user, but under sustained questioning, and facing the prospect of a body X-ray, he admitted to being a courier. Wearing a sealed plastic 'bunny suit', the man was made to sit on a lavatory until nature took its course, when the cocaine, wrapped in cocktail-sausage-sized packets, was automatically retrieved and repackaged for use as evidence. We later learnt that the courier had secreted forty-six packets of the drug inside him. For us, at least, it was a fascinating introduction to the world of drug detection.

My fellow course members were a friendly, urbane bunch. When not in court shadowing drugs cases, we spent the time debating contentious subjects such as abortion and the right to silence. Jonathan, an Oxford student, paired up with me and after work we'd stroll together from the Customs office on the South Bank to nearby Waterloo station, where he'd catch a train home. On one such walk he suggested that many people on welfare didn't need the benefits and could find work if they really wanted too. His solution was to tighten up the benefits system and force them to work.

'You've never been hungry, really hungry, have you, Jonathan?' I asked him.

'No.'

'Never been without clothes or a place to sleep?'

His face took on a curious expression. 'No.'

I stopped dead in the street and turned to face him. 'I have. It's appalling. It robs you of everything: dignity, self-respect. Come over here a minute.'

I led him to the grim concrete walkway under the raised roundabout known as the Bullring. Down below, stretching as far as the eye could see, were dozens of cardboard boxes, each one occupied, some by whole families.

'See that. Most of them can't claim benefits, because they've no permanent address. Because they can't get benefits, they can't even get basic accommodation.'

'I hadn't noticed that.'

'You look but you don't see, Jonathan. You've been walking past this spot for over a week. I saw it the first morning I made my way into the office.' I looked down at the huddled mass of unfortunates. 'Don't let this expensive suit delude you, Jonathan. I came from people like that. I never had to live on the streets, thank God, but it was close at times. The next time you start to talk about cutting benefits, think about the people under this bridge, and maybe then it might not seem such a good idea.'

I got my exam results through while I was on the attachment: straight firsts in all the exams I'd sat. I was ecstatic. I also had a new lady in my life, Chrissie. We'd been introduced through a mutual friend, who'd described me as a policeman, a traditional Mr Plod, and we had been seeing each other on and off for over a year. She was slim, with one of those endlessly attractive faces that defy age. At the beginning of 1992 I'd invited her to live with me and to my great delight and surprise, she agreed. We have been together ever since. She fills my days with laughter and my nights with warmth.

It was my final year at university. Five subjects to master, each one counting towards my overall grade at the end of the year. Among the options I took were evidence, which I thought would be essential as I wanted to be a criminal advocate, and jurisprudence, the philosophy of the law. Of all the subjects I studied for my degree, this was perhaps the most thought-provoking. Through it I was able to explore the fundamental building blocks of the law itself: why we have laws; why people obey them; whether the law has a duty to enforce a moral point of view. It was endlessly stimulating.

Having made the decision that I wanted to become a barrister, through the summer I sat various additional exams set by the Council of Legal Education and designed to weed out those unsuitable to undergo the training. Among these was a critical reasoning test, to see if you could think through and solve problems quickly. I had no idea how I'd done. The exam week approached. The end of a long, hard four weeks. Everything I'd worked for during four years was on the line. Strangely, I felt more excited than nervous. It was just another challenge, different from the others I had faced, but I relished it and felt like I was eighteen. I put the pen down after the last paper was completed and let out a satisfied sigh. With a nod to the officer I walked out into the bright sunshine and lit a cigar. It was in the hands of the examination board now.

I had three days off, then began to write this account of my life. When I'd first approached my agent about writing it he'd asked me: 'How does the story end?'

He had me there, I had to think. 'I suppose with me getting a degree.'

I immersed myself in my writing through June, not wanting to think about the exam results. In the first week of July I made my way to the university and stood in a small, silent crowd waiting outside the Law Faculty hall for the results to be posted. The senior course tutor emerged at noon precisely and pinned a series of sheets of paper on the board, stepping quickly to one side so that he was not trampled to death as the throng pushed forward. I searched for my name. Around me there were whoops of joy and groans of disappointment. Then I found it. Henry McCallion: 2.1 pass. I jumped as high as I could in the air. Henry McCallion LL.B (Hons), with a double first in Jurisprudence. Life just doesn't get any better.

I waited to find out if I could now go on to the next stage of my legal training, the CLE's Vocational Course, the necessary step to becoming a barrister. Competition just to get on to the course was fierce. Even a 2.1 in law was no guarantee that I would be accepted.

On 4 June 1994 I received a letter franked with the stamp of the Law Society. On opening it I let out a shout of joy. I had a place on the Vocational Course! Only a limited number of places were to be offered, so getting one was in itself an achievement. I called everybody I knew in the world to tell them my good fortune. The friends I had made locally decided on a celebratory drink and we all went to a wine bar and discussed with some relish the kind of barrister I would make. I felt as if I had won the pools.

When I got home, the light was flickering on my answering machine. There was a message to ring a friend in Ulster. Despite the fact that it was after midnight I did so. Suddenly all the joy I felt evaporated. There had been a helicopter crash on the Mull of Kintyre. Among the dead was my old friend Ian Phoenix. I sat staring at the wall, my mind numb. Eventually I got up and poured myself a drink. Anyone who had met Ian could not have failed to be touched by his warmth and generosity. I remembered him, a superintendent, coming to my house when I was injured to take me out for a drink, giving up his precious spare time to help me when I had needed it so much. I found it hard to comprehend that a man so full of life could be dead. What should have been one of the happiest days of my life was shrouded by the loss of one of the very best comrades I had known. I remembered his roguish smile, his sheer love of life. Friend after friend called; none of us could come to terms with the loss. How long I sat, I don't know, but eventually Chrissie came and led me to bed in the early hours of the morning.

The next week I went to Ian's funeral in Belfast. Six SAS men carried his coffin from the family home. The cortège stretched well over three hundred yards as mourners, who had travelled thousands of miles, said goodbye to a very special man. At the cemetery, six uniformed RUC men carried the coffin into the church. The president of the Parachute Regiment Association in Ulster read the eulogy. He spoke about the kind of man Ian was: a man who had cried after Loughgall, the attack on the RUC station that had left eight IRA men dead, at the absurd waste of human life; about a police officer dedicated to the fight against terrorism; and about the father and husband lost for ever. A bugler from the 2nd Battalion Parachute Regiment played the last post. I fought to hold back the tears.

We went to Ian's house, where, in true Irish style, a wake was prepared. I tried to speak to his lovely widow, but the words just wouldn't come. She smiled at me.

'I know, I know, but Ian always said that if he died nobody was to cry at the wake. Go and get yourself some champagne.'

Ian had left a legacy in his will, dictating that champagne should be served in plenty. We toasted Ian and gave him a good send-off. We talked of the helicopter crash and the great loss of RUC and Army personnel. Nobody knew why the giant twin-engined Chinook helicopter had crashed. It had been flying low, in bad visibility, but the journey was a routine one and the pilots experts. If the cause of the crash was a mystery, its effect on the fight against terrorism was not. Also dead in the crash were the current head of Special Branch, his deputy and most of the leading

RUC specialists in counter-terrorism. MI5 operatives and leading Army intelligence chiefs had also perished.

Good men could be found to fill their jobs, but what could not be replaced was the years of accumulated trust these experts had built up together. The crash had been the single most devastating blow against the intelligence community since the Troubles had begun. The very heart and soul of the RUC's Special Branch had been ripped out. It could have been even worse, for the current head of the SAS and two other leading SB men had narrowly missed joining the flight, held back due to operational requirements. It was some small solace. A few hours later we were joined by my long-time friend Bill, who told me about the day after the crash.

'We all went to headquarters. There was little work done, Harry. We all just sat around dazed, drinking cup after cup of coffee. Nobody could really come to terms with the loss. One inspector got a call from the chief constable that morning telling him to get his staff together for a pep talk. He replied: "What staff? There's only me and a sergeant left." ' Bill shook his head. 'It's the same everywhere: departments devastated, everybody just numb.'

I nodded. The enormity of the loss had come home to me. RUC Special Branch is a small, almost family unit. Losing ten senior men in one go was almost too catastrophic to comprehend.

'Right at the end of the meeting,' continued Bill, 'somebody mentioned your name. Even people who have never met you had heard about you. They wanted to know if you would be coming over for Ian's funeral and how you were doing in your studies. I was able to tell them you'd passed your degree and been accepted on the Vocational Course to become a barrister. You know, Harry, we're all very proud of you.'

I felt a lump in my throat. At a time of the utmost grief, men who were in the front line of the battle against terrorism had spared the time to think of me, to feel pride in my accomplishments. I went outside into the cool night air. I felt both sad and happy. But more than anything else, I felt proud. I had a sudden image of myself as a ragged-arsed kid from the backstreets of Glasgow. I looked at the moon, large and bright and full of promise, and raised my glass.

'You've come a long way, Harry McCallion, a long way indeed.'

GLOSSARY

AK47 Russian Kalashnikov 7.62mm assault rifle firing 750 rpm

APC armoured personnel carrier

Armalite American 5.56mm assault rifle firing 650–850 rpm; official designation M16

ASU Active Service Unit of **IRA** or **PIRA**

badged accepted for entry into the **SAS**, after successful completion of **Selection** and **Continuation**

basha originally an improvised waterproof shelter made from a poncho and available materials; by extension, barracks, house, bed or other accommodation

bergen backpack carried by British forces on active service, carrying everything necessary for survival

blue-on-blue accidental clash between soldiers fighting on same side

Bren gun light machine-gun of 7.62mm calibre firing about 500 rpm

Browning High Power American semi-automatic 9mm pistol with thirteen-round magazine

casevac casualty evacuation: removal of injured to aid post or hospital, usually by helicopter

claymore anti-personnel land-mine detonated by trip-wire or remote control

CO Commanding Officer

contact engagement with an enemy force

Continuation course taken after **Selection** in which recruits are instructed in SAS patrol skills

crow inexperienced soldier or rookie

DCM Distinguished Conduct Medal
Det military detachment
DMSU Divisional Mobile Support Unit (RUC)
DS Directing Staff: in charge of SAS training
DSO Distinguished Service Order
H hour scheduled time of commencement of a military operation
HMSU Headquarters Mobile Support Unit (RUC)
INLA Irish National Liberation Army. Republican paramilitaries
IRA Irish Republican Army. Republican paramilitaries
Killing House the SAS's Close Quarter Battle training building at **Stirling Lines,** Hereford
LUP lying-up position: secure resting place used during a military operation
LZ landing zone
MM Military Medal
MO *modus operandi*: method of operation
MP5 German Heckler & Koch 9mm sub-machine-gun particularly suitable for close-range use and favoured by the SAS in hostage-rescue situations
NCO non-commissioned officer
OC Officer Commanding
op operation
OP observation post
OTR on the run
PIRA Provisional IRA. Republican paramilitaries
point (man) soldier positioned at front of four-man operational group as lookout
QGM Queen's Gallantry Medal
R&R rest and recuperation
RPD Russian light machine-gun of 7.62mm calibre firing 650–750 rpm
rpm rounds per minute
RSM Regimental Sergeant-Major
RTU returned to unit (of origin)
Rupert SAS term, normally disparaging, for officers
RV rendezvous point; to rendezvous
SADF South African Defence Force
sangar protective wall, usually curved or circular, built of stone or sandbags

GLOSSARY

SAS Special Air Service

Sea King medium-lift helicopter designed to carry twenty men (depending on the weight of their personal equipment)

Selection four-week SAS course held at Hereford and in Wales which all prospective recruits must pass before acceptance for the **Continuation** course

SLR self-loading 7.62mm rifle firing 650 rpm, now replaced within the SAS by the SA-80 assault rifle

SMG sub-machine-gun

SSM Squadron Sergeant-Major

SSU Special Support Unit (RUC)

stag guard duty

Stirling Lines Regimental Headquarters of 22 SAS at Hereford, and named in honour of the Regiment's founder, David Stirling

Tail-end Charlie soldier positioned at rear of four-man patrol as lookout

three-tonner Bedford cargo truck

tout informer

UDA Ulster Defence Association. Loyalist paramilitaries

UDR Ulster Defence Regiment. Loyalist paramilitaries

UFF Ulster Freedom Fighters. Loyalist paramilitaries

UVF Ulster Volunteer Force. Loyalist paramilitaries